Search and Placement!

A

Handbook

For

Success

For
Search, Recruiting, and
Placement Professionals
ONLY

Search and Placement!

A Handbook for Success

Copyright © 2004
Steven M. Finkel

For information write to :
Placement Marketing Group
P.O. Box 410412
St. Louis, Missouri   63141 USA

or

Professional Search Seminars
11330 Olive Boulevard
Suite 106
St. Louis, Missouri   63141 USA
Website: www.larrynobles.com

ISBN 0-9669693-1-6

Printed in the United States of America

ABOUT THE AUTHOR

Larry Nobles has been conspicuously and consistently successful in the search, recruiting and placement industry for more than 25 years.

As a consultant, he has completed searches at every level from secretary to CEO, in every industry from Office Support to IT to Engineering to Sales. Beginning with a national franchise, Larry ranked #16 out of 1500 consultants in only his second year in the business.

As a General Manager, Larry built his firm from small to #3 out of 250 offices in only his third year in operation. Opening another new office, he developed it to #3 out of 43 regional offices in his second year.

As Director of Training for a major franchise, Larry Nobles opened scores of new recruiting firms across the U.S. with remarkable success. Of the thirty offices he personally trained and developed (none of whose managers had any background in our industry), every office not only remained in business, but was in the top 25% of the franchise system within five years.

An internationally known trainer with extensive experience on three continents, he has been the top-rated speaker at (US) National Association of Personnel Services for 5 consecutive years!

The Fordyce Letter has referred to him as "Trainer Extraordinare." And Steve Finkel, our industry's leading trainer, has described him as "an absolutely top-flight speaker with outstanding industry knowledge and a clear, straightforward presentation of quality material based on rock-solid sales principles."

He is widely-regarded as the best developer of new people in the history of the search and placement industry.

Search and Placement!

A

Handbook

For

Success

by
Larry Nobles

with
Steve Finkel

DEDICATION

As Larry requested, his book is dedicated to his beloved family of whom he spoke proudly and often.....his wife Janet Nobles, son Conor and daughter Lauren.

The portion of this book done by Larry's editorial assistant is dedicated to my deranged brother David Finkel, brother Michael Finkel, and sister Susan Dykstra.

"One friend in a lifetime is much; two are many; three are hardly possible."

— ***Henry Brooks Adams***

ACKNOWLEDGEMENTS

Despite the substantial body of work from which this book is drawn, no book of this substance writes itself. As Samuel Johnson said, "Sir, what is written without thought will be read without profit." The great profit you will see from the information presented here is a direct result of the hard work put into it. There were two (or perhaps three) who worked, consulted and supported to get this to you whose names do not appear on the title page.

First we have Angelica Traas, my office manager. From transcribing audios to personal notes, from draft after draft, rewrites, multiple edits and bad handwriting, she hammered this book out, both at home and at the office. Bookwriting is tedious at best and maddening at worst; Angelica saw both and kept at it. To her is due much appreciation.

Secondly, we have my business consultant and psychological counselor Covey McFinkel the Gordon Setter, and his admiring understudy Shadow. Bird hunting partner, top field trial competitor, obedience, house and office dog, my pal Covey has helped me through the loss of his loved predecessors and other traumas for nine years. His confidence in me, his good sense and good advice, his brilliance and his craziness have kept me amused, learning, awed by his talent and working hard regardless of stress or turmoil. Thank you, Covey and Shadow, for everything.

TABLE OF CONTENTS

CHAPTER   **PAGE**

	Foreward	
	Introduction	1
1	Organizing For Success	13
2	Operating Your Desk	23
3	Goal Setting: What's Right For You?	37
4	Problem Solving By Analysis	49
5	Guiding Your Success: The Daily Plan	55
6	Foundational Matching	63
7	Beyond Basic Matching	71
8	Marketing: The Bedrock Presentation	83
9	Marketing: Post-Presentation	97
10	Recruiting: Finding The Best	119
11	Recruiting: Building The Presentation	129
12	Recruiting: Rebuttals and Responses	137
13	Candidate Analysis: The Other Side of Matching	151
14	Avoiding Candidate Problems	167
15	Writing Searches: Critical Key	173
16	Candidate Preparation	189
17	Client Preparation	203
18	EIO – A Profitable Interjection	213
19	Candidate Follow-up	221
20	Client Follow-up	231
21	Negotiating The Offer	241
22	Closing	251
23	Developing Clients	263
24	Client Development: Issues and Education	271
25	The Client Development Program	281
26	Post-Fee Development	293
27	Performance Time	311
28	Afterwards	315

FOREWARD

By Steve Finkel

I first met Larry Nobles over 20 years ago. He was speaking at an industry conference which I also was addressing. As is my habit, I hid out in the back of the room, just one of the audience. I was familiar with his extraordinary achievements developing new offices in his own firms and as Director of Training with what was, at the time, a very fine franchise. But frankly, I was not expecting to be impressed.

The reasons for this had nothing to do with Larry Nobles, and everything to do with the "industry trainers" that I had heard before and since. Coming from an extended background of the best classical and corporate sales that exists, I listen a bit differently than does the average search consultant. As the old joke goes, I listen for three things....content, content, and more content on a bedrock of solid sales-proven principles that will increase effectiveness for anyone. This foundation is lacking in our industry. Most "trainers" are in fact simply <u>speakers</u>, focusing on presentation rather than content, copying material taught to them by their managers, stolen from their clients or others, and presenting material that is useful — if it is useful at all — only for one personality type.

It took me less than half an hour to see that Larry Nobles was different.

I was amazed! Here was a man with a warm pleasing manner of speaking who focused on solid industry-specific material that would increase anyone's production. It was evident that he understood his material, could break it down into individual steps, and explain it in a manner that made sense to anyone at any level. And all of it was equally effective for people of different personality types, resting on a foundation of valid classical sales principles. Who <u>was</u> this guy?

Afterwards, I walked up and introduced myself. We shook hands, and looked at each other. No one ever accused me of dishonesty. "Larry," I said. "I have to admit it. Other than myself, that was the best presentation for new people

I've ever heard." He looked at me. "Steve," he said. "I've heard you speak and heard a great deal about your in-house programs. For experienced people, you're the best I've ever heard." And we both broke into laughter.

Larry and I met often over the years. Sometimes I'd be at the same conference as he. Other times the phone would ring. He'd tell me he would be in my home city, and we'd get together. Or I'd be in Tulsa. We are different people, with different personal interests. So the talk would always turn to our common interest — sales.

In the beginning, I could not understand how he came by his extensive in-depth knowledge of genuine salesmanship. Here was no parrot mimicing what he had been once taught or had heard. Here was no shallow speaker, addressing new people because he could not do anything else. Here was an outstanding professional sales trainer with a real foundation. How did he get that way?

Larry Nobles had some uncommonly good fortune early in his career, but he made the most of it, and had the right mind and character to do so.

The name Jack Maxwell is not much known in our industry these days. But those who knew him will not forget him. Throughout the 1970's, Jack Maxwell was a legend. He was Larry's first manager.

Jack was originally a degreed certified mechanical engineer with seven years experience in two Exxon Refineries. You and I both know that engineers are not the most sales-oriented people around.

But they have their good qualities. The best are logical, organized, planned and disciplined. Jack Maxwell bought a Dunhill franchise, and set out to educate himself in sales with the same effort and focus he brought to his engineering endeavors. His second year in business, he was the top consultant in the 250-office Dunhill System. But that was not enough. He kept studying classical salesmanship with great enthusiasm. Over a period of time, he developed talks, speeches, seminars and an audio cassette series entitled, "Closing the Close Ones". He was generally equal in exposure to the old-time industry speakers of his generation —Art Pell, Lou Scott, Tony Bruno, and Phil Ross — with less flash and dazzle, but with a far better classical sales foundation. When you have an engineer who masters selling, that's an unusual individual….and a great mentor.

After mastering the <u>sales</u> facets of our industry, he found the star he needed to build his firm in Larry Nobles. The discipline, logic, focus and dedication I've learned after twenty years in hard-core martial arts has been of enormous professional benefit to me. Larry got his in a different classroom — flying helicopters under enemy fire for two tours in Vietnam. The results of natural talent, trained discipline, surprisingly good initial training, and a strong desire to study and learn selling yielded a remarkable individual. His results and accomplishments as General Manager of Jack Maxwell's firm, his success running his own firm and his remarkable record of developing others may be read at the beginning of this book in the "About the Author" portion.

We kept in contact frequently via phone. I am of the opinion that initial training is best done by the owner of the firm. But not everyone feels up to doing so. When I received frequent calls to train new people, my response was "buy my videos and books. Then call Larry Nobles. Here's his phone number. Then call me back in six months to a year."

Sometimes my phone would ring, and someone would say, "Larry Nobles is coming to our office. He told me to buy your products." Or "Larry Nobles trained my new people. He told me to call you in two years about in-house training. So now I'm calling."

When Larry came out with his excellent audio cassette programs, I was pleased to recommend them. Anyone in our industry —especially someone who commutes to work — would be wise to own them.

And then one day, I received word that Larry Nobles was gravely ill and not expected to live.

By the time I called, he had gone through tests, had procedures, trips to The Mayo Clinic, the things you do under those circumstances. What emotional trauma he may have suffered leaving behind a beloved wife and family, he never discussed with me. He seemed to have come to terms with it. Men don't whine, at least not to other men. And Larry Nobles was the right kind of man.

I arranged to distribute his four recently-made audio cassette products for him. We discussed the idea of a book. His mind was clear. He was excited. I pulled together the material, drawn from his 21 hours of audios, 17 articles that he had written for *The Fordyce Letter*, my notes from eight of his programs that I had attended. He mailed me outlines of his in-house training, his notes from his speaking programs that I had not attended, and we discussed the critical Introduction and last chapter. I drew up an outline, asked questions about various topics, his thoughts about the future of our industry, uses of the internet. What an experience!

And then Larry Nobles passed away.

Every word, every thought, every recommendation, every comment in this book comes directly from him. I wrestled with the question of what to do when Larry's opinions conflicted with mine. But it was an easy decision, really. This is not Steve Finkel's book. It's Larry's, and the Author's Royalties will go to his family. This book should be owned by every new <u>and</u> experienced person in our industry.

It is the clear and cumulative knowledge of a remarkable individual in our industry.

Read this book. Underline it. Re-read it. Recommend it to others. You cannot fail to benefit significantly. And your production will soar. When it does, give some thanks to Larry Nobles. There are quite literally thousands of highly successful search consultants who have already done so.

LARRY NOBLES

Is there a single final farewell?
My songs cease, I abandon them.
From behind the screen where I hid,
I advance solely to you.

My friend, this is no book.
Who touches this touches a man.
It is to you I speak.
I spring from the pages. Call me forth!

— *Walt Whitman*
<u>Leaves of Grass</u>

INTRODUCTION

*I*know the best business in the world. Yes, I do. And not just for me. Not just — depending on where we are in the economic cycle as you read this — for the over 50,000 others in this profession. For you!

I am referring of course, to Search and Placement. Or, if you prefer, Third-Party Non-Internal Recruiting.

If you've been in our business for awhile, you already know the truth of that statement, though this introductory chapter may remind you of some things you have forgotten.

But perhaps you are new or inexperienced, or you are just not sure about your future in Search and Placement. If that's the case, you're undoubtedly questioning my initial statement. "He doesn't know me", you're thinking. "How can he make that statement?"

I can make it because I have been observing all businesses for over 25 years as a recruiter. I've worked all desks — and what you have in front of you is the Best profession in the world! And I can prove it.

QUALITIES OF THE PERFECT BUSINESS

Let's take a look at what makes the ultimate profession. We'll have to be reasonable, as openings for Rock Superstars or Heavyweight Boxing Champions are sort of limited. But, within the limits of good sense, what do you want?

First of all, I think you want to stay interested — and even challenged! We're not talking about a quick six months, but a Lifetime Career. If you're bored, the rest doesn't matter.

Secondly, it's important to consider an absence of negatives. We can joke about being a Rock Star all we want, but a 40 week-a-year travel schedule gets a little wearing. And there are certainly interesting corporate jobs, but many require frequent relocation if you are going to climb that corporate ladder. Moreover, some professions have lots of positives, but if you have to work 60 hours a week, is it worth it?

Thirdly, it would be nice if we were doing something good for people and, yes, beneficial to society. We all work to support ourselves and our families. But there is much to be said also for being proud of your business and feeling good about yourself.

Fourthly, you've got to factor in the amount of time (and cost) required to get into a productive state. Being a doctor is a pretty good job for some people, but the time and cost to get there are both astronomical.

And finally, we have income. How much do <u>most</u> people make? How much <u>can</u> you make? How much is <u>reasonable</u>?

Let's take a look at the modern Search and Placement industry, and see how we stack up.

CHALLENGE

What is the Search and Placement business?

At bottom, it is the most complex sophisticated intellectually-challenging multi-step <u>sales</u> job in existence!

We are not just "intermediaries" or "distributors", as would be the case if we handled industrial steel or printed circuit boards. We are not just "consultants", as in business or HR consultants. We are all of these... and much much more. We are unique.

Does this mean you need a hard-driving sales personality to be successful? Of course not! The variety of personalities that can be outrageously successful in our industry is endless. Including yours.

It <u>does</u> mean that the depth of intellect and knowledge required to totally master this business is vast.

Think of it this way. In the mid-70's, a well-known trainer of the times named Phil Ross produced an audio series entitled, "The 28 Steps of the Placement Process". According to Mr. Ross, there were 28 distinct portions to "putting a deal together" and earning a fee. Moreover, a competent search consultant must perform effectively *at every one of them, every time,* or risk losing the fee.

Wow! Complex? Challenging? Long "learning curve" involved? You bet! But learnable? Absolutely!

ABSENCE OF NEGATIVES

Here's another strong positive.

If you are an outside sales rep, you may be "on the road" constantly. Even if you work a local market, you spend a huge amount of time in your car in traffic, travelling from call to call.

Many jobs where the incomes matches ours require 60 hours-a-week, work on weekends, or being "on call" constantly. In the corporate world, relocation — sometimes frequent — is the norm if you want to move up.

How much of that applies to us? None. None at all.

Oh, sure, many people in our industry do put in long hours. As we'll discuss, you have to <u>learn</u> <u>this</u> <u>business,</u> and that requires reading books, watching videos, taking notes, listening to audios while driving to work or at home. There is no business that you are born knowing. Talent is <u>not</u> enough!

But once that is mostly done, this business can generally drop to around 40 hours a week, more or less. Some work more, but most of the time, it's because their inefficiency in the office forces them to do so. That's why this book starts with the not-too-exciting subject of desk management and planning. If you're sensible, you'll enjoy all the enormous benefits of our business — without any inherent negatives.

PERSONAL SATISFACTION

What do we do? We help people. We help candidates. We help clients. And we even help "source companies".

We are <u>not</u> social workers! Don't be confused. You must be a hard-nosed practical effective business person and well-educated salesman to maximize income in this industry. But you <u>can</u> "do well by doing good". And we do.

Zig Ziglar, surely one of America's finest motivational sales speakers, is the author of the life-changing quote: "You get what <u>you</u> want by helping other people get what <u>they</u> want!" He could have been talking about the Search and Placement business.

Let's look at the three entities involved in the Search process, and see why they all benefit massively by our efforts.

Client Company

First, we have the client company. The hiring manager has a problem. The more productive his staff, the more likely <u>he</u> is to be promoted. No highly productive employees means reduced success and promotion for him. But what type of employee does he seek?

Generally, the need is for a person with a narrow specific background, and experience and accomplishments that directly relate to the position and goals that must be achieved. But where is such a person to be found?

Only a good search consultant can <u>consistently</u> produce candidates with the narrow credentials and experience to jump in and do a job right now, with no time needed to learn or "ramp up".

Does the client company benefit? You bet it does! Does the hiring official have his or her own career greatly enhanced by hiring the best possible talent? Absolutely!

The Candidate

Now here is an area where we <u>directly</u> <u>and</u> <u>substantially</u> improve people's lives!

If the candidate is actively looking, by definition he gets what he wants. Your efforts result in the right position for him.

But the real thrill is when we get to be "corporate fairy godmother". The reality is that <u>many</u> people are not happy at all in their careers, but "fear of change" keeps them from taking steps to leave. There is limited challenge, limited income, limited growth. The phone rings... and their lives are dramatically changed for the better.

And we even get paid! What could be finer?

The Source Company

Don't kid yourself. The firm from which you obtain the candidate benefits too.

If the candidate is actively unhappy, they are better off with a more optimistic and motivated employee.

But even if that is not the case, a position must be developed. Every person eventually gets in a job rut of doing things in the same way, revolving around current strengths and knowledge. A new holder of the position keeps the previous strengths and adds more.

The best example of this is sales. Even in a very good territory, a new sales rep will not only keep existing accounts but will obtain a lot of additional customers and distributors. It is not that the new rep is better; he just develops the territory differently.

Apply that to your area of specialization, and the same beneficial results will be seen.

YOUR INCOME POTENTIAL

This is a difficult area to address, strictly as a result of inflation. I can remember when a thousand-dollar fee was respectable, and I've met some "old-timers" who remember $200 fees! So take a look at the copyright page of this book if you think my numbers are low. Twenty years from now, I'm sure they will be!

Niche

First of all, I'd like to say that the field you are in, i.e. your area of specialization, doesn't matter. That's right. The best producers achieve the same production levels, regardless of their niches. A good example of this is when I was in attendance at a Texas Association Annual Conference banquet, and they gave out awards to the top producer in "professional" and in "office support". The difference in average fees would have been dramatic. But the difference in total production between the top person in "office support" and "professional" was $2000! What makes you successful is not your niche; it is you!

Average

So what can you expect to produce "on a desk", as we say in Search and Placement?

The best validated survey is that produced annually by *The Fordyce Letter*, the only monthly publication in our industry. An economic downturn can definitely affect things for a few years, but that's not the norm. So we'll assume at least a pretty good market.

Putting aside those people with less than two years of experience, the average production for the remainder was around 200K per year! By definition, of course, that means half did better. Now it is possible (or even probable) that *The Fordyce Letter* subscribers produce better than the rest of the industry. But they have a <u>lot</u> of subscribers. And that is not an unreasonable number.

Maximum

Let's put aside the half-dozen or so top retainer people who pay major money to public relations firms to get their names bandied about in major financial publications. A very few such people do exist, but it is unlikely you'll do business in that way.

Among the contingency crowd, there are probably a half-dozen people who, in a <u>very good</u> market, bill a million dollars. There is very little to be learned from such people, and they may be viewed as an aberation, that is, a radical departure from normality.

The reality is that raw luck can strike; a great niche in a boom market combined with lucking into a very few rapidly-expanding clients can yield high short-term billings. Such production plummets dramatically in a recession, and never return to previous levels. Then, too, every field has some rare geniuses, but you can't count on being one. There is nothing to be learned from such people. Babe Ruth and Mickey Mantle were not very good batting instructors. And unless you have Ted Williams' eyesight and reflexes (ex-fighter pilot, who flew wingman for John Glenn in the Korean War), it won't do you much good to emulate his swing.

You should also realize that many claims of <u>unreasonably</u> high production are due to blatant falsehoods, accounting gimmicks, or massive support masquerading as "total production".

A Reasonable Maximum

So what <u>can</u> be achieved? Let's assume you are a generally smart, articulate, hard-working sort of person with some sales talent who is willing to study and learn. What can you reasonably expect to produce over time in Search and Placement in a decent market? How much <u>can</u> you produce?

For the answer to that, we turn to a specialist. There is a problem in getting real numbers on potential top production for normal good people in our industry. The difficulty is that <u>all</u> speakers and trainers in our industry, myself included, have historically focused on new people.

The reason for that is two-fold. First, most of us got our start with franchises, or we are descended from franchises. Franchises, by definition, take people who know nothing about this business, and develop them to a degree of adequacy. They, in turn, hire new people and develop <u>them</u> to a degree of adequacy. Some people, of course, eventually do much better than "adequacy", but they do it on their own. The trainer or manager is on to new people by then.

Secondly, trainers, like anyone else, have to be paid. That means they need as large a market as possible, and an owner who will pay for his people to be developed. In a normal growth market there are <u>more</u> relatively new people than relatively experienced people. Further, the manager will <u>far</u> more readily pay to develop new people, as the better ones are "already doing all right".

Obviously, foundational material will benefit <u>anyone</u>. But from the trainers of many years ago to franchise trainers to the current new "wanna-be's", raw rookies is what most people with national exposure see. What <u>can</u> experienced well-trained people produce? Really, they don't know. That's not their job.

So Who Knows?

For the answer, we turn to the only person who has ever specialized in developing not new people, but top producers — Steve Finkel. Steve has taken a different path than myself or anyone else, and this is what he knows. He has developed some terrific products for newer people, but his in-house training programs have, for over twenty years, started with decent producers and progressed from there.

I am writing this book — me, Larry Nobles. I expect to get some literary proof-reading help from Steve, but this is <u>my</u> material, and it will benefit you enormously. But I am not shy about asking for help in this area, and I did. Here is Steve's answer.

How Much? The Answer

"It is my belief", says Steve Finkel, "that the Search and Placement business, or Recruiting, if you prefer, for most people offers the best possible income in the least time and the most pleasant working conditions in the world. And that a normal person with good talent can be <u>trained</u> to achieve that income."

What does that mean in hard numbers? He continues, "Over time, I can train a good recruiter to bill upwards of $400,000 per year. Some support in terms of one or two part-time recruiters (a tool Steve promotes) can increase that number significantly with relatively low cost."

"Depending on individual talent and motivation, a person can feel absolutely confident of achieving those numbers over time with the proper training, <u>regardless</u> of the area of specialization. Some people will do better, but they have unusual personal qualities which cannot be replicated. But that 400K in consistent personal production is realistic and achievable, based on a good market and on-going training, in today's dollars."

Wow! Not bad! Now you'll obviously have to translate that into your compensation structure to see what that means in earnings for you. And not even Steve can develop that production overnight. We are speaking of years. But I think you'll agree that combined with all the preceding favorable factors we've mentioned, as a long-term career opportunity, Search and Placement offers the best deal around!

WHAT DOES IT COST?

So what does it cost, this terrific lifetime career? Can you just wander in, get some exposure to your manager, a little training and then go out and be successful? No.

The reality is that the "turnover rate", the percentage of people who are not successful in our field, as in any sales field, is high. Why is that? What can stop you from outrageous success? Or perhaps you are already in our business, and not where you want to be. Maybe the production level quoted seems high to you. Why is that? What is stopping you from the success that should be yours?

Ronald Reagan was noteworthy for many reasons, but a main one was that he was highly successful in four different careers, spanning his entire life. He made the right decisions. And he had a saying that applies here. "There are no easy answers", he said. "But there are simple answers". Here's how to achieve this outstanding lifetime career.

Discipline

One might say this is a metaphor for life. The reality is, as noted sales trainer Zig Ziglar said, that, "Winners achieve by doing things that losers will not do". That really says a lot.

Let's take some examples. I don't like planning. I don't like organization. I don't like checklists or paying attention to detail. That just isn't me. I'll bet it isn't you either. But you know what? It doesn't matter what I like. I flew helicopters for two tours in Vietnam. I saw that people who weren't planned and organized, and who got sloppy about checklists and details <u>after</u> they got good …just didn't come back.

You, too. It's easy to fill out your Daily Planner at the end of the day when you are new. It takes awhile, but you know you have to do it. Your manager will show you or you'll read about it here. He'll show you the second day and the third. You won't like it, but you'll do it. But how about after a few weeks or months? Or years? Doing what you don't like to do because you know you should is <u>discipline</u>. You can skip checklists and get sloppy for a while. But one day, you won't come back either.

Or how about keeping track of numbers and analyzing ratios in this business? It has to be done to maintain your work pace, and to identify problems at an early stage. It's tedious stuff, but highly important. If you drift away from doing it, you lose.

The same with conversations around the office, personal calls, just staying on the phone. It's easy to get distracted and accomplish less than you should, especially when you think you know this business. It's also undisciplined. Stay disciplined, even when it's boring.

Lifetime Learning

This business is a highly complex sales business. "Selling" is not a personality trait. It is a hard and specific set of skills. It must be learned and to do well, it must be mastered. It ain't easy.

Ask any experienced manager about individuals who say they will do well in this business because "I love people". If you love people, perhaps you will do well in the ministry. This business is for people who are willing to learn a profession.

Or take those who claim they "love to sell". I've hired a few of those people over the years, and listened to them on the phone. They fail. They don't love to sell; people who love what they do are excited about learning more, and implementing what they learn. These people just love to talk.

"Born salesmen" don't make it in this business long-term, though they frequently get off to a quick start. Why not? Because they have a short learning curve. They peak early; they start fast, and then "know it all". If that is you, quit now. But if you are willing to really study long-term and invest the time and thought to do so, you will do better than you ever thought possible.

Toughness

I'll be straightforward with you. This business can — and will — be frustrating and disappointing at times.

Calls are not returned. Clients hire someone other than your candidates at the last minute. Offers are turned down. You are going to hear "no's" when you would far rather hear a "yes".

Can you reduce the disappointment? Absolutely! Can you eliminate it? No. No matter how good you are, some will happen.

That's called "big-ticket selling". A deal you think is put together will fall apart, causing you anguish and costing you money. Will you get through the disappointment, and stay focused?

That is this business. The rewards — both emotional and financial — are enormous. What does it take? It takes on-going long-term learning. And it takes toughness.

THIS BOOK

So what will you get here? You'll get what you need. Effective organizational skills on a desk. (Sorry. But it is critical). Obtaining Clients. Selecting. Recruiting. Presenting Candidates. Coaching. Follow-ups. Closing. And then when we've put the deal together, we'll talk about <u>developing</u> clients from a one-time placement source to serious repeat business.

If you're new, you'll get a great foundation. If you're experienced, you'll see things you may have missed along the way, and will be reminded of things you may have drifted away from over the years. What will you get? Increased production!

THE KEYS

To attain that result, there are two keys.

First, you must <u>own</u> this book. You hold in your hands an enormous amount of material. It is impossible to absorb this in one or two readings. Moreover, in two or three months, (and six months and a year and ten years), you'll have a different level of knowledge that you do at present. Re-reading this book will yield you much more.

Secondly, you must <u>underline</u> or <u>highlight</u> this book. Doing so will help greatly to <u>fix</u> this information in your mind, just as in a college textbook. Moreover, periodic and on-going review will be essential. Interestingly, if you use a different color to underline or highlight at a second or third reading, it will surprise you how your perceptions will evolve along with your knowledge of our terrific industry.

We spoke of a willingness to learn. This is what it means. Only by doing so will this book become for you what it should… a handbook for success.

The best business in the world? You bet it is !

Let's begin….

ORGANIZING FOR SUCCESS

1

*W*hat are the most important elements in maximizing production in our industry? Well, yes. Industry-specific selling skills. No question about it. Without selling skills, you are like a man shooting and firing blanks. You will get no results.

But what is the most important factor beyond that, and one which will help you to maximize your skills? Desk Organization, Work Flow, and Time Management! Without that, you can have all the ammo you want in your gun. But if you are just firing wildly, what good will it do you?

Now if you are the kind of sales-oriented individual you ought to be, I'll offer you a warning and a promise.

The warning is that the next section will be tedious for you. Don't expect excitement. We like selling. It is exciting! We do not like planning. It is boring. If you wanted to be a boring person, you'd have been an accountant or a computer geek. I know it, and you know it too.

But here is the promise. If you'll pay close attention to the next few chapters, and underline, highlight, and review, this "Business Operational/Daily Planning" portion will increase your production far more that the same time and effort spent in skill improvement!

A QUIZ

Two search consultants, equal experience and intelligence.

Consultant A has only decent selling skills, but is extremely well-organized, plans thoroughly every day, understands how to "operate" a desk.

Consultant B is a genius at selling, but is disorganized, plans poorly and rarely.

Who produces more? And more consistently?

You know the answer. Consultant A will <u>double</u> the output of the poorly-planned consultant B, and will do so regardless of the marketplace.

I've seen your desk. Or if you're new, I've seen your desk the way it will be if you don't use the material you'll find here. I've seen lots of desks like yours. It looks like Europe after the War, doesn't it? You are losing some serious money through disorganization and incorrect work flow! But fear not; there is help available. And no, you won't find it on a computer.

It will not be exciting. But it will be profitable. Let's start at the beginning.

The Source of Our Income

Let's backtrack a little, and establish some things. We make money by making placements. OK, that's simple. Now how do we make placements? By setting interviews. Interviews happen from certain telephone calls, placements happen from certain interviews, and dollars happen from placements.

Basically, interviews are the beginning of our money. Now, if interviews are the beginning of our placements and the beginning of all money, where do interviews come from?

The Source of Interviews

There are only two kinds of telephone calls that will set an interview. What are they? Well, obviously, candidate marketing is one. Marketing the Candidate is defined as a call to a company making a presentation on a candidate's background <u>without</u> knowing whether that company has an opening. Some in our business refer to this as a cold call. But we call it a Marketing Call to indicate that we are marketing a candidate's background. Sometimes when we market, make a good presentation, and have a great candidate, the company will say to us, "Fantastic! I like the sound of that person. Can I see her at a certain time?" And they bring her right over and they hire her, though perhaps at a second interview.

But there is one other kind of call, and one that is a lot more likely to yield an interview. That call is called a "Matching" Call. Some call it a "presentation" call. What it means is that we have an existing Search Assignment. On that existing assignment is a set of specifications, and we have matched a candidate's background to that information. That's why I call it a Matching

Call. You've matched the candidate's background to an existing set of position specifications, and you call that company, knowing that they have an opening. You present that candidate, and attempt to set an interview.

Thus, there are only two kinds of calls that set interviews. <u>Marketing</u> <u>Calls</u> in which you do not know that they have an opening, and <u>Matching</u> <u>Calls</u> in which you do know that they have an opening. Those two calls set all of our interviews, which result in all of our placements and all of our dollars.

Is This Organization?

Now, why are we talking about calls when this is supposed to be about desk organization and work flow? Because matching a candidate's specifications to a company's search specifications is an administrative organizational paper-matching process! It is <u>not</u> a sales technique!

Fees From Matching?

How much of your production comes from that technique? Of all the placements you will make in a year, how many fees come from by matching a candidate to an existing order? How many times do placements come by marketing cold into a company, resulting in a hire of the person you were calling about?

What happens frequently is that you market the candidate, and the client interviews, but does not hire. Or you may obtain a search, but not an interview. Then you send them someone else, with a more appropriate background. That candidate gets hired.

That is a placement made by matching. You <u>got</u> the search by <u>marketing</u>. You <u>made</u> the placement by <u>matching</u> candidates' backgrounds to an existing set of criteria. So what number are we talking about when we ask how much of our money comes matching a candidate to an order?

The number I get all across the country is 90%. Meaning 90 percent of the placements we make actually started with a <u>match</u> of a candidate to an existing search assignment. And only 10% results from a placement made by pure marketing where they hired the person we were calling about. Think about it. ***90% of your income comes from your ability to match a candidate to a set of criteria.*** And that is an organizational function. You need an administrative system to make those things happen. If you are not in control of the <u>administrative</u> functions of your desk, you lose!

Without this, there will be fees on your desk that you don't know about! I proved it to myself when I was a young consultant. I know computers well, and have worked IT extensively. But as I learn new systems of organization, new technologies and techniques, those simply reinforce some of the things that I did in the past that cause me to understand how important the original systems are.

A Sad Example

Almost any experienced search consultant, no matter how computerized the office, can tell you stories of losing fees due to the lack of ability to match candidates and orders.

I remember years ago when my boss would follow up with me. We would talk about the search that I just took. And he'd say, "What are you going to do on it?" And I'd reply, "I want to recruit on it." And he would frequently respond, "Well, that would be good, but why don't you send them the two candidates that you interviewed last week? Remember Candidate A and Candidate B?" Here was my boss following up with me who had a better memory and knowledge of the people on my desk than I did! I was not <u>organized</u> well enough to use my inventory to make myself placements.

BUT WHAT ABOUT...

I know. That was old stuff, and now computers have solved our organizational problems. Well, no. They haven't.

When computers first became readily available at reasonable prices to small businesses, it was thought that they would correct many such problems. They were going to cause you to <u>never</u> lose a candidate, <u>never</u> miss a follow-up call, <u>never</u> be disorganized. Sure. Just as they were going to put accountants out of work. They haven't. And they won't ... Why not?

Let's listen to the Founder and President of Intel, the world's largest chip-maker, on the subject. Here's Andrew Grove in his fine book, <u>Only The Paranoid Survive:</u> "The first thing that you should realize," writes Grove, "is that everybody with a gadget hawks and hypes it and consciously or unconsciously works double time to make the product as important as possible. Under the circumstances, you ought to be suspicious. When you explore these developments first-hand, you'll discover that mostly they aren't what they're cracked up to be."

It is important to separate functions, to realize what computerization <u>can</u> do effectively, which is information storage and retrieval (though there are some negatives), from what it <u>cannot</u> do, which is the planning and organization of your desk and day.

Your owner has determined what level of techno-stuff is right for your firm and market. However, the basic business organization structure addressed here will be of enormous benefit to you, <u>regardless</u> of whether you are looking at paper or a computer screen.

All of the top producers that I know can put their fingers on any information in 5 seconds because they are so organized they have things where they want them — without a computer. They can react to any business situation that comes up. They <u>never</u> <u>ever</u> miss a match or miss a placement or possible interview from organizational problems.

WHY IS THIS A PROBLEM?

Why do we have the problems in organization and systems that cause us to lose fees, regardless of our level of computerization? Because we are sales people! We're the deal-makers. We are on the phone, we're hot, we got to move, and we've got to make something happen. We don't have time to plan. We are the shuck-and-jive crowd. We are ready to move, and "Watch out, world. Here I come!"

<u>It's</u> <u>not</u> <u>our</u> <u>basic</u> <u>nature</u> <u>to</u> <u>be</u> <u>organized.</u> If that was our basic nature, if that is what we liked to do and to do all the time, we'd be administrative people or accounting people or IT people. Those people have that controlled organizational ABCD type mind. We don't. We have to work to overcome our weakness in those particular areas, so we can end up getting the results that we want from our desk.

The Mechanic

I've known some people who are top producers who really did not have great sales skills. Most people who succeed do develop good selling skills. It is <u>highly</u> important! But not all. Knowing our business and having an organized business strategy count for a lot, too.

If you give my choice between the super-glib person who likes to talk and talk and talk and is disorganized, and the hard working mechanic who is willing to work a good mechanically-oriented system and is willing to work hard and sell when they can, I'll take the mechanic every time. They will <u>always</u> out-produce the first producer consistently. Obviously, really good producers are organized <u>and</u> have a solid foundation of sound selling skills. You should too.

WHAT YOU MUST LEARN

To effect more placements, we must talk about daily planning, and we must talk about your desk. We are going to talk about a matching system that will literally put more quantity of interviews together for you, and it will put more <u>quality</u> interviews together for you.

Your Desk

Let's talk about your desk. If we are going to produce inventory (that is, either searches or candidates) that is going to set interviews for us and maximize production, *we need to have a desk that supports that system.* We start with a clean desk. That's easy if you are brand-new. But what if you've been in business for a while, and have an incorrect disorganized system?

I have seen the following system increase so many people's production that I say to you if you don't want to spend the weekend trying to clean off your desk, take some lighter fluid and a good ole match and just torch it. Start all over again, and when you do, you'll find that you can take this system starting from scratch and make far more money than staying mired in a mass of paperwork or computer screens.

Stay with me on this! We'll give you dazzling sales stuff later.

IN-BASKET

Upper left part of your desk I want you to put an "in-basket". This becomes a very important part of your desk, as you will see when we discuss maximizing results from the normal day by proper utilization of this tool.

PLANNER

In the center of your desk there is a manila-folder file that you should have DP written on. That file is your Daily Planner. Within that Daily Planner is a list of all the calls you are going to make that day. When you make those calls, it's going to produce inventory and other pieces of business that you are going to have to handle during that day. Your Daily Planner has a list of all the calls.

Take all the candidates and orders that you are going to call on and put them in a stack in the order that you will make the calls right <u>above</u> your Daily Planner. When you get to call three and it says, "Call John Jones at ABC Company", the search assignment form or file will be lying right there in front of you. You do not have to look for it. You are ready to go. You are off and running as far as calling is concerned, and can make the most intelligent informed best call possible.

Tickle File

In the center of your desk, there should be some calendar or "tickle file" to record future phone calls, because during the day things will be said to you like, "Call me in two weeks. We think we might need somebody then." Or, "Call me in two months or "Call me tomorrow".

Can this be computerized? Yes. But transfer the next day's calls that your tickle file brings up in <u>writing</u> to your Daily Planner at the end of the day. Writing things down is <u>commitment</u>! Write it down or lose it.

The calendar or tickle file should be right above your Daily Planner where you can quickly enter future appointments by phone that you arrange, as people request follow-ups.

MPC/ SA FILES

In the upper right-hand corner of the desk are two more files. On one of the files it says MPC and on the other is says SA. Now what are these files for?

MPC means the <u>Most</u> <u>Placeable</u> <u>Candidates</u> file. In this file, I want you to place your top 6 candidates. The SA file stands for Search Assignments. I want you to place your top 6 search assignments. If you do not have enough, put in <u>only</u> those you do have that meet the criteria we'll discuss later. Do not compromise!

These are very important files. I call them your DM. What does DM mean? Decision-Makers. And as you fill them, they will make the decisions for you as to what to do to maximize your income, as you'll see later.

Can these be computerized? Not really. They are decisions you must make. They require judgement, not computerization.

BACK INVENTORY

Next step is a lower right-hand desk drawer, in which you have a set of pendaflex files. In those files you have people or search assignments broken out in areas in which you can retrieve them. I have an entire right-hand desk drawer for candidates and searches.

Why do you need two files on top of your desk? Isn't this redundant, since we have candidates and searches in our file drawer? No. There is a difference between the files on top of your desk, and the lower right hand drawer. That difference is one word. It's a word called Action.

The candidates that we put in the lower right-hand drawer and the searches have been graded by our criteria as being not worth our time to spend actually making calls on. The candidates are active, but not MPC. The searches are open, but not Recruitable. Later, we'll discuss why. They are going to sit in that desk drawer and wait for something to come along, so that we take action on them.

For instance, a candidate is put in that file, and as we create new searches, we keep looking at that candidate and pretty soon "Oh, good! She matched this one!" When she does, we set up an interview and we start into the placement-making process. But other than that, the information lies in the lower right-hand drawer and waits for a matching search assignment to come along. We do not take action specifically to represent her background unless that happens.

Now on top of your desk, in the MPC files are those 6 candidates that have been graded as being so good that we are going to take action on their behalf. That means we are going to physically pick up the phone and make calls trying to find an opening for those people. The reason these are so important is because trying to find something to work on in this business is not difficult. In fact, many of us are awash in a sea of paper or computer files. *The people who are most successful in this business know what to work on and with whom to work.* That is the key.

Even if you put the wrong candidate in the MPC folder one time and you market that candidate and it turns out to be a bust, that's fine. Why? Because you learned something. You learned that type of candidate is not good for the MPC file, and you will put other and better candidates in there in the future.

In a very short time, those files will teach you how to separate the superior candidates and searches from the average ones. That's why you should not computerize what requires judgement. This is critical for you to make a lot of money. That is why you need two candidate and search files.

THE DEAD FILE

There is another critical repository that is not on your desk; it is over in the corner. This is a stand-up three-drawer file cabinet that many people call "The Dead File." Well, we call it the Gold File, because there is a lot of business created out of that file.

In this section we keep inactive files of people, and search assignments that are no longer active. We also call it our "Good luck, Charlie" file where we put people that may not fit our specialty, or whom we have never been able to place. Rather than keep them on our desk cluttering things up, immediately stick them in that file even though they are active, because odds of doing anything with them are very very slim.

How should that cabinet be organized? When you start to create that stand-up file cabinet, it should have exactly the same type of file as your lower right-hand desk. Suppose you have a file in the lower right-hand desk that says "Industrial/Commercial Sales Reps, Midwest". You should have a file in that stand-up three-drawer that says the same thing. You can thus take people out of the active desk and lower right-hand, and move them over to inactive in the stand-up three-drawer file cabinet.

Why call it the "gold file" when there is nothing but a bunch of dead people (or searches) in there? Well, they're really not dead, of course; they are just inactive. They have found a job or taken themselves off the market, or they have gotten a promotion or various things have happened to them. We update their file when we find out they are inactive, and we put them away.

What that file is not for is finding active candidates: active candidates are in your lower right-hand drawer. These files are for marketing and recruiting lists.

Think how it increases production when you are looking for somebody to call, to be able to walk over to a file and pull out 50 candidates with exactly the background that you want to find! Those people will sometimes resurrect themselves and say "Hi. I'm ready to look now". Alternatively, they will be able to refer somebody to you. They know you, you've worked with them, talked to them in the past, and it's a great set of contacts. That's why we sometimes call it the "gold file".

Review of "Dead Files"

Can you computerize your "dead file"? Sure. If your firm has done so, that's the way it is. But one reason you should <u>own</u> this book is to <u>keep</u> reading it when you are experienced. When you are, get in the habit of rummaging through this file occasionally when planning.

An experienced person will frequently find a candidate he or she knows and remembers, but who does not "match the specs". Matching is critical, and the innovative methods we will discuss later will be mandatory. But experienced people (not new) know when to "break the rules". I put together about two deals a year, just rummaging around on other searches. When you are experienced, you will too. Multiply that times your average fee times your anticipated years in our business, and that's a lot of money. If you <u>only</u> rely on a computer, it will be lost!

Emergency Phone Number

We'll cover this under "candidate interviewing", but you will have an emergency phone number <u>other</u> than their current home number and their work number. Thus, you can call and trace them, and find them where they are. This will make you a great deal of extra income.

There is nothing worse than having a recruiting assignment and no one to call, unless it is pulling 95 people out of that file, 94 of whom you can not find. It is a simply a waste of time and added frustration. We'll show you how to avoid this later in this book.

What Next?

We've got your desk organized, clean, and it looks like an executive's desk. Now we are going to go through a normal day's operation and see how we <u>operate</u> that desk. We have your desk looking right, organized and ready to go. Let's see how you <u>use</u> that desk properly to maximize production.

OPERATING YOUR DESK

2

*A*ll right. We have our desk organized, and we are ready to roll. Let's talk about early Monday morning.

Here's a common scenario. If you've been in this business for awhile, it has happened to you. If you're new, here's what <u>will</u> happen…unless you follow this chapter.

We've got that Daily Planner ready. Our files are intact. We have the list of calls. We get to the end of the day, we look at our results, and guess what? We've made a great fifty-call program for ourselves the day before. But when the day is over, we look down and we've completed ten of the calls! What <u>happened</u> to the day?

Have you been told that Daily Planning is the secret to production in this business? Wrong. Sorry. That is <u>not</u> the secret to production in this business! <u>Execution</u> of the Daily Plan is the secret. Unto itself, daily planning is a time-wasting administrative exercise unless you make the flipping calls. You meant to, you put fifty down, and were all set to make this great call program. How do we did we end up with only ten of them actually completed?

THE IMMEDIATE RESPONSE TRAP

It is critical to understand what will naturally happen in this business without a clear and distinct effort, or we will never get through our day. Here we are with a Recruiting Call list and a Marketing Call list. We've decided that we need two Search Assignments today to keep us on our production level. And we are out there calling and on the fourth call, we get that order! Fantastic. Isn't that a great feeling? You're in there marketing, and somebody says, "Let me tell you what I need." You yank out the form, and you think "Oh boy! I've just made a deal! The client has no problem with the fee. It looks like a good assignment. I'm ready to go and make a placement." We feel so

good, we jump up. We run around the office. We bother all the other consultants showing them the search, and get them all off the telephone. And
what do we do?

Well, we walk back to our desk. We put our hands together and we start hunting right in the right-hand desk drawer (or in your computer), which I call our
Wah-Wah. It's so much more fun down there looking for a candidate to fill
that new assignment than it is to go back to that fifth cold marketing call. But
the effect of what is happening is that you are burning telephone time. When
you are doing file searches, that is <u>adminstrative</u> <u>work</u>. That's why we said
matching is administrative earlier. And you cannot do it during sales time or
during telephone time. If you do, you are not going to be effective in your job.

Telephone time is not the time to be looking for a candidate. That's why
you made a list of fifty calls… so you could <u>make</u> fifty calls. I see it every
day. As soon as non-efficient consultants get that new order, they jump down
to that lower right-hand desk drawer or start wandering around on their computer, and we see papers flying out of there or computer screens flickering.
They are going to find that candidate. They will put that match together and
make a placement! But in reality, they are just playing in their Wah-Wah.

Self-Control

To avoid this problem takes discipline and self-control. One of the top companies that I ever worked with generated two million dollar plus in sales.
Every consultant in it with over two years in our business does well over two
hundred fifty thousand dollars in production. And they have only <u>one</u> <u>rule</u>.
Do you know what that is? ***If you are not on the phone making sales calls
during prime telephone time, you are goofing off!*** I do not care what you
are doing; it does not matter.

There was one lady who had joined that firm who had no experience in
recruiting, and no experience in IT, which was her "specialty". Yet she did a
hundred and eighty-four thousand dollars in sales in her first year. Was she a
skilled sales person? Not with just a year in business, she wasn't.

I asked her how she had done so in her first year. She replied, "My manager
gave me some basic training, a book to read, two video series to watch, and a
dictionary of IT terms. They speak in initials, rather than words. Like CICS
and MPS. All the different words that they use are initials, and you have to
know what they mean. CICS means Customer Information Control System,

for example. But I did not know that. So I made some calls. A guy gave me an order and he gave me a list of initials, and I didn't know what they meant. I was looking them up in my directory."

"One of the other consultants walked by — not my manager — and he handed me the phone and said, 'You know, if you don't talk into this thing, you will never make any money.' And I explained to him I was looking up a term I didn't know. He said, 'There are after-hours and lunch time for looking up terms. Now you need to call people and sell them something.' Greatest lesson I've ever learned."

THE PURPOSE OF A PLAN

The reason why we make a Daily Plan is so we can follow it and execute it and call people and sell things. Think of it this way. *You can not make any money while the phone is on the hook.* Instead of making hard productive calls, it is easier to be down in our Wah-Wah, and papers or computer screens are flying out. We are going to find that candidate.

I know a lot of Office Personnel specialist consultants are saying, "Sometimes I have to react quickly to a position opening, or I'll lose it." You are exactly right. All we are talking about is priorities.

When <u>would</u> you burn telephone time to be searching for a candidate in a file? When <u>would</u> you give sales time to do administrative work? When you <u>have</u> to react, because you only have a couple of hours to make the referral or the company is going to hire someone else. Office personnel specialists only: do this. Go get in your file. Find the two candidates you want to refer. Call them quickly and qualify them. Then set the interviews and then do what? *Get back to your daily plan.*

Back To The Future

See, that's what we never do. We never get back. In fact, when I was first trying to learn this concept, one of the ways that I thought about it was to remember a band called "The Beatles". They had a hit called "Get Back". I loved it, and I used that thought in my head every time I got off my Daily Plan. That little song kept playing in my head, "Get back, get back, Larry. You are burning time. Get back to it."

If you get a great search on the fourth call of the day, that is great! It's OK to get up and feel good. Then what do you do? You get back. You get back to call number five, and you quit burning sales time.

You've got to be honest with yourself. Some of us know we are burning sales time; it's just a darn good excuse to get off the telephone. Well, if that's your attitude, maybe you need to look into an hourly-wage job. We need somebody here that enjoys talking to people about solutions to problems, who loves selling this business and working with people. If you're new, have the discipline to force yourself to do your job right now. You will like it a lot once you get good. Be honest with yourself. Get up and feel good! But don't show other people your Search Assignment now unless there's a purpose to be served. Get back to your desk.

Where To Put Interruptions

What do you do with the Search Assignment? That's what your "in-basket" is for. Take the Search Assignment form, and put it in your "in-basket." And I'll say this to you. Don't worry about it for the rest of the day. If that order gets filled this afternoon before you get a chance to work on it later, you should not be working on it anyway! If that candidate you recruited takes a job this afternoon before you get a chance to look at him or her and plan at the end of the day, you don't need to be working with that candidate.

As we go through our Daily Plan and produce inventory (searches and candidates), we toss the results in our "in-basket." That "in-basket" starts to hold our brand new inventory .

MULTIPLE PLACEMENTS

The things we need to look at have a tendency to match! Why? Because we are working in a narrow niche market. Matching similar searches and candidates is where multiple placements come from. You see, when you are recruiting on an assignment and you find a candidate, how many placements can you make? One. If you are marketing a candidate and you get an open assignment for a candidate you are marketing, how many placements can you make? One.

Where do multiple placements come from? How do successful people get six, eight, ten things going at once? It comes from matching the secondary objectives of their inventory production calls. We will cover multiple sec-

<u>ondary</u> <u>objectives</u> in the "Marketing" and "Recruiting" chapters. But briefly, when we are recruiting, we are trying to find a specific candidate to fill a specific opening. But at the same time we are trying to find other candidates who do <u>not</u> fit the opening that we are looking for. We'll toss those people in our "in-basket" and match them against existing assignments when phone time is over to send them on interviews.

When we market a candidate, we market to get Send-Outs (1st interviews), but likewise we market to get searches. Those searches won't always fit the person we are marketing. But we will put them in our "in-basket" and match them with the ones in our files. Then we can send candidates on interviews on that particular new assignment.

Multiple placements are made by matching those search assignments and candidates that you produce during your sales time that do <u>not</u> fit the current thing on which you are marketing and recruiting! That's how important matching is. That's why it is 90% of our income. That is where multiple placements come from.

<u>Only</u> with an organized plan can we make the most high-priority calls possible during the time our clients are the most available. A lot of people say they make night calls; others get in early in the morning or stay later and call other time zones. Well, that's good. But I want you to understand, when we have time to call our clients, we need to <u>utilize</u> that time. <u>Anytime</u> we burn the best telephone time to do administrative chores, we are simply losing money! To us, <u>time</u> <u>is</u> <u>money</u>.

HOW MANY CALLS?

Now how many calls should you be making? I've had that question asked all across quite a few nations. Well, that's not an answerable question. Different people have different talents. Different people are in different geographics and have different marketplaces. And it requires a different number of calls to achieve what they want. Some people have higher goals than others.

The number of calls that is correct is the number of calls that helps you reach your goals. In inventory production. In interviews and in placements.

Yet, even though I can not give you a specific number, there are ratios that work, and we will talk about them later in this book. But the average call for the average recruiter is <u>planned</u> at two-and-a-half minutes. Obviously, I know sometimes you are on the phone for 30 minutes taking a complex search. Sometimes you are on the phone for 30 seconds when you didn't reach the party you were calling. Or you reached the party and there was a quick "I don't need anything today" or "Can you call me tomorrow?" and a hang-up, and it was a minute. What you have to say to yourself is how much telephone time should I <u>prepare</u> for myself? And then how do I utilize it?

Well, you <u>plan</u> to make a call every two-and-a-half minutes. That's right. Two every 5 minutes. Or six every 15 minutes that you are going to be working. So you have about 24 – 25 possible calls an hour that you can make. Will you get through every time? No. Of course not. That is why you plan on such a high number of calls. Top producers have easily 60 –100 call programs during the day and they make a lot of money.

The Result of Poor Planning

The average consultant that produces less than 100, 000 dollars a year spends less than two hours a day on the telephone total time. Yes, less than two hours a day total time. And computerization changes nothing in terms of phone time. Why? *Because they are disorganized, and are easily distracted.* They can't find the paper, they lost the phone number, they must look through multiple computer screens and evaluate. They don't have a plan. They don't have a number of calls in a row where they continue to call one after another. And they spend their day running around the office looking for something to do, and waste hours of production time a day doing it. Or they spend phone time composing pointless e-mails.

The Daily Plan is to help you get through a normal day and <u>achieve</u> the number of calls you need to make.

Now if you try to organize your day but don't give yourself time to do administrative work, you'll find yourself <u>getting</u> disorganized. So let me give you a routine that will help you.

THE ROUTINE AND HABITS

When we are in our "Wah-Wah", we are violating a critical performance rule: you are doing administrative functions in prime telephone time; you are goofing off. So how do we avoid that?

Let's take a normal 8 to 5 work day. Yes, I know there are recruiters that work more hours. But if you are organized and you are effective, you can work an <u>eight</u> <u>hour</u> <u>day</u> and get the amount of work done you need to get done in that work day — if you'll only <u>work</u> while you are there!

Here is a routine for you. Try it. Or if you're new, start this way. Try it for 60 consecutive <u>working</u> days and you'll never know how you lived any other way. And you will be astounded at your results.

BREAKING HABITS

There are set of rules for breaking habits.

One is start the first chance you get. All of us are going to start a diet on Monday. We all have heard that one, right? The rule is to start the first day that you <u>can</u> start, whatever that day is, and get it started.

Rule Two: <u>no</u> <u>exceptions</u> until that habit is formed. So if you are quitting smoking, that means no sneaking one behind the barn. When you are dieting, that means not sneaking the pie at midnight. It means <u>no</u> <u>exceptions</u> until the new habit is formed.

Rule Three: Tell every friend that you know and admire to watch your smoke. <u>Tell</u> <u>them</u> <u>what</u> <u>you</u> <u>are</u> <u>going</u> <u>to</u> <u>do</u>. Tell them "Watch out! Here I come with this new program of planning and discipline." Do you doubt the benefit of this? Well, *Men's Health* magazine found that 80% of men stayed on an exercise program for six months when they bet their friends fifty dollars or more! Sometimes it's a little bit of pressure we need personally, because we don't want to look foolish in other people's eyes if we give up our new program.

Do those three rules. <u>Start</u> <u>today</u>. <u>No</u> <u>Exceptions</u>. <u>Tell</u> <u>people</u> to watch out. I guarantee you that those 60 days in a row of that habit will form the <u>new</u> habit. And, really, life is nothing but a string of habits.

Our habits and how we form them will dictate us where we are going and how to get there.

THE HABIT IN ACTION

So what <u>should</u> be our habits at work to maximize time invested?

Let's say 8 o'clock to 8:30 you need to have time to relax to have a cup of coffee, to say hello to your friends and people in the office, and to prepare for the work day. You may have to make sure your plan is ready to go or look up last-minute phone numbers, or put something in your plan that you produced last night on a telephone call. So 8 to 8:30 is hello, coffee, and minor last-minute preparation.

The Day

Once 8:30 hits, it is time to be on the phone. 8:30 to 11:30 is prime telephone time. All we are doing is spinning the dial, one time after another. Dialing for dollars, they say. Smiling and dialing. (All right. Push the buttons. But it doesn't rhyme.) Keep a mirror in front of you to help you maintain warmth and enthusiasm in your voice; keep a smile on your face, and <u>call people</u>. Talk to them about this wonderful business of recruiting and employment; you are changing people's lives! You are moving people up the corporate ladder. You are increasing people's salary. You are putting them in more stable companies. You are solving corporate problems, and helping the careers of managers. That is one of the reasons I love this business. <u>Enjoy</u> calling people and <u>enjoy</u> talking about it. You will find when you do, you will make more calls!

Now, one of the things you need to be doing at this time is marketing for new clients and interviews. There should be a time set aside to be doing marketing.

Too many of us get distracted by other kinds of calls, and do not realize that <u>marketing</u> is the <u>guts</u> of our business. We will discuss this later extensively in the marketing part of this book. But we must regularly call client companies that are going to pay us.

So 8:30 to 11: 30 is telephone time. Do <u>business</u> in that time. Spin the dial. (OK. Push the buttons.) Take anything that you produce, a candidate, a search, and toss it in your "in basket". I'm going to tell you how to use that later.

11:30 to 12 is administrative. Send resumes, go to the fax machine, or e-mail (if you must), redo resumes, rewrite searches, or do file searches if you <u>absolutely</u> need to find someone in particular.

Why 11:30 to 12? Because that is the least effective time in the morning. Many people go to lunch early, or if you are calling in a different time zone, they are already at lunch. That gives you the necessary time, 30 minutes, to deal with all the administrative things that you produce during the morning sales time. By allocating this specific time, you don't have the excuse that "I have to get off the phone and do this administrative thing first thing in the morning." You've got time set aside to do that.

12 to 1 is lunch. Go have a good one. Sometimes it is good to get away. Long lunches are not known to be productive. Go at 12 to 1, relax your mind and get set for a powerful afternoon, and come back. 1 to 1:15 is afternoon preparation. That is the time to do last- minute chores that help you get pre-pared for the afternoon. Presentations, reviewing daily plans, looking up phone numbers, etc. Get focused!

AFTERNOON

From 1:15 to 4 o'clock, you should be back on the telephone.

Now we are talking about some <u>serious</u> <u>telephone</u> <u>time</u> about five hours and 45 minutes. That gives you enough time for well over 100 telephone calls per day. Are you hitting that number? If you are averaging about 20 or 30 calls, you can see that you are only about 20% effective in your work. ***That's because you are mixing your administrative and your phone time***.

4 to 4:30 is matching. It's matching? Yes! Didn't I say that 90% of our income is based on our <u>ability</u> <u>to</u> <u>match</u> <u>searches</u> <u>to</u> <u>candidates</u>? Well, if that's the case, when do you match? You must have a certain amount of time set aside for <u>specifically</u> that purpose, or you will not get it done. And we do that from 4 to 4:30.

From 4:30 till the end of the day, 5 o'clock or 6 o'clock or whenever you leave the office, is daily planning and administrative. It's getting administrative functions done that resulted from what you produced during the afternoon tele-phone time. Plus, it's making a <u>new</u> <u>plan</u>, getting ready for tomorrow.

Stay In Control

Have you awakened at 3 o'clock in the morning with opening eyes and sweat running down your forehead worrying about this business? That's mainly out of lack of <u>control</u> of our business. You are generally thinking about placements, what you are going to do tomorrow, or where you are headed. One of the greatest things that ever happened to my head and my income was using one rule: that is, ***being ready with my Daily Plan for tomorrow before I left my office today***. We will cover this plan later in this book. But it is the key to control.

OK. Now we have gone through a regular day. We've accomplished our plan. We use the <u>Get</u> <u>Back</u> idea to get back to our plan, and make sure that we <u>complete</u> a Daily Plan. If you do not complete a Daily Plan, you have to ask yourself "Why am I not effective in executing daily plans? I'm effective in making them, but not executing them." After you finish this book the first time, read this chapter <u>again</u> for the answer!

THE "IN" BASKET

So we are at the end of the day, and we have two new search assignments and three new candidates in our in-basket.

Some of us have much more, because we have "exchange partners" who mail us stuff. (I know; some of you do e-mail. Same thing. Leave it to the <u>end</u> of the day.) Some of us may have partners in our office that put things in our "in" basket. But let's say that we have two new search assignments and three new candidates at the end of the day. What do we do with them?

At four'o'clock, we <u>match</u> them. The key is to pull them out one at a time, and see if anything in our office matches it. So we pull out that search assignment and we say, "Is there any way to match a candidate to this order so I can set an interview tomorrow?" And we look where? We look in our MPC folder, because that is where our best candidates reside. Then we look in our lower right-hand drawer for active candidates that might match those orders. If we find one, we take that candidate out and call him tonight or plan on doing so tomorrow (write it down!), qualify him and find out some information that will help us sell the company on setting up an interview. That is called Candidate Qualifying, and we'll cover it later.

<u>Don't</u> mail resumes. <u>Don't</u> send e-mails. <u>Call</u> your candidates, ask them about their backgrounds, and specifically what relates to the search that you are going to refer them on that will help you set an interview.

PROBLEMS IN MATCHING

Let me tell you about those people that have habits that cause them to break down in the matching process. Those are people we call pack rats. These people have piles of paper all over their desk. They have stacks of everybody they have ever seen. I used to have a lady that worked for me who not only had stacks all over her desk, but she had all her drawers full and went down to the grocery store for cardboard boxes. She would keep reams of candidates under her desk. She had people in her desk who were no longer alive. Now that kind of mass of ineffective paper is going to kill your production. You have no chance of good solid matching when you have a pack-rat syndrome.

So you think that's old stuff? You think your computer has solved the problem for you, and this no longer applies? You must be pretty new in the business, my friend, or brainwashed by the software hustlers or techno-geeks. Here's a question. *What percentage of the candidates in your computer files are up-to-date?* Not very high, you say? Pretty low? If that isn't the case, it will be if you're not careful. That computer is your three-drawer file cabinet we mentioned in the previous chapter. It is the <u>Dead</u> file. (Didn't pay attention, did you?) You think the PC is The Answer? Wrong. Read the previous chapter again when you finish this book.

If your manager has computerized, that is fine with me. But please don't make the mistake of thinking that you are now organized as a result. A computer cannot plan and organize your day; only you can do that.

People who jumble everything together in files or in their PC have lost all possibility of finding the right candidate! That's because it is impossible to match two or three searches against eight hundred out-of-date candidates. You'll never get it done. You'll be there till 11 o'clock at night still going through all those pieces of paper or computer screens. And guess what? People who try to do so shake their head, come back to life, and start all over again. Why? Because there is such a mess to be matched, they cannot do it all.

SOLVING THE "PACK RAT" SYNDROME

So how do we stay out of the pack rat syndrome? How do we keep this matching alive? All we want on our desk are active, ready-to-be interviewed candidates, and active ready-to-be filled orders. <u>More</u> is not better in this business. <u>Less</u> is. <u>Only</u> <u>active</u> on our desk. That's why we have the three-drawer stand-up file cabinet that we call the dead file. That is the place to put inactive materials.

I know that you pack rats out there are starting to get worried and begin to shake at the thought of any of that material getting away from you. When you file in that three-drawer file cabinet or your "dead file" computer section, I want you to know that it is not all gone. It's just in a different place. You can go over there and play with it any time you want. And as mentioned, if you're experienced, sometimes you <u>should</u>. But once you get it off your desk, you don't have to look at it every day simply because it is there.

So here's a simple solution. Once a month have a "purge day" on your active desk. Take every search assignment out that is old, and every candidate out that is old.

Now what is "old"? I don't know. That is determined by what desk you work. Obviously, people in the higher professions and dollar ranges last longer on the marketplace than people at lower ranges of dollars, or clerical people. In my business, I take out every search assignment that is two months old, and every candidate that is four months old. But I take them out. Don't go and stick them back in the file on your desk!

Purging Your Desk

Here is what you do. Put those on your Daily Plan for the next day. And call them all. Call every candidate that is old and every search assignment that is old, and <u>requalify</u> them. If they are still active, put them back in your lower right-hand drawer. If they are inactive, put them in the stand-up three-drawer file cabinet. That way you will process inactive stuff out of your desk. Everything you have will be active, and ready to be interviewed or ready to make you placements.

This purge is good for business. Don't think of it as busy work. When you put those people or search assignments on your daily plan for the next day, they update themselves! Candidates refer other people to you. When you call previous potential clients, sometimes the order has been filled. But guess what? They'll say, "I'm so glad you called. Yes, we filled that, but here is what I do need." And they give you a different order you weren't working. Perhaps the original search wasn't very good when you took it, and it is now two months old. Now, the hiring official is desperate and this particular order has become hot, and you are going to be recruiting on it tomorrow. There is a lot of business produced from this purge.

DEVELOP AND EXECUTE!

Here is what I want you to see that is going on now. You are <u>developing</u> a Daily Plan. You are <u>executing</u> every call on that Daily Plan by <u>utilizing</u> effective telephone time. When you <u>produce</u> things during the day, if you must react to them, react to them quickly. Then <u>get</u> <u>back</u> to your plan.

Remember the secret is not in daily planning, but in <u>executing</u> the darn thing. So when you make your daily plans, make it a habit to execute it in it's entirety. As you execute the plan, you will produce new candidates and new orders on a daily basis. Put those in your "in-basket". At the end of the day, you have time set aside to match every single piece of inventory that comes across your desk.

The System That Never Fails

Think about it. You will never ever with this system miss a possible placement. You will evaluate every order and every candidate on a timely basis to see if you can set interviews and make placements. Visualize this new paper entering at your "in" basket. Sometimes I call the in-basket, your "port of entry". That means nothing comes in or on your desk until it passes through the "in" basket, and it gets matched. <u>Don't</u> allow people to stack things on your desk. <u>Don't</u> allow them to throw things on your desk. Make them put <u>every</u> new item in the "in" basket so you can match it, and it goes through your port of entry.

See the flow! Inventory comes into your in-basket. At the end of the day, you match it. If you can set interviews with it, you make qualifying calls to the candidates. You write presentations (covered later), and the next day you <u>make</u> presentations. If you can not match them, you put them in the stand-up three-drawer file cabinet, if you can not use them. Alternatively, they go in the lower right-hand drawer because you are waiting for a match. Or you put them on top of your desk. Candidates may go in your Daily Plan because you are going to make calls on them tomorrow. Or you put them in your MPC or SA files, because they are top candidates or top search assignments and you are going to work on them soon.

As you work on them, you purge monthly and then put them into the stand-up three-drawer file cabinet.

You must see your desk as a processing plant of inventory, not a repository of one. Inventory comes in to your port of entry, gets processed, gets worked, and gets moved out. Utilize this system of <u>processing</u> candidates and searches, rather than a system of stacking of papers or adding computer screens and piling them or putting them all together.

Follow this thought process and plan of organization of your desk. Implement your plan, and maximize your day. By doing so, you will find yourself getting the absolute most out of the industry-specific selling skills you must <u>also</u> have to succeed in our terrific business!

GOAL SETTING: WHAT'S RIGHT FOR YOU?

3

*D*aily planning, desk operations and how we utilize the physical facilities at our disposal to reach the production levels that we want are only the beginning. To be the producer that you want to be, you must understand how to <u>get</u> from point A to point B by <u>goal</u> <u>setting</u>.

Why do you think you hear so much about goal setting? Because that's the way the world works. To get anywhere, *you have to know what it is that you want. You have to know how to bring it about, and you need a plan of action that makes it occur.* So let's lose some of the natural reluctance we all have about goal setting. Let's figure out how it really works.

I want to help you set a production level that starts you down the road to the production that you want, and then increases on a quarterly and yearly basis. We <u>must</u> do so to get you where you want to go!

A major problem in this process stems directly from not understanding the goal-setting mechanism. Since we do not, we set an objective we can not reach, that we know we are not going to reach, and that we do not attempt to reach. And at the end, we say to ourselves, "Well, if I had <u>really</u> worked or had <u>really</u> tried, I probably could have done it". No, you couldn't. It was the wrong goal.

The problem with that approach is it tends to set a "failure syndrome". It has no method of inspiration to help us get where we want to go. Why set goals that are so high you are not going to reach them? I know it's nice to talk around the office and tell other people "Watch out! Look what I'm going to do." But goals by themselves are so much hot air. In reality, your real value is measured by how much money you actually put on the board.

And so it is for yourself. You value yourself based on whether you set and <u>reach</u> goals that are valuable to you. Stay with me for a bit while we talk about reaching production goals.

Goals With No History

What objectives should you set if you are brand new? If you have no past history, you might talk with your manager or other consultants as to the history of the desk that you have taken over. Find out what other first-year consultants have done on an average to get a reasonable figure if you are totally unknowledgeable of what number is realistic. Then use that number to set your first- year goal.

Too High A Goal?

But what if you have a year or two under your belt, and you do have a production history? The biggest mistake that people make in setting goals is trying to set one so much higher than they have achieved.

Let's say you did 100K in your first year, perhaps 35K in your first six months and 65K in the last six months. Now you desperately desire to do 250K. I don't want to rain on your parade. It's great to make that kind of a leap forward, and it is not unusual.

Many good people do it, because they have seriously understood the way this business works. They have obtained a lot of clients in their first year. They have worked hard on their sales skills and their knowledge. They have a base of candidates and clients that allows them to double their production. It could happen. But I have to say that in my experience that is the exception, not the rule.

People who try to double their production level of the last six months must understand that to do that, in general, they also have to double the number of interviews they set. They have to double the number of candidates they recruit. They are going to have to double the number of searches that they are going to take. Those things expend an enormous amount of energy in phone calling if your quality of your work has not <u>also</u> doubled. But while your skill level will certainly improve, doubling is not likely. Improving skills is a long-term process.

On the other hand, you could do more work on your own. Perhaps last year, a lot of your work involved split placements for which you received half-a-fee, and you are now going to work at full-fee. Then for the same amount of placements, you will receive more money. Or perhaps through your skills, you have decided to work on higher dollar-volume fees. Then with the same number of placements your fees will be bigger, because the percentage will be based on a larger salary. Thus through the same effort expended, and the same numbers — candidates, search assignments and so forth —, you can achieve higher production.

A REASONABLE GOAL

But for a rule of thumb, let me say that I believe in <u>increasing</u> your goal, not doubling it. For most of us, an increase of 25% above last year's performance (or the last six months if it is your first year) is appropriate. It is a stretch. We have to do more, and get better. We have to work harder and sell better to reach that goal. But it is definitely attainable.

This presumes, of course, a roughly similar market. If you started in a Recession and now the economy is resurgent, that should be factored in.

When you are starting out and you are trying to improve your productivity, do not compare yourself with anyone. One of the most difficult things for new recruiters to do is to sit in a room of experienced people. They try to do what the real professionals do and say, and pull off what they are able to accomplish. Without the same talents and experience, it can't be done. One of the senior consultants that sits beside you may be able to produce in 15 calls what it takes you fifty to produce. Stop comparing yourself with anyone. There will always be people better than you. But it is only <u>temporary</u>. You will get there. This book, a few other products mentioned here, your manager, and your own hard work and talent will help you to do so.

Any comparisons are only injurious to your own self-image. Take your <u>own</u> production history, your <u>own</u> abilities, your <u>own</u> efforts, and try to improve them. If you do so, you will feel successful, and you will be successful. Drop the idea that you have to measure up to anyone else in this world. It will only hurt you. Improve your skills. Don't try to beat the other guy.

GOALS?

So how are we going to improve ourselves? First of all, you have to understand goal setting and what it is. Goal setting is a highly <u>emotionally</u>-charged state. It is not simply a set of figures you are going to produce on a board.

You must understand the difference between the words "goal", "dream", and "objective". If you understand these differences, then you are going to have a much better chance of achieving your economic desires.

Most of us don't set goals, though we think we do. What do we set? We set objectives. And objectives alone have no power to help us reach the goal when times get tough. And times will get tough.

A Dream

Let's talk about that. What is a dream? Let's define the term. A dream is a vision. It's a thought. It's a wish. It's a fantasy. It's something that exists in the cerebral state. It's not real. It's in the mind. We think about it and we draw up images, visions, ideas, thoughts, and fantasies of a cerebral nature that we may want to achieve. What is the one-word difference between a dream and a goal? That one word is the word action.

A dream becomes a goal only when we put action into that dream, and make plans to actually bring about that dream.

Let's say it this way. Imagine your mind is a manufacturing plant. Then realize that everything you now see, the pen or highlighter you are holding, the paper you are touching, the clothes you are wearing, all began as a thought in someone's mind. Through a series of logical steps, they developed them into material reality. That's what you do when you set goals that you can obtain. The car you are driving today was once a thought in someone's mind. Through a series of logical steps, he developed it or manufactured it into material reality. The difference between dream and goal is the word action. Your dream can become real with the proper action.

Let's see if we can determine the critical steps of reaching your goals, and the difference between the words "goal" and "objective". What's the one-word difference between those two? The difference is the word emotion.

AN OBJECTIVE

An objective is an unemotional step toward the end result or goal. But the goal is an emotional need. It is something we want, something we desire, something that makes us feels good. It is that emotion that powers us, that causes us to work in hard times to overcome obstacles and work around things that come in our way. We try to write a number on a board and make ourselves feel good and say, "We want that." In actually, we don't want that. It's an objective. There is no emotion to it. It doesn't do anything for us.

An Example

Let's take the goal of climbing a mountain. Why do you want to climb mountains? What is the statement that George Mallory made in 1922 after the first serious attempt to climb Mount Everest? "Because it is there". What does that mean? Does that mean Mallory wanted to put his foot on a different piece of real estate? You can go into your neighbor's yard to do that! There is something emotional that causes certain people to overcome the mountain. Suppose you are one of them.

Let's name some <u>objectives</u>. These are <u>unemotional</u> things that you must <u>do</u> to climb a mountain. You have to get in shape. You've got to pick a mountain. You must go out and buy equipment. You have to train and practice, and then go and climb the mountain. Getting all these things together necessary to achieve the goals are <u>objectives</u>. They are <u>unemotional</u> steps on the way to the <u>real</u> goal.

Now once we climb the mountain, we are indeed standing up there. You have seen those pictures of the mountain climbers on TV, where the helicopter swings around behind them and the camera shows them from their back looking out over this breath-taking vista. They are standing with their arms in the air looking out over the land. They have finally told you why Mallory tried to climb the mountain. He wanted to reach the goal.

But it is <u>not</u> for the mountain; it is for the feeling. He climbed the mountain for the emotion of doing it.

Should you climb Mount Everest? No. Mallory died in 1924 on his second attempt. He didn't make it. But you will!

I ask in all of my seminars, "How many of you out there have a production goal for this year?" They all raise their hands. Then I say, "No. You don't have a production goal; you have a production <u>objective</u>".

WHAT DO YOU WANT?

The goal is, *what will that production get you?* What do you want worse than anything? Do you want an educated child? Do you want to buy some life insurance? Do you want to start a retirement fund, buy a new car, a new home? Do you want to move up in the world? Or is it not even material? Do you want to be the number-one recruiter in the office, the number-one recruiter in the region, in the association, in the state? Or do you just want to feel good about yourself when you look in the mirror in the morning and get ready and saying, "I'm doing it! I'm getting there! I'm real, I'm right." That's the emotional goal — NOT the objective of just money!

You must center on what it is you want emotionally. What is it that production level will get you? That is what drives you; the rest of it is just objectives. When you write the number on the board as your goal for next year, that's only the production level that gets you your goal. You need to sit down with yourself and take the time to determine what you really want.

You are in the best business in the world, a business that will allow you to achieve what you desire. It is truly remarkable to realize that if you want to give yourself a raise, all you have to do is work a little harder, learn a little more, get a little better. Be a little more effective, and then you can do whatever it is you want to do with your life.

Most people in the work-a-day world don't have the ability to give themselves a raise. They don't have the ability to knock down thousands and thousands of additional dollars if they become more effective at their job. No matter how effective, no matter how hard-working they are, they will get the same paycheck.

BACK-TRACKING

Once we know what we desire emotionally, let's set a production level that will get that. Let's say that we have decided that for no other reason than you want to feel good about yourself and consider yourself a competent recruiter, you're going to set a first-year goal at $108,000. I picked that only because it equals $9000 a month, an easy number to work with. Perhaps you feel that to be a low number. I do not suggest it to be right for you. Feel free to increase it as you see fit.

Now how do we go about achieving that goal? Just because we write that number on the board doesn't mean we know how to achieve it. Here's how....

Once you set a yearly figure that provides you with the income to reach the real goal, then you work backward to set up the monthly, weekly, and daily benchmarks you need to make sure that figure comes about.

THE BENCHMARKS

Here's a couple of numbers and ratios that you are going to need to work with to be able to understand how to make things happen for yourself. One is an average fee. We need to know what our average fee. Once we do, we know how many placements to make in a year to be able to do $108,000 your first year in business.

The average fee is the total production divided by the number of placements. So let's say an average fee of 7,500 dollars. Your average fee may be five thousand. Your average fee may be fifteen thousand. Keep in mind that if you have a lot of "splits", your fee of fifteen thousand split is seven thousand five hundred. That is not the point. The point is understanding how to reach an average fee.

Once we know that, we have to know our send-out-to-placement ratio. Our send-out-to-placement ratio is the number of placements that we make for the number of interviews set. If we set sixteen interviews and we make four placements, we have a four-to-one ratio. That means we need four times as many face-to-face interviews as we do placements to get where we want to go. Through these two numbers, you can plan your needed activity levels so you can come out with the money you need to progress towards your goal at year's end.

I suggest you also keep track of every candidate that you recruit. Every search assignment that you take. All the presentations you make, whether it is a resume referral or a verbal referral. And the telephone interviews that you set.

Once you keep those, those are the ratios you can use later on to determine if the goals you set for yourself are obtainable. They will help you understand how to plan your daily activity, so you'll know what to do.

Determining an Attainable Goal

First of all, let's give you an example of how to determine an obtainable goal, and whether or not it is obtainable. For example, you have chosen 108,000 dollars in yearly production next year to reach your real goal. This is the objective you set to reach the real goal of feeling competent your first year in business, and gaining the income that you really want. And you have figured an average fee of 7,500 is your average fee. That's with splits and everything. It doesn't matter. Focus on the total amount of production. Then divide it with the total amount of placements, and you have an average fee of 7,500.

Let's assume a closing ratio of eight-to-one. For every eight interviews you set, you make one placement.

How do we figure out the number of face-to-face interviews per month to produce to have made 108, 000 dollars? Well, if you divide 108,000 dollars by 7,500, you come out with 14. 4 placements next year to be able to do 108,000. And you divide that by 12 months, and you get 1.2 placements per month. Now to produce 1.2 placements per month, how many interviews do you need to set to do that? Since you assume an eight-to-one closing ratio, you simply multiply the 1.2 placements by eight interviews and that comes out to 9.6 face-to-face interviews per month that you need to do. 2.4 per week. That's a first interview set every other day.

It is possible that your manager considers eight-to-one too low or too high for your market, your niche, your firm. For a brand-new person, it might well be too low. For others, it might be too high. That's fine. Adjust these numbers in accordance with your manager's experience.

Evaluating Progress

Now ask yourself, is this reasonable? Do I possess the skill? Do I have the experience and the abilities to do 9.6 interviews per month? If I do, I have a realistic goal. But what if you have set only 5.0 interviews per month after three months, and you must double the number to achieve your objectives? Then you have to ask yourself, "Am I really setting myself an obtainable goal that will make me feel like a success? Or an unobtainable goal that will make me feel like loser when I don't reach it?"

It is much better to set smaller goals and <u>reach</u> them. By doing so, you will thus set a success pattern for your career and your life. If you constantly set big goals that are never met, you set a failure pattern, and you never ever have reason to celebrate what you are doing.

FURTHER RATIOS

Let's talk about candidates, and search assignments. Referrals (meaning presentations of candidates to clients) and phone interviews. You must keep track of them, so that you will know those ratios also.

For instance, once you keep track, you will have a certain number of candidates you have to recruit for every interview that you have to set. That ratio may be ten to one, ten candidates for every interview set. Or five to one. The ratio doesn't matter, as long as you know what to do to set that interview.

It takes a <u>minimum</u> of three months worth of numbers to be accurate. One month could be skewed low or high. You can have a poor month, and it does not really tell what your real abilities are. Or you can get hot and really hit the nail right on the head and make a lot of things happen right. Based on that month, it will appear to be a lot easier than it really is.

Keep a full quarter's worth — three full months — of numbers before you try and use this system. Only then will the numbers be truly indicative and accurate.

Know the number of candidates-per-interview. The number of searches-per-interview. The number of telephone interviews that happen. It really doesn't matter what those ratios are, so long as they tell you what you have to do on a daily basis to reach your face-to-face interview goals. But the face-to-face interview goals are the <u>cutting edge</u> of productivity. You can recruit one hundred candidates, and never make a placement. You can take one hundred searches, and never fill one. But it is very difficult for you to set a hundred interviews, and not make a placement!

BENCHMARKS

We are going to keep track of candidates, search assignments, referrals, and telephone interviews. However, we keep them only as a benchmark to tell how to go about setting the interviews that we need to reach the production objective that we have set for ourselves. Only by doing so can we <u>reach</u> the real goal of security, a new home, the financial stability or whatever it may be that you <u>emotionally</u> care about that will drive you. Figure out the number of candidates

and the searches you need to help you to set your daily plan The Daily Plan —
which we will cover — tells you what calls you must plan to be able to reach
face-to-face interview levels you need.

Candidates

For instance, how many calls do you have to plan to recruit three candidates?
I don't know the answer for you. In some niches or markets, not very many,
because there are plenty available. In some, a lot, because there are very few
available. It depends on very different factors. But <u>knowing</u> that allows you
to set down your daily plans. Go back to the last chapter when we talked
about telephone time and it's effectiveness, and how many calls you have to
make. ***That is what daily planning is all about.***

Remember that you have 24 to 25 calls per hour that you can <u>attempt</u>. With
the program outlined in the previous chapter you have about five hours and
forty-five minutes of possible telephone time to reach the numbers that you
need. Keep track. As you historically analyze what really happens, then you
can really plan your day.

Keep in mind that if you decide that you need 22 candidates to set up the
number of face-to-face interviews necessary for you to reach your goals, how
many of them do you have to have a day? One a day. There are 22 average
working days in a month, not thirty. Thirty includes the weekends and holidays and so forth. Be careful that you are using accurate numbers to set up
your quantity.

Connects

On average, I will tell you that most recruiters tell me that they have about 50%
connects. That is, they reach the person for whom they are calling 50% of the
time. Why is that number important? It's important because if we connect with
15 candidates and recruit one, as an example, then how many calls do we have
to plan to recruit one candidate? We have to plan thirty. If we have a 50 %
connect ratio, then thirty calls will result in 15 presentations or contacts. 15 will
be "not in's" or "leave messages" or whatever. So we have to plan thirty to
connect 15, to recruit the one candidate that we really need. That's how we
work backwards from the yearly figure that we need to produce the goal we
want and do it and plan it on a daily basis.

Do Numbers Lie?

These <u>daily</u> <u>numbers</u> are the key to success, not the yearly figure! I'm going to tell you a secret that I think you will enjoy. ***I've never had the numbers lie to me.*** Once I set the numbers using my historical figures and work backward to set my goals, I have not missed more than 10% of my end result! If you try it on a daily and weekly basis, reach your daily activity minimums of candidates and search assignments, you <u>will</u> reach your interviews. If you reach your interviews, the numbers prove that you will reach your placements.

Read this chapter again when you finish this book. Implementing what we have discussed here will allow you to achieve not just your objectives, but your <u>goals</u>... every time.

PROBLEM SOLVING BY ANALYSIS

4

Improving Quality By Analysis

*C*an keeping track of numbers improve the quality of your calls? Yes. What does quality have to do with numbers? There are two sides to numbers in our business.

One is that quantity is history. As we talk about numbers and setting goals, we are talking about history. Yesterday, last month, last year. That's the reason the numbers don't lie. As stated, if you are new, you will have to ask your manager to set realistic objectives for you.

However, if you do your daily work and strive to improve, you will exceed your goals because you get better. The quality of your work goes up. You get better organized. You listen to cassette series every morning while driving to work (www.larrynobles.com). You read books and watch videos. The owner of your firm may decide to bring in a professional industry trainer. You get new clients. You get better in your sales skills. You understand your niche better, and learn where to go and who to talk to. As those quality items increase for you, the same numbers produce more money.

Analysis

But it takes more than that. It takes conscious analysis!

Let's talk about quantity a bit, and see if it can help us in the area of quality.

One great thing about analyzing numbers is that it tells you where you can focus your efforts to get better results. How can numbers help you to improve the quality of work that you need to do? Numbers are an indicator of various performance problems that you will need to address.

Let's say you are looking over your numbers for the past year and you are trying to plan next year. One of the questions that you should ask is, "Where do I need to improve my skill base to make sure I am doing better work next year?" Look at the numbers. The numbers are indicators of areas of weakness that can be strengthened through various techniques.

We will cover how to develop or improve skills in each of these areas in later chapters.

Low Inventory

Let's say you have low inventory (candidates and search assignments), and few interviews. If I saw a consultant with very little inventory being produced and very few interviews being set, then I would say that person has low marketing and recruiting skills. They simply are not producing enough inventory to produce enough matches to set interviews.

Alternatively, it is possible that the consultant is simply not making the phone calls. Those areas need to be checked; quality or quantity? Number of phone calls being made is quantity. Low marketing or recruiting skills or techniques is quality.

High Inventory, Low Referrals

Let's say you have high inventory (a lot of candidates and searches) but few referrals, meaning presentations to clients. That person has low matching skills. The problem may be an inability to see what candidates fit what orders. Or he is not asking the right questions of the candidates or clients to know what matches should be made.

Alternatively, he may just not be aggressive enough in focusing on <u>interviews</u> as the key to success. He may be overly-selective in presenting candidates.

High Inventory, but....

Let's say someone has high inventory. She is good at getting candidates and search assignments. She makes a lot of referrals. But few interviews result. That consultant probably needs to improve presentation skills when she calls the company to present the candidate. She is not doing a good job in convincing or closing to set date and time for these people to get together.

Or perhaps what is needed is better matching skills if the response from the client is consistently "no". Again, we'll cover solutions to these problems in later chapters.

High Interviews, but.....

How about high interviews? I have seen consultants that obtain an awful lot of searches and candidates and set a lot of interviews, but nothing ever seems to happen. One consultant that I was working with had set thirty-four con-secutive interviews and made <u>one</u> placement! When that occurs, the person has low <u>qualifying</u> and <u>matching</u> skills. They produce a lot of inventory and they put together a lot of interviews. But nothing ever happens. No offers are made. No placements occur.

That means they have not qualified a search well enough to know what the company is looking for. They have not qualified the candidate well enough to know what the candidate is looking for, or maybe what the candidate is really good at doing. And they can not match those two together to make things really happen.

It is pretty easy to get people to get together and talk. The skill of having them complete the cycle with a hire and a start date is a critical function. Check the qualifying and matching skills when you have high interviews, but few offers come of it.

It is also possible that Follow-up after Interview with Client is weak. See chapter on this subject for specifics.

Interviews and Offers, but.....

Now on the other side of the fence, what if you have high interviews and you are getting the offers, but still have few placements? You may be working with low closing skills. This indicates an inability to get the people closed on accepting the offer. Sometimes that relates to qualifying problems, in that we did not know what the candidates wanted in the first place. In that case, no amount of closing will help.

It is also possible that the source of your candidates is a problem. If you are pulling candidates off the internet or through responses to your job postings there, you can count on a lot of "turndowns". You are not the only one they are dealing with! Or are they poor offers? Selecting the Search could be the problem.

Actually, this is a complex scenario. For the total answer involving all possibilities, see the chapter in Steve Finkel's book *"Breakthrough!"* entitled "From Good to Great!" which addresses this entire subject more fully.

However, low closing skills or fear of closing are certainly also options. The fear of giving these people the information that is needed to make the correct decision about their careers and to <u>direct</u> them properly needs to be considered.

To Determine Problems.....

Numbers can indicate where we need to focus our efforts to improve skills. You should go back on a quarterly basis and go over your numbers. Compare to past quarters to see if there is an increase or decrease in your numbers or in ratios. If you have gone from a nine-to-one closing ratio to a five-to-one ratio, you have become considerably better in your skills. It means you are making more money if you are still setting the same number of interviews. Go back and see if there are any areas in which you are slipping.

VETERAN'S SYNDROME

This works especially well for many of the experienced consultants who have difficulty with what I call the "Veteran's Syndrome". There is a cycle through which many go in this business. In the beginning you are trying so hard to learn the business that you are really are consciously incompetent. You <u>know</u> you do not know what is going on, but you are working hard to improve that.

Then you begin to learn the game. Your skills improve. You begin to understand how things occur, and how to make them happen, and you begin to be good at what you do. Pretty soon you have said something so many times that it comes out of your mouth like silk. You can say the same thing over and over again without even thinking about it. And you begin to make placements like it is second nature to you. You keep numbers, you analyze, you plan, you study videos, you read books, and listen to audios. You become competent.

But slowly, you quit doing what made you that way. Your numbers and billings slip. You don't know what is going wrong. You seem to be doing the same things. But nothing seems to be occurring any more. That's what we call the slump or the "Veteran's Syndrome".

The numbers will help you. If you will go back and compare past numbers and ratios, it will point to areas where you have become sloppy or areas where you are not paying attention to the basics.

Somebody said to me one time, "Why do we have to continue to review the basics? Why do people learn the basics over and over again in this business?" It's not that people forget the basics. It's that they <u>get</u> <u>away</u> <u>from</u> <u>them</u> by being a veteran. There is much much more to this business than "basics". Those who say there is not — and believe it — are shallow in their thinking. But without them, you have a major problem. When you have a slump, go back and analyze. Keep copious records on yourself, even if your manager does not.

It is one of the greatest indicators of performance problems and will help you to turn things around when times are tough. Knowing and analyzing your numbers will allow you to produce the amount of activity and money you want, consistently, year-in and year-out, throughout a long and successful career.

GUIDING YOUR SUCCESS: THE DAILY PLAN

5

*N*ow to be able to implement the previous chapters, we must be able to operate a Daily Plan that gets us where we are going. Let's talk about daily planning and what it really is.

I want to say this; daily plans are highly misunderstood. A Daily Plan is not a form. People keep calling me and saying, "Larry, do you sell daily plan forms? What daily plan form do you use?" Don't worry about the form. If you must have one to help, Steve Finkel has a very good one for sale. It is explained in Chapter 6 of his book *"Breakthrough!"*, which I highly recommend.

However, an effective daily plan can be done on a yellow legal pad if it is done correctly. A form is only a way for you to organize your thoughts and put things down so you can remember how to use them. If you want to make or buy something formal after really understanding the <u>order</u> of planning, feel free to do so.

A Daily Plan is also <u>not just a list of calls</u>. Too many people feel a Daily Plan is simply a list of marketing or recruiting calls. Even that is more that most people do, though few will admit it. Many people list only the calls in which they are going to make a placement, and then they write down a note saying "market candidate tomorrow" or "recruit for ABC Search". They don't write down the companies that they are going to call. They don't write down their phone numbers. All they write down is an instruction to themselves. Well, I'm sorry. You have to look up those phone numbers sometime, and guess what? You are going to take telephone time or write them down tomorrow, because you did not do it during planning time today.

So What Is It?

A daily plan is a fully-planned and completely laid-out sales approach that you execute the following day that gets you the objective you are looking for. It's not just a list of calls. It's not just a form. To maximize production, you must see it as a daily operational mode that causes your desk to perform.

Running a desk is like running a company. That desk has everything a small company would have. It has a profit-and-loss ratio. It has a fixed-expense ratio. It has operating expenses. It has a CEO at its helm — you sitting in that chair — who decides how hard the company is going to work. How many attempts to market the product or service are you going to make? How hard are you going to sell when you get somebody on the line? What is the correct ratio of marketing and recruiting calls? How many different types of calls are going to be made?

If you see it in that respect, if you have always said to yourself, "I could run a company", you have the opportunity to do so. Your first step is to formulate a plan.

Formulating the correct operational mode will absolutely bring about whatever production level that you want, and whatever profit or income level that you choose. You have the ability to do so.

Let's talk about that plan, how it is an operational tool, and how it helps you put those numbers together to help you reach your goal.

THREE LEVELS OF PLANNING

Level One

A Daily Plan has three levels to it. Level One has <u>one</u> objective, and that is to make placements. Level One is calls you write down at the top portion of your daily plan, which refers to *follow ups on existing activity*. It's defined as calls that move placements <u>forward</u>. So any call that occurs after the first interview has been set is a follow-up on existing activity, and belongs in Level One.

Let's say that on Tuesday you set a telephone interview, which has started existing activity. Yes, I understand that face-to-face is what we've said is the real activity. And you are right. But telephone interviews are so close to real activity that they belong in Level One. We must treat them with the importance that they deserve. Too many of us think of a telephone interview as something that is <u>going</u> to happen. We think it is two people who are going to get together to know each other before they <u>really</u> get together. No. It is an interview.

Level One may be defined as any call that exists <u>after</u> the first interview has been set. It can be a call as simple as a company calling you saying, "I had so-and-so coming in on Friday, but I can't meet with him." The rescheduling for Monday by you is Level One. Even though the interview has not happened yet, it is clearly a Level One call, because it's a call that exists after the first interview has been set. It has not happened, but it has been set.

Level Two

OK Let's talk about Level Two. What is the objective of Level Two? The objective of Level Two is singular: ***to set an interview today.*** Too many times we just call around and talk to candidates and companies, and kind of see what happens. We have to <u>make</u> things happen. A strong focus on setting up interviews is the way to do it!

As mentioned earlier, there are only two phone calls that set an interview. Under Level Two "I am going to set an interview today", you will plan to do both.

First Type – Level Two Call

Remember what is the most frequent way that we set interviews? Matching! We set more interviews by matching a candidate to an existing assignment, and then calling and making a presentation on that person. Under Level Two is matching. How many matching calls can we make tomorrow?

When you are planning, you will see how important it is to stop at the end of the day and do your matching out of your in-basket. Where do you think Level Two calls come from? They come from doing a matching of new inventory on a daily basis. "Inventory" is new candidates or new searches. No new inventory eventually means no new interviews! Every day you have to try for one matching call, so you can try and set up an interview.

Some consultants develop a pattern of low interviews, and end up setting only three or four interviews a month. It is probable that their <u>focus</u> is wrong! Ask yourself, "is it because I'm not planning for matching at the end of the day, and I am therefore not making matching calls <u>every day</u>?"

Think about it. Twenty-two working days in a month. If you only make one matching call a day, then you are going to have twenty-two opportunities to set that interview. If you are only fifty- percent effective, then you are going to set 11 interviews a month. A five-to-one ratio means you are making over two placements a month. That will probably yield the money you are looking for. So under Level Two, the first step is to set and plan as many matching calls as possible.

Second Type — Level Two Call

Secondly, under Level Two, there is another matching call. It's what I call the resume follow-up call. In many instances, we call and make a matching call, and the person will not set an interview. All they want to happen is for us to send a resume. And so we do. We fax, mail, or e-mail it and wait one day after arrival of resume. Then we call, follow-up on the resume, and see if we can get these people to meet our candidate. That is still a matching call. We are still matching a candidate to an existing opening. But we are follow-ing up on a resume.

In general, sending resumes on a wholesale basis or even immediately upon request is to be avoided. You do not want to become a "paper-mill operator" or, even worse, a "spam merchant". We will address how to avoid this later in this book. But there are limited conditions when this is indicated. Those limited circumstances are what we are addressing here.

The only main difference between these two calls is the first-type Level Two call is matching the person with no mention of the resume. In the second-step matching call —"the resume follow-up"— they do have the resume, but it is still a matching call. The two first calls are both matching calls. One is called a matching call, and the other is called the resume follow-up call.

Third Type — Level Two

What is another type of call that sets up an interview? The Marketing the Candidate Call! That means we are going to call companies that we do not know have a particular opening. Then we are going to market an individual to them, and try to motivate them to see that person. If they do, we set an interview.

It is critical to plan enough calls under Level Two. Without doing so, nothing will happen! There are only three types of calls to be planned on Level Two.

These different types of calls intend to set an interview today and reach our objective. One is matching. Two is resume follow-up. And three is marketing. Focus on Level Two, trying to set up an interview today!

Level Three

Level Three of your Daily plan is Inventory Production. I realize that term is misleading as we use it here, and requires an explanation.

Inventory Production means both marketing and getting search assignments, and recruiting and getting candidates. However, that is not targeted enough to help you reach your organizational and operational goals. ***The objective of Level Three is to set an interview tomorrow.***

We are going to do that by marketing and getting assignments, and by recruiting and getting candidates. We may also do that by purging our files and calling existing candidates to see where we are. We may re-qualify old orders. We may do candidate re-qualifying of those who are not at the "purge" stage, to see where they are. And we are going to use the inventory produced to set interviews "tomorrow".

Set Interviews Tomorrow?

What do I mean, "set interviews tomorrow"? Why is <u>that</u> an objective, rather than just "producing inventory of assignments and candidates"? Because if we use the third objective of Level Three, the objective of setting an interview <u>tomorrow</u>, it makes us think "What is the best thing I can do tomorrow that will produce the inventory that will allow me to set an interview tomorrow?"

If we decide that we need to market and we want to set up an interview <u>tomorrow</u>, where are we going to market? We are going to market in that area in which we <u>already</u> <u>have</u> <u>existing</u> <u>candidates,</u> so we do not have to go out and find them.

Suppose you have five good candidates in a particular area. You go out and market in that area, and pick up two new search assignments. You now have two orders and five candidates. Success! You have an opportunity to make one or more matching calls <u>tomorrow</u> to try and set interviews.

But if you just go out and market for <u>any</u> opening, regardless of whether you have any candidates or particular inventory in candidates to match that, all you are doing is producing inventory. And you will see no matches because of it.

Level Three — when you say "set an interview tomorrow" — means to market in the area in which you have existing candidates. It also means recruit in an area in which you have existing search assignments. That will help you set interviews <u>tomorrow</u>.

Two Objectives of Marketing

You have probably noticed something. We have marketing listed on two levels. We have marketing listed on Level Two. And we have marketing listed on Level Three. Now what is the difference?

The difference is the <u>objective</u> of that marketing call. Level Two marketing is very targeted. We may be only making ten calls, because we have only one candidate that we know is committed to move and highly in demand in the marketplace. We may know ten companies that can use that person now, even though we do not know whether they have any openings. We will almost certainly have spoken with the hiring official previously. But when we call, our objective is to close hard, ask for the interview, and try to get the person to see this candidate or talk to them by phone.

In Level Three there is a different objective. In Level Three, we are using a candidate that we hope will produce search assignments for us. One is a very targeted, "I want to produce an interview", which is Level Two. The other one is not quite so targeted in that our major sub-intent is to produce new searches in a given area. That is Level Three.

THE UPWARD FLOW

Now look at these levels very closely. Level Three produces inventory that at the end of the day. With your organizational skills, you match. <u>The next day</u> those go up to Level Two into the matching call. Through your presentation skills, you make a matching call and you set an interview. Now you have moved it up to Level One. And you make follow-up calls on that interview until you make a placement.

You can see this is not just a list of calls, or some form. It is an <u>operational</u> mode. If done on a daily basis, it will allow you to succeed. It contains all three portions of our job.

They are done <u>every</u> <u>day</u>. If you do not do Level Three every day, you will not produce the foundational inventory that you are looking for. But when you do plan and produce the inventory, that creates the matches that comes out of the top of this form in production dollars.

Every day, <u>all</u> <u>three</u> <u>levels</u>. Implemented properly, it will produce more activity than you can even imagine. This single thought frequently triples activity levels and production levels, by using the three levels of daily planning on a daily basis.

BITA

Let me leave you with one last thought on numbers and maintaining activity levels. There is a critical number you must always know; we call it a "BITA". "BITA" stands for Balls In The Air. What that means is how many possible projects can you keep in the air at one time? If we only have one interview going, we can only make one placement. More BITA equals more placements.

I saw a juggler juggling balls once, and I thought, "How many can he keep up there?" Well, guess what? That is what we do! We define one ball in air as one possible placement. It's not an interview. It's a project.

Projects

For instance, you have one search assignment and three candidates interviewing. You do have three interviews, but you have only one project. It can only result in one placement. Let's say you have one hot candidate. And you have that candidate interviewing with three companies. You have three interviews, but guess what? That person, even though they get three offers, can only accept one position. So only one fee can result.

A <u>Ball</u> <u>In</u> <u>The</u> <u>Air</u> is a project that can result in a single fee.

Now these are real-time numbers. These are numbers we are looking for every day. What you must do is set yourself a specific number of projects that you will keep going at one time. Let's say that number is four. You have promised yourself that you will keep four projects in the air at all times. This tells you on a daily basis what to do. You are no longer working with historical numbers. You are working with "now" numbers.

Let's say you have four BITA's on Tuesday, and you know on Friday, you have an answer to an offer. Guess what is going to happen to your "BITA" number on Friday? It's going from four to three. I don't care that the person accepts, and you put a 12 or 25 thousand dollar fee on the board. Congratulations! But you still are down to three. Even if the great things happened, <u>you</u> <u>need</u> <u>another</u> <u>BITA</u>.

You still must, between Tuesday and Friday of that week, start a new project so you can <u>keep</u> it at four.

Why is this important? Let me ask you when is the time you love this business the most? When you are hot! That is when you have more going than you know what to do with. You are a deal maker, and you can't wait to get to the office and call the next client or candidate!

And when might you get depressed? It's when you have nothing going, and you looking at fifty gut-busting cold calls just to get something going.

Remember the "BITA" number. It will level out your production. It will always keep you high. It will always be interesting. You will <u>always</u> love this business on a daily basis, because you <u>always</u> will be on top of the world. Constantly keep the correct number of projects going. Never let your projects get to zero.

You now have the daily, weekly and monthly operational mode you need to reach your yearly goals. Re-read these first chapters repeatedly, even though Planning, Goal-Setting and Organizing is not your idea of thrilling reading. It will work for you. It always does, when combined with skill. Just go and do it.

FOUNDATIONAL MATCHING

6

*W*hat is your niche? Do you have one? Is it the right one? Too broad? Too narrow? Have you thought it through? Most people in our industry evolve into a niche, but unless you have done so logically, it may be costing you a lot of money. If you're new and you're not careful, it will for you as well.

Even if you have the perfect niche market, how do you "match" candidates with clients? Most people in our industry, even the most successful, have never really been taught to match properly. When you first started, how much time did your manager spend on this subject? My guess is .... not much. And yet doing this properly will have a significant effect in lowering your send-out to placement ratio, thus resulting in much more production. And it will do so with no additional effort. Let's take a hard look at these two critical areas.

THE NICHE

Specialists are always are going to make more money for the same amount of effort than generalists. Why? Because their production and inventory tends to match more.

Let's say that you work healthcare and you decide to go out and recruit hospital Chief Financial Officers\Controllers on Monday for a specific search. You are a good recruiter. You recruit three of the top Controllers but only one matches the search. On Tuesday, you are marketing and market a Director of Nursing. You don't set up an interview. But you have an excellent presentation, good sales abilities, and you wind up with a new search for an Emergency Room Supervisor Nurse. The problem is that even though you are good at inventory production, none of those Controllers can take that ER Supervisor position. That's what it means when our inventory is not matching.

Specialists tend to make more money because they are working with a particular type of person. Let's say all they recruit are mechanical engineers. The only area of industry that they work is mechanical engineers. Thus, they have a greater chance of their inventory matching.

OVER-SPECIALIZING

Can you over-specialize? Yes. You can over-specialize to the point that you jeopardize your career or your income, because you are working too narrow of a market.

When I came back from working as Director of Training for a major franchise in New York, I rejoined my original firm in Tulsa. I started working only exploration geologists in the oil and gas drilling market. All I worked with was geologists that explored the oil and gas field. All I talked to was exploration geologists, and the only people I marketed to were exploration geologist managers. Every search that I took and every candidate that I recruited were exploration geologists. A perfect niche, right? Wrong! They still didn't match a lot of the times because I had a shallow-drill person and my client wanted deep-drilling areas. There were still more areas of experience differences in the specific basins that they worked that caused my people not to match. But I thought I was well set even though some of them did not match, because I was working that specialist area.

In the early eighties, the OPEC cartel thought they were going to glut the market with oil. All the oil companies in Oklahoma quit hiring. Guess what happened to my business? Yes. It went south badly! If I had also worked with accounting or sales within the oil industry, I could have used that inventory to move to other industries. But I was out of the luck.

You must remind yourself and evaluate your niche as follows: "When I specialize, I must specialize enough that the people that I recruit and the search assignments that I take tend to match. But I don't want to specialize in such a narrow area that it can die on me completely and I cannot move my inventory elsewhere".

SO WHAT IS BEST?

Let's take office support people as an example, and see if we can look at a way of specializing, yet not over-specializing. Let's say you want to spend a lot of your marketing and recruiting time in the legal field. You become an expert in legal. You get to know all the legal attorneys. You get to know who are the good law firms and who are the poor ones, who people want to work for and for whom they do not. You get to know most of the legal secretaries; you get to tell the difference between a commercial legal secretary, and a bankruptcy or a litigation secretary. You get very knowledgeable, and you market and recruit in that particular area. Then a lot of your people tend to match a lot of the openings that you get, and you can easily set interviews.

But even though you specialize there, it does <u>not</u> mean you have to give up dealing with other office-support types. You should also work with book-keepers, executive secretaries, some variety of entry-level IT, etc. within legal. But also you should work somewhat outside the field, because these types of candidates are useful in other areas. You are a generalist who <u>works</u> like a specialist.

What I would do is select a specialty <u>within</u> my broad specialty, and tend to do most of my work in that area. If you work in IT, you may do most of your work in data base analysts. Even though you specialize in that, you can still work the programmers, the systems analysts, and so forth. In that way, you still get the advantages of the matching process without the disadvantage of being so overly-specialized that some client or industry can stop hiring and really hurt your business.

WHAT IS CORRECT MATCHING?

There are two levels of matches that I feel that most of us make. Those two have been made for years, and then we make a referral. That's not good enough. I want to give you two other levels of matches to add to it. The <u>four</u> matches literally tell us the health of our placement before we ever make the first phone call. You can project with these principles whether or not you have put a good placement together. Not only will it tell you the health of your placement, but if you cannot answer all of these principles, it points <u>directly</u> to areas in which you lack knowledge about either the candidate or the position.

Without this knowledge, you are in danger of not having enough information to cause the placement to happen. That's right…to <u>cause</u> the placement to happen. I want to say this to you: placements are made by the skills of the consultant. Period.

Now, the facts are that we provide far better candidates than can be found by clients or HR departments on their own. We find candidates that are precisely evaluated, tailored to the specific position, and that they would <u>never</u> see in any other way. But let us put that aside.

Suppose quality <u>were</u> equal. Why do you think that your candidates would look better than the ones that walk in off an ad or internet posting? They do so because of your ability to prepare them for what they're going to encounter in the interview. Yes, other candidates who walk in off an ad or job posting may be equal to yours (though it is most unlikely). But all they know is one quarter of a small piece of newspaper or computer screen that says "We want this"; they don't know what to talk about, they don't know the history of the company, they don't know the problems involved in that job, they don't know what area of their background to emphasize. Thus your people <u>look</u> better because of your skills. That is why I say, placements are made by the skills of the consultant. Matching is a <u>critical</u> skill!

Many people fall into the "wishing and hoping" stage of consulting. Sending a resume, wishing and hoping that the company likes it, setting an interview and letting these two fine people talk to each other, wishing and hoping that they'll fall in love. That's not the way this business works. It works because we match candidates to orders correctly. We learn what it is that causes companies to hire and candidates to move. Once we know that, then we are set up to really understand and execute the placement-making process.

FOUR MATCHING PRINCIPLES

Let's talk about those four matching principles. What is it that we match when we first look at a search assignment and a candidate?

The General Pass

What are we first looking at? I call it the <u>General Pass</u>. The first pass where we look at this and this and this, and we say, "Yeah, this one's possible — I can put this one together."

What do we look at in the General Pass?

<u>Skills</u>. We look at the candidate's skills versus the company's job requirements. In other words, we're looking to see if we have a mechanical engineer and is the company looking for a mechanical engineer? Do the skills of

the candidate, the things that they have been doing in the industry, match the requirements that the company gave us to fill? Candidate skills versus job requirements is the first step in the General Pass. Do we have a possible placement here?

Now there are other areas besides just the skills and the job requirements under the General Pass that we will need to match. We need to match the experience level. Just because they have the right skills, they may be a two-year person and our client is looking for a ten-year person. Thus, the candidate does not have the seasoning or experience to pull off some of the projects or duties inherent in the job, even though they happen to have the basis of the skills our client is looking for.

We also need to match the education level. Is it appropriate? In some instances, a customer will want a Ph.D. because they are doing research. They may require an engineering degree or a technical degree. Or they will take someone with no degree, depending upon the requirements of the job. In that instance, a person need not have a degree, but must have appropriate education for the position that we are trying to match them to. Degree or no degree is not the entire question. It's appropriate experience level for the position trying to be filled.

Obviously, we also need to worry about the salary level of the person. Even though they may have the experience level and the education and the right skills, can our client afford this person? Is the salary area an issue?

In some instances, it depends how you qualified the candidate as to whether or not you could make this match. Too many times you may have a fifty thousand-dollar job and a fifty thousand-dollar candidate and not put them together. Why not? Sometimes your candidate would move laterally in money to get that job without hesitancy. It would advance his career in a location he wanted, and present a challenge he wanted. However, by failing to qualify the candidate well enough, you may make the wrong judgement call. When in doubt, present the opportunity to the candidate! Call the candidate and say, "Here is the situation I have. What do you think?" Give them the right to say no, rather than saying no for them.

Also, depending on the position, you may want to think about the amount of travel involved. When you are talking about travel, find out about not just the percentage of travel, but the specifics. For instance, does "fifty percent travel" mean a day gone and a day in, a week gone and a week in, a month in and a month out, six months overseas and six months home? All of those are "fifty- percent travel", but you need to know more than just the percentage to make an accurate match.

If there is no relocation involved, how about the length of commute? Some candidates won't cross town, and some won't work downtown. Or they are on the east side of town, and may refuse to commute to the west side.

In my particular instance, relocation is a frequent situation. We have to talk about where the person would go. This includes where preferences are and where home is, where their parents may live, and where they went to school. We must know if we have an area of the country that is acceptable to those people.

So we are going to do the first pass of matching skills vs. job requirements. In addition to that, we match the experience level, the education, the salary, the travel, and the relocation. Now that is what I call the General Pass match, or "is it possible"? Is this the right person? Can they do this job? And does everything pretty much match?

IMAGE MATCH

If that is the case, then we want to move on to the second match. What else do we match, in addition to the technical aspects of the person and the company? Sales recruiters and office support recruiters match this much more than technical recruiters. Yes, it is an image match. Some people call this "chemistry" or "personality". I would like to call it an "image", because each corporation has a corporate culture or a corporate look about them.

Believe me, if that person doesn't come in there and look like that corporation, they can interview great, but they are going to have a hard time getting hired "because they don't seem to fit". A lot of candidates that fit perfectly on a resume do not fit at all in person.

You have to know what the corporate culture of your company is. That is why I always encourage people to visit their clients if possible, because they begin to see that. (Note: this means clients, not customers or prospects! See Client Development chapters for clarification.) What do I mean by corporate culture or image? Have you ever heard of the IBM image? These are images that you get when you say those words, that kind of corporate three-piece-suit candidates you are looking for. In the accounting field, they talk about the big 6 image....or they used to, anyway.

An Industry Example

In Oklahoma, we have two different kind of oil firms, and they hire two different types of people.

We have one type of person where the rich oilman has sent his son out to Harvard. They may have had an oil background to start with, but they come back in three-piece-suits all ready to run an oil company. Then we have the good ole boys down the street that have the pointed cockroach-killer boots and belt buckles and their big hats. They are oilmen too. And they are very good at what they do.

But they do not mix. One type of person would not fit well in the other's environment. They would never get hired; I don't care how good their resume looked. If you didn't understand the appropriate images and sent the wrong one too many times, you might lose the client.

THE "PLAYING GOD" SYNDROME

One thing you have to consider is whether you are using your image to screen people out. You are not hiring for you. You are referring them to someone else. Your idea of what a good image is like and their idea of what a good image is like could be totally different.

I remember one time that my boss had me interview an engineer that came into the office. I was going to interview him and send him straight over to the hiring authority, who was just across the street from us. It was a high level and important position in the company. And this guy came in, and I was on the floor! I mean this guy had hair that was too long to be short and too short to be long. He had these coke-bottle glasses that make your eyes look great big. He had a plaid shirt and striped pants. He walked like…well, let us say that he was amazing. None of his answers matched any of my questions. When he left, I had tears in my eyes, I was laughing so hard. I would never send him to my top client. But since my boss wasn't there and I had to do the job for him, I sent him across. I couldn't wait until the next morning when my boss got in, and I could tell him about this candidate that he sent to his top client.

Came the morning and I said, "Your engineer showed up yesterday." And my boss said, "Yeah, I know. He got over there and interviewed quite well. He accepted the offer yesterday." I said, "What? He accepted the offer last night?" He replied, "Yeah. They put him in a room, and wouldn't let him leave until they concocted an offer for him, because they wanted to make sure they got him." The guy had three important patents in their area of product. No matter what I thought of the guy's appearance or demeanor, <u>they</u> could not have cared if he had two heads. He was a great engineer to them, and my prejudices could have cost me a sizable placement, and someone else — the candidate — a good career path. What is the moral? Be careful in how you judge the requirements on image that your companies give you.

Let's say that somebody says to you, "I want someone that's 'promotable'". Now what does that mean? Do you know how to recognize a promotable person for a particular corporation? Here's the point: what you think is promotable and what the company thinks is promotable could be two completely different things.

So here's the rule, when it comes to Image Matching: ***when in doubt, make the referral***. This is especially true when you are new, or dealing with a new client, even if you are experienced. That referral will tell you whether or not you're on target for the word "promotable". And it will <u>take</u> you a few referrals to a particular company before you find out the type person that they hire, until you learn what to refer or how to judge those images that the client is giving you. Be sure to make notes on the client file. A short pencil is better that a long memory!

Now those two matches are foundational. They are critical. But there is more to this business than "foundational". Let's address what comes next.

BEYOND BASIC MATCHING

7

*T*hese two basic matches in the preceding chapter are what most recruiters make. They match the candidate skills versus the job requirements. If that works and all the other things are in line, they match the image they think is the right type of person. Then they make the referral in the hopes that the company will like what they see. Well, that's not enough. That only tells us whether or not to make the referral.

There are two more matches - the advanced area - match three and match four of this area that will help your production significantly, and will tell you how to make the placement. It'll tell you the odds of getting an offer or an acceptance. If you can make these two matches, it will tell you the health of your placement before you ever make the first phone call. Moreover, it will point directly to those areas of knowledge you need to acquire before you get to the end of the placement, because at this point you may not know enough to cause the placement to happen.

So let's go on to Number Three, and talk about the area of matching that will tell us about the placement rather than just about the referral.

MATCHING : PRINCIPLE 3

One of the things that we have to ask ourselves is "Why do companies hire people?" Why? Because they need somebody to solve a particular problem that results in making or saving money for the corporation. Everybody in a corporation only has one of two jobs: they either make the company money or they save the company money. If they can't do one of those two things, they do not have a job very long. Have you ever heard of a salesman who hasn't made a sale in six months who still has his job?

No. Why not? Because he's hired to make the corporation money — and he's costing the corporation money.

Everybody has one of those two jobs. What do presidents do – make or save? They do both. What do salesmen do? They make money. What do accountants do? They save money. What do engineers do? Well, mechanical engineers make, industrial engineers save. Even the receptionist, guess what — she makes and saves — both!

When we know why people are hired, we know what job they have to do. Then we have to know how they will specifically impact the company monetarily. By doing so, we will know how to match them with a particular opening.

"GENERIC" MATCHING

Think about the matching criteria. Remember it is a tremendous amount of our income. This goes back to the questions we ask and don't ask when we take the initial search.

Sometimes we match candidates and orders and set them up with interviews, and nothing happens. One of the reasons is we are doing what I call generic matching. That means someone told us that they want a candidate with five years of engineering experience. We sent them somebody with five years experience, and nothing happens. Generic matches inevitably result in the inability to be specific in your match. You can recognize this by the answers you get from your hiring official. Have you ever heard, "Yes, he kind of looked good. But, you know, I can not put my finger on it, but I don't think it is going to work"? The problem there is you have a hiring official who does not know what he is looking for to begin with. And you have not helped him to be specific. Without specifics, you are forced to do generic matching.

When we get into that area of taking search assignments and helping people know what they are looking for, we will cover how to target a match and get them to hire that candidate.

The generic search is rampant in our industry! If you pick up almost any order on any desk, it will say the same thing. So many years of so much experience in a certain industry. Five years of engineering experience in a high-speed manufacturing environment. Three years of secretarial experience in a front-office corporate environment. Two years of programming experience. It just goes on and on and on. The same "generic" over and over again.

How I Learned

I got taught not to deal on this basis by a hiring official who really helped me in my career. I had taken a search for a five-year engineer with five years of mechanical engineering in a manufacturing environment. However, when I informed the client that I had found one, he replied, "Gosh, Larry, that sounds good, but what has he been doing?" And I replied, "Five years of mechanical engineering experience in an industry just like yours." He said, "I know, Larry. You just said that. Tell me what has he been doing." I said, "for five years, he has been an engineer." And he kind of snapped at me and said, "I don't care how long he has been alive. What in the heck has he been <u>doing</u>?"

What did the client really say to me? He meant, "Does this guy have five years of experience, or does he have one year experience five times?" What he actually said to me was, "Larry, there are forty thousand five-year engineers out there. Why did you bring me this one?" Guess what? I could not tell him, because <u>I</u> <u>had</u> <u>not</u> <u>tried</u> <u>to</u> <u>discern</u> <u>the</u> <u>difference</u> between this five-year engineer and any other five-year engineer.

Hey, that is what the order said! It said bring me five years of engineering in my industry. That is what I brought him. What else could he ask for? He could ask for a lot more. A lot of times our matches don't work, and we wonder why not. Frequently, it is because we don't know what the candidate or the company is looking for! That's why we have focused so much on specificity in this critical chapter. As you will see mentioned in future pages and chapters, to a great degree, the art of selling is the art of <u>differentiation</u>. Later on we'll show you how.

GAINING FLEXIBLITY

Many in our industry believe in "gaining flexibility". What does that mean? The idea is the broader you can get the specifications on the order, the more candidates you could fit into it. So they ask someone, "Well, can I send you somebody that is non-degreed, even though you want someone with a degree? Would you pay fifty-five thousand if I find somebody, even though your tops is fifty? Would you take somebody with chemical experience, rather than just refining? Would you take this? Would you take that?"

It's called "gaining flexibility", and it was a standard in our industry for many years. It is a hold-over from our "employment agency" days. However, in the modern world of search and recruiting, such a technique is no longer appropriate.

The <u>broader</u> the specifications for the job, the <u>harder</u> it is to make the place-ment. You do not know what fits, the hiring official does not know what fits, and after numerous interviews, confusion still runs rampant through the situ-ation. You have no way of closing the hiring official, no way of convincing the hiring official that your candidate is better than another. Nor can you advise your candidate on what to talk about or emphasize in the interview, because you <u>don't</u> know what's going to look good in that situation.

As we mature as recruiters, we need to <u>quit</u> gaining flexibility. What we need to do to help the client is to <u>define</u> what it is about their job that's going to cause them to hire.

MATCHING NEEDS

We have to search for the company's <u>specific</u> need. We must match the accomplishments and achievements of the individual against the company need as it relates to the dollar-making or dollar-savings that they are hiring this person to do. That is going to sometimes be difficult. I once had a client say, "Larry, do you know why it is difficult for you to get a complete search for me?" And I said, "Well, no. Why?" And he replied, "You ask me questions I don't know the answers to." Good! That is what I should be doing. You, too.

What he had told me was, " I need an engineer, and I am going to pay him $60,000." And here was Larry with 45 minutes worth of questions that he had not thought through. You need to understand that when you start prob-ing for the <u>specific</u> need within that job description, the client may not have thought of it. You need to help him along.

An Example

Let me give you an example of accomplishments and achievements vs. the specific need of a company, to show you how this helps us to find and sub-mit the <u>correct</u> candidate for this particular client need.

Let's say the company has given us the generic description of five years of industrial engineering experience in a high speed-manufacturing environ-ment. Well, we see those kind of openings every day, in a "tech" or engi-neering specialty. How do you fill somebody that broad? You don't even try. Instead, you <u>narrow</u> the focus.

What kind of industrial engineer is going to make or save them the most money? I know what qualifies an industrial engineer in this third matching level; they do plant layout, time and motion studies, efficiency reports and studies. So where should this particular engineer be expert? Ask. "Well", says the hiring authority, "I want him to be good in all of them. I want a well-rounded engineer." Whoa! Trouble ahead! Obviously, he has not thought through what it was that he wants this person to do. You cannot identify the right candidate.

I had a situation just like this once and another consultant in my office chose to work on it against my advice. After submitting four candidates, all were interviewed. Two went to a second interview. They ended up hiring an ad response!

When you find out what the <u>specific</u> need is, you know <u>which</u> candidate to refer. If you have three five-year industrial engineers in high- speed manufacturing environments, I think you can rate them one, two and three and be mostly right. You should know which of the three is better for your client. But all the average producer does is refer the three resumes and say, "What do you think?" He <u>hopes</u> that somehow this person will be able to read a resume and be able to make a selection.

Consulting

That is not how you consult. You must <u>evaluate</u> and <u>make</u> <u>recommendations</u>. But you can't evaluate until you know the specific need of the client. But how do you get to the specific need?

Let's say we find another hiring authority who wants five years of industrial engineering experience. This time, however, the conversation goes more like this. "Is there anything that this individual will do for this company as soon as they get on board? Are there any specific projects that this engineer will handle?' And he says, "Yes. We are going to redesign our plant layout, and this person will need to be able to give us a hand in that area." Your response may be, "Well, how many other industrial engineers do you have?"

Let's say you get an answer of two. Ask, "Do either one of them have plant layout experience?" If the answer is "no", focus his thinking with, "Wouldn't it be nice if I not only find you an industrial engineer with five years of high speed manufacturing experience, but someone who has done a plant layout in their past and knows how to manage one of those projects?"

Now you know what you are looking for. And so does the client. This one we can fill! But before you submit candidates who look good "on paper", <u>call</u> the candidates and get more information.

CANDIDATE RE-QUALIFYING

This is called <u>candidate</u> <u>requalifying</u>. You may not have thought to ask these candidates about their plant layout experience when you first interviewed them! Now it is time to call them back and say, "Have you any experience in this area?" Number one says, "Well, I have studied it in college and I got an "A" in it, but I really have never done it." Number two says, "I did it my first year in industry. I was a gopher in the project." But he had never really managed it or really run one. He had gone over the procedure, but had not done one. The third one says, "Larry, yes. I just redesigned the layout for my present company."

Ask, "How did it come out?" You see, it is <u>not</u> <u>enough</u> to know that he did it. We have to know is he any good at it! He could have burnt the plant down when he had done it! Now we are going to refer him to our client sure in the knowledge that this person knows about plant layouts. Since we have to talk to him about what he is doing, we also get the accomplishments and achievements that were obtained in that project.

THE HIERARCHY OF ACCOMPLISHMENTS

Are all accomplishments equal in terms of how the client perceives them? No. There is a clear hierarchy in terms of the "worth".

When you are asking a candidate about accomplishments and achievements, you want to get it if possible in <u>dollars</u> <u>and</u> <u>cents</u>. If you can't get it in dollars and cents, then ask about <u>percentages</u>. If you can't get it in percentages, then you want it in <u>any</u> <u>form</u> <u>that</u> <u>infers</u> <u>the</u> <u>making</u> <u>or</u> <u>saving</u> <u>of</u> <u>money</u>.

What do I mean <u>any</u> <u>form</u> that infers a making or saving of money?   Well, there are lots of people that can not make a dollar-and-cents judgement on what they have done for their company. For instance, sometimes programmers cannot tell you how much money they have made or saved the company. Why not? Because no one has ever told them! But there should be some way of telling the good ones from the poor ones.

Some Examples

I had a mining engineer one time and I had asked him about his accomplishments and his achievements. Had he made or saved his company any money? He really did not know. I asked about percentages, and had he ever come under budget? He had no percentages or hard budgetary information for me. So I am down to number three; "Give me something that will tell my client that you are a good mining engineer." He said, "Well, tell them I hold the world's record for sinking a declining shaft mine in the shortest time in history." I yawned, and said, "Well, OK. I will tell them."

But guess what? When I called mining managers and I told them I had this individual, they were jumping through the telephone trying to set up an interview with this guy! Why? Well, I didn't know that declining shaft mines are expensive and cave in a lot, and they frequently go over budget. I had the world's record holder of sinking one in the shortest time, and that inferred he would make the company millions of dollars. Or <u>save</u> them millions of dollars in helping them with their mines.

Any time you can get an accomplishment or achievement in a form that tells this company your candidate is good, you have achieved your objective. But we want to get it in dollars and cents or percentages if at all possible.

Let's go back to our industrial engineer example mentioned previously. Ask the candidate, "How did your new plant layout come out?" He replies, "Well, we are now producing 22% more products then we were before." Now is that hierarchy level one, two or three? That's two, percentages. So my next question is to say, "How much in dollars and cents did that mean to the company?" He says, "Well, we project five million dollars in gross revenue increase next year through our sales, because we are putting out more product." So now we have somebody that truly has the accomplishments, achievements and abilities to solve the client's industrial problem.

When you are matching people on level three and four, you must see yourself as an ***industrial problem solver***. What problem does the client have, and specifically how can your candidate cure that problem or impact that problem monetarily? Then you have a good match!

THE DIFFERENCE IN PRESENTATIONS

Look at the difference between these two presentations. Listen to me when I call my client without this matching information, and the way you can call now with this information.

Generic!

"Hello Bill, this is Larry with the Reality Group. I was doing that search for you on industrial engineers and I came up with one with five years of industrial engineering experience in a high-speed manufacturing environment just like yours. He has a BSIE out of Georgia Tech, and is currently working on his Masters. I think he would be interested in talking with you about joining your staff. Does that sound like a person you would like to talk to? Yes, sir. I have his resume."

Have you heard that phone call? It is the presentation of a generic five-year person, and the hiring official doesn't know whether he wants to see him or not. The candidate may be good at what he does, or may not be. I have simply not told the hiring official about that.

Matched!

Now listen to this phone call.

"Hello Bill, this is Larry with the Reality Group. You know, I was on the search for the industrial engineer you wanted me to find and I have talked to a lot of industrial engineers. A lot of them are really good. One, however, stood out head and shoulders above all the other engineers I had talked to for your particular situation. He has five years of the high-speed experience you are looking for, plus he also has a BSIE out of Georgia Tech and is working on his masters. But specifically, the reason I selected this engineer for you is that he has just redesigned the layout in his present company. That resulted in 22% more product output and they project five million dollars in increased revenue because of that design. I felt certain this is the man you want to handle the project you've got coming up. What are your thoughts? Yes, sir. I have his phone number."

Now that is a real call! What did I sell? I sold value. I told the person he had an industrial problem, and I had the engineer or candidate that could resolve that problem positively.

THE ANSWER TO (COMPANY) PROCRASTINATORS

Accomplishments and achievements are company closing power! This is a major key to the closing power you need to convince the hiring official to hire.

Why <u>do</u> hiring officials procrastinate? Why do they not just jump in and make a hire? Why do they want to see other people? Frequently, it is because they have a fear of failure. Procrastination in hiring is based on a <u>fear</u> <u>of</u> <u>hiring</u> <u>the</u> <u>wrong</u> <u>person</u>.

When you have a procrastinator, understand that this is an expensive venture for that person, and they may be on the line to make that decision. They have got candidates. But they don't know which one to hire, whether they should hire at all, or whether they should see some more. They are <u>fearful</u> in making a decision.

Some people may believe that the appropriate response is to put the arm up behind their back and bash them over the head with statements like, "You better hurry up and hire this person. If you don't hire this person, they are going to be gone. I've got this candidate on other interviews and if I don't hear from you by Friday, then this person will be placed somewhere else."

Well, here we are with a fearful hiring official trying to make an important decision for the company and we are slamming him around with too-drastic sales techniques. It only moves him <u>further</u> from the decision, not <u>closer</u> to it.

If I have the accomplishments and achievements, I have closing power. I can say, " Bill, I know that you have that project coming up that is highly important to your department, to say nothing of your career and reputation. I feel like you would want a person who has done it in the past successfully. In fact, this candidate has made his company five million dollars with that design. I would suspect that this is the person you would feel comfortable moving forward with. Do any of the other candidates indicate that they have made their company almost five million dollars?"

"Well, no, Larry, they have not."

"Well, I think that you will feel comfortable that this man can come in and handle this for you. When would you like to proceed with an offer, or what level of an offer would you be thinking about?"

It is important to make the hiring authority <u>comfortable</u> with making the right decision. <u>Use</u> that word! Help him make the decision by not driving him further away.

Remember that on our third matching level we are doing the accomplishments and achievements of the candidate ***as it matches the specific need the company is looking for***. Accomplishments and achievements are dollars-and-cents, percentages, or any form of that infers the making or saving of money. With that knowledge we now have <u>company</u> <u>closing</u> <u>power</u> to be able to help this person make a decision.

PRINCIPLE 4: MATCHING CANDIDATE CONCERNS

Now let's talk about number four, the reason that candidates change jobs. Why do people leave companies? As recruiters, we have always had the wrong idea there. We have been saying "Look at this great opportunity that I have out there for you." Doesn't this sound sweet?" And they go over and look and they <u>do</u> think it looks great. Then, unless you have strong overall industry-specific selling and closing skills, they turn the offer down.

Why does that happen? Because we as recruiters have been frequently working on the wrong end of the problem. People leave companies because they have a problem where they are, and again we become industrial problem solvers. If we <u>resolve</u> that problem, then that person will leave and we will have an opportunity to make a placement.

The way to tell the difference between shoppers and serious candidates is that serious candidates are not <u>only</u> moving to anything; they are also moving <u>from</u> something. If they are truly happy where they are, you can not pull them out of there with a team of wild horses. When we call them and try to recruit them what do they say to us? "No, thanks, Larry. I am happy where I am." If you are Direct Recruiting, which is a complex methodology if done properly, rebuttals will work <u>very</u> effectively to get the candidate thinking. But even after doing so, the serious candidates have concerns about their present position.

Serious candidates can <u>define</u> their Reason for Leaving, though you may have to assist them in defining it. Only then will we know that they are serious. But what do we match that against? What do we have to know about the company that helps us know that this candidate matches this company? If you have three openings that this candidates basically matches, you should be able to tell which one of these opportunities is better for your particular candidate. Only one of the three really may be workable for the person.

Frequently, we take a person out of one company and we move him down the street and we put him in another company just about the same. It may be a similar industry making a similar product. And guess what? We get him a job with the very same title that he had. And yet it is absolutely the right move for him, and he is thrilled! Why?

When we move people out of companies with the same titles that they just came out of and at similar money, what are we selling? We are selling opportunity. We are selling the <u>opportunity</u> to have more. But we also are selling the opportunity to <u>solve</u> <u>the</u> <u>problem</u> they are having at their present company. If we don't solve that reason for leaving, then they won't leave. However, if the client has the same problem as their old one, we call that a turndown. If they realize that company has the same problem <u>after</u> they accept the offer then, we call that a fall-off.

What we are doing is solving problems that candidates have, and that is how we know they will accept. By meeting their expectations, they will be a far better employee for the client as well. Matching means putting the right client with the candidate, just as much as the right candidate with the client.

Correct Matching

Let us look at these four matches again.

Number <u>one</u>: candidate skill vs. job requirements tells you whether or not this person can do the job and whether the match is possible.

Number <u>two</u>: image tells you whether or not they are the right type of person for the job.

Number <u>three</u>: matching the accomplishments and achievements against the company's specific need tells you how likely this person is to get an offer over other candidates.

Number <u>four</u>: matching the Reason for Leaving of the candidate against the company's opportunity tells you how likely that candidate is to accept that offer.

Now that is matching! That is consulting. If you will match all four, you will be able to put a tremendous amount of placements together, because you will have the information necessary to affect that close and affect that company's offer. So remember the four matching principles and use them.

Ideally, you will know all four of these pieces of information. But what if you don't? If you don't know all four, go ahead and make the referral. You can learn these things as you go along with the placement process. But you have an indication of what you need to learn to be able to make the placement.

If you use these critical techniques, you will find yourself setting many more high-quality interviews, resulting in more major fees that most people in our industry even think possible...with <u>no</u> extra time on the phone!

MARKETING: THE BEDROCK CALL!

8

*W*hat are the two most exciting areas of our business? I believe they are marketing and recruiting. Oh, exciting? Marketing? Are you kidding me? Those gut-busting cold calls that we have to sit down every day and work our way through. Absolutely!

Marketing and recruiting are the absolute foundation of our business. It's what gets us the results we want to move forward to reach our goals. I love this business. And you will, too. It is <u>fun</u> talking to people about new opportunities. Talking to companies about new candidates, and going "on the hunt" for new searches and clients gets me excited!

When we are sitting there looking at that list of marketing calls, sometimes we make it life or death. Of course it isn't. Rather, it is interesting to talk to people about new areas of their companies or divisions, their careers as managers, about expansions, problems they have that we can resolve, and the kind of person that we can find for them. Do you want to help people improve their lives and careers, and make money besides? You came to the right place!

VALUE-BASED MARKETING

What types of calls do we make to potential clients? Broadly, we can say that they fall into two categories: Marketing a candidate, and marketing your services.

By marketing a candidate, of course, I mean presenting a specific individual; marketing your services refers to who we are and what we do.

Which is best? The answer is that both are necessary. However, when I market a candidate, I am presenting immediate value to my client. Presuming you have selected the right candidate, you are showing them that you have someone right now that can come in and make them money or save them money.

On service, we are <u>information</u> based. We are presenting long-term value.

There is no doubt that this is extremely effective for a well-trained advanced search consultant if it is done properly. Steve Finkel has an entire module in his in-house training programs on "expanding your client base". He has conducted these programs for a number of my client firms after I have laid the foundation for them, and the results are truly remarkable. However, in my opinion, for newer people or less- experienced people, the place to start is absolutely with candidate marketing, and even Steve believes that it should selectively used on an ongoing basis for consultants at <u>every</u> level.

Moreover, the later chapters in this book on Client Development will help you to transition from a one-time fee obtained by candidate marketing to multi-placement accounts.

The Philosophical Foundation

My own experience sometimes tells me what is effective in sales. I say to myself, "When I get calls from people, how do I respond to them? What makes me listen, sit up and take notice of a person?"

As a small business owner, I get frequent calls from stock brokers who want me to invest, start a retirement program, or put money away for my kids' education. But mainly the way that they approach me is, "Hello Larry. I am so-and-so, and I am with a certain stock brokerage company. We can do a great job for you". Well, who cares who he is with? I don't know him from Adam, and all of a sudden he is trying to tell me his firm's name, and wants me to assume that they know what they are doing. All is he says to me is his name, who he is with, and do I need his service? I listen and ask for his card. Guess what I do with the card when it comes through the door? Yes. I pitch it.

But once, I had a stock broker call me and said, "Larry, I know you are the owner of a small business. I want you to know that I happen to have the top-rated retirement program for self-employed and small business owners. It has the least risk with the greatest return of anything on the market today. I can get you into this program quite inexpensively, and allow you to get started with your retirement. I know it will have value to you to be stable financially when you retire. I was wondering if I could send you this program and talk to you about it". Did I hear that? Yes. Was I interested in talking to him? Yes, I was. Did I keep the material that he sent it to me? Yes. Why? Because he was selling <u>value</u>. And when he was selling value, I heard him. This might make or save me money. I <u>wanted</u> to hear about it. But when people just call up and say, "Hello and this is who I am, this is what I do, and I want you to know about my company", I do not hear them.

Paul Hawkinson is the editor of our industry's only newsletter, <u>*The Fordyce Letter*</u>. In a recent survey they found that <u>candidate</u> presentations rather than service presentations are <u>65%</u> more effective in creating initial business! Now this does not refer to the sort of advanced sales-oriented material that has been mentioned. And "initial business" is important, but long-term business is even more important. Still, for most people in our industry, it is accurate. The reason is when we call people, there is immediate value in what we say, and it causes them to act.

If the client at the other end of the telephone is picking and choosing amongst the people that call, how does he make the decision on which to choose? Sometimes we get a very cold reception. And sometimes we have a very warm reception. What is the difference?

A Warm Reception

Once, I was calling and trying make a client out of a top executive of a Fortune 500 companies. I kept calling this lady and she was fairly restrained. I could never get her to warm up. I made presentations of candidates, and there was never really anything there. After a three-month period, we had talked about half a dozen times, but nothing ever really occurred. I persevered.

One day I presented a candidate to her right in her own backyard who happened to have a certain experience. And she was just as cordial as she could be all of a sudden! "Gee, Larry. What about him? Who is he? Let's talk." We had a great conversation! While we ended up deciding that the person wasn't exactly what she was looking for, she gave me the perameters for somebody who would fit an opening she <u>did</u> have. I later turned it into a repeat account. I thought to myself, what is the difference? Why all of a sudden cold, and then — boom! I am her best friend. It has to do with the word "value". If I can present value to the client, I have an opportunity to gain their attention and have them cooperate and talk with me. Doing a value presentation with the <u>right</u> candidate is the key.

Marketing the right candidate, <u>combined</u> with <u>perseverence</u>, gets you in doors. Marketing creates business. Marketing a candidate with immediate value causes them to give <u>you</u> the order when they are turning everyone else down!

When I market a candidate, why do I think clients want to use me? Because when I market a candidate, I always try to market the right candidate. He or she has specific qualities that will appeal to and interest potential clients.

That particular type of presentation says two things about you.

First, it says you represent good people. If this prospective client is looking for a candidate, that might tend to make them give you the order rather then someone else.

But it also says you know what is going on in that marketplace. In fact, in a lot of your marketing programs, you will have potential clients say, "Gee, that does sounds like a good person. Boy, those people are hard to find. Every time I am looking for one, I can never find them" And it leads into the obvious close of "interview now while this person is available, because soon you will need one, and you will not be able to find them."

CLIENT PERCEPTION

We had a group of HR people on a panel I was chairing at a national conference one time and we asked them about the marketing call. Does it bother them for people to call up and present candidates to them? And they said, "No. Actually it does not. In fact, it helps us keep aware of what is going on out there. What is available? Sometimes our managers do have an opening. We would like to hear about that".

And I asked, "What about those companies that just say they are a great company and they are a specialist in your area? Does that bother you?" And they said, "Well no. It bothers us if they are just touting their company and how good they are, and they don't say anything about how they could best be of service to us. If you are going to make a service call, the value is to say, 'How can I be of best service to you?'"

This is not to suggest that you should be dealing with HR. For most niche markets, you should not. But the perceptions of hiring managers are the same.

VALUE-BASED SERVICE CALL

Make sure that your value statement says something about service to the <u>client</u>, not "continuing to spread our wings" about our company. That sort of comment indicates a very low level of thought or selling skill.

The type of service call you should make would go something like this. "Hello, Bill. This is Larry Nobles with the Reality Group. The reason I called you today was to introduce my firm to you. We happen to be contingency recruiters in Tulsa, Oklahoma and we specialize in your profession. We handle chemical engineers in both refining, gas and the chemical marketplace. I wanted you to know that if your needs in the near future include putting top chemical engineers on your staff, then we've done this for years. As a matter of fact, we've been in business for 18 years. Our staff has a total of 43 years in experience among the four of us. We would like to have a chance to do business with you.

Let me ask, even though we think that we can handle all of your assignments for you, <u>how</u> best could I be of service to you? What is the best thing my firm can do to help you get the best staff on board when you are looking for someone?"

That adds some sort of value to the call and allows the client a way to express their needs, rather just talking about you and how good your company is. <u>Value</u> needs to be included in any kind of a presentation.

Objectives of the Call

It is frequently thought that the purpose of a Marketing the Candidate Call (which we refer to as a Marketing Call) is simply to get an interview. While true, that's only one purpose. If you focus too heavily on it, you will lose much of the worth of the call.

Rather, there are actually <u>five</u> objectives of a marketing call. Here is what we do when we are trying to make this call.

<u>One</u> and most important, we are trying to get a send-out on the candidate that we are presenting.

<u>Second</u>, we would like to get a search assignment. If the person doesn't need the candidate we are presenting, do they have other needs that we can work on?

<u>Third</u>, we want to get market information. We want to get information on the particular group or type of companies we are calling that will tell us whether to continue to call them.

<u>Four</u>, we need to get client development information. This information helps us to decide if we going to try to develop this company, or are we not going to call this company again. That allows us to put that company in our client stack, or in our source file. We either place people with them, or recruit people from them. We can not mix the two.

And the <u>fifth</u>, is that we want to get is advertising for our company. We advertise sometimes for candidates, but many times we don't have a good program that keeps our company's name in front of those hiring officials that might want to use us. The best form of advertising is your <u>telephone</u>. Call them up and introduce yourself, and send them a card. Send an introductory letter and send them a <u>printed</u> brochure. Don't think your website will do the job! <u>Continuing</u> to <u>call</u> <u>them</u> is the advertising you are looking for. Don't even consider e-mail "spam". You won't think it's that, but they will.

Always remember to end your marketing call with your name and your telephone number, so they can return the call to you if they have something that they need. It will surprise you, but they <u>will</u> keep your number in many cases.

So there are the five. One is <u>send-out</u>. Two is a <u>search assignment</u>. Three is <u>market information</u>. Four is <u>client development</u>. And five is <u>advertising</u>. And of those five, number three — market information — is one of the most important areas for you to pay attention to in the early stages of your marketing.

Qualifying A Client Base

Let me give you an example. Many years ago I was expanding my business in Tulsa, and there was a lot of oil business being done in town. It was a market we had never worked, but my boss suggested I should call some of them and see what kind of accounting needs they might have. Accounting was my field at the time.

My first step was simply to go to the yellow pages in Tulsa and look up oil producers. There were almost 700 companies listed there. Let me tell you that at thirty conversations a day (plus my other work), that is a lot of days calling those companies and a tremendous time investment on my part. But it had to be done.

In calling them, one of the things that I wanted to know was "Who is your controller, and how big is your staff?"

Why did I want to know those two statements above anything else? Because I quickly found out most of those firms were not large oil firms. They were little two-man drilling rigs. They were small pools of people that had a couple of wells, and they really didn't really have their own accountants. They were using outside CPA's to do their accounting. I had <u>no</u> chance in making a placement with those people. Which was which? There was only one way to find out!

As a matter of fact, there were sixty-eight possible companies that I could do business with in the future. So my first pass in this industry, market information was <u>more</u> <u>important</u> than trying to get send-outs or job openings. Obviously you <u>do</u> want to get send-outs or search assignments. If it is there, a good candidate and presentation will get it. But for me to have tried that without <u>first</u> qualifying, I would have had to again go back through those 700 companies trying to make placements with people who could never utilize my services.

In your initial pass, do everything you can to get the information that tells you who to call back. After you have done so, your calls can be much more targeted.

In that specific instance, when I found out what size the firm was, it still did not tell me what kind of people worked there, and what kind of people did not. I has to find who had lube units and who did not. Some only produced gas, and some produced both gas and lubricates. If they didn't have a lube unit, there was no reason to call them about a lube specialist. It is the same on your desk and in <u>your</u> field. Once I qualified the market, I found fifty firms I could actually do business with. And I did a <u>lot</u> of business by focusing on my <u>real</u> market.

You must be constantly refining and defining your marketplace, so that your marketing in the future can be more targeted. Otherwise, it will be time wasted marketing wrong candidates to them, and will make you look ill-informed.

When you go out and market, ask questions to try and get all five of these objectives met.

The Right Candidate

Ideally, you must have a marketable candidate when you go out there. You are not going to get a send-out if you don't get anybody excited about the person you are calling about. Later in this book, we will talk about all the criteria that we use to judge a candidate. But for marketing purposes, let's talk about these three.

First, you need to know the candidate's accomplishments and achievements. He or she must have some valuable qualities, hopefully in dollars and cents, that you can use to impress a company and want to see this person.

The most obvious example is sales. If you call up and have the number-one sales rep who has been 250% of quota every year and has just caused a million dollar territory to rise to three million dollar, you are making some very positive monetary statements to this hiring official. That is so much better than just calling up and saying I've got a salesman. We need to know how good that person is and what are his accomplishments and achievements.

Secondly, candidates to market need to have a Reason for Leaving. If I am going to spend my time marketing individuals trying to get them employed, I need to know that they are a serious candidate. I can tell if they are a serious candidate by making sure they have genuine professional reasons for leaving. Also when I know that, I will have a better idea as to which company to put them in.

Three, there needs to be demand for his services. You must market those people who are hard to find. The more demand there is for the person, the better response you will get. Only a small percentage of the people we call are actually going to want to see this person. What you are going to try to do with this marketable candidate is to impress this hiring official enough that he will enter into a business discussion with you. If hiring managers enter into a business discussion with me, I know how it will end if it is a good firm. Sooner or later I am going to do business with them.

Make a thorough call. Get off the "do you want to see this person, do you have an opening, hang-up call". Talk about the market, and their company. How do they deal with people? Do they use people like you? Advertise yourself with a good presentation and the right candidate, then give them your name and number. Accomplish your objectives! A marketing call is so much more than dredge-up-a-job-order. There are five objectives as we've discussed, and you need to try and reach them on every call.

THE MARKETING SCRIPT

Let us talk about the script that you might use, the things that you might say, and how to put together a script that will be meaningful in terms of having company respond to you.

A script should have three parts to it. It has an <u>opening</u>, a <u>body</u> and a <u>close</u>. And the entire script <u>should</u> <u>not</u> <u>last</u> <u>longer</u> <u>than</u> <u>thirty</u> <u>to</u> <u>forty</u> <u>seconds</u>. I know that sounds too brief. But if you are well organized and you are presenting value, you can say plenty in thirty to forty seconds.

If you go longer than that, people simply quit listening.

Psychologists tell us that people can only pay attention for about seven seconds before they make some kind of judgement in their mind about the caller or the subject of the call. If you don't quickly get their attention and say upfront exactly what you are talking about, you are going to lose them. If they quit listening, you could have the greatest presentation and the greatest candidate .... and nothing will occur. You will get no results.

Let's remember that our opening is meant to gain their attention. It's meant to get them to listen to us so that they hear the rest of the message. Don't fake it; you need a script.

The Opening

What is an opening? And what is contained in an opening? An opening is very simple. It is to the point and it says who you are, who you are with, what you are doing, and who you are bringing to them.

It would go something like this, "Hello so-and-so, my name is Larry Nobles. I am a technical recruiter with the Reality Group in Tulsa, Oklahoma. The reason I called you today is that I have recently recruited a _____". And after the "a", I want you to put a job title. Nothing else.

You are calling because you have recently recruited an insurance actuary. You recently recruited an electrical engineer. You recently recruited a controller. You put a <u>job</u> <u>title</u> in there, because if you use descriptive terms such as a "fine young man", or a "top candidate", you are not telling them what you are talking about! Thus you instantly lose their attention, and the rest of the presentation goes downhill from there.

Now you have their attention. They know who you are and what you are doing. They know what you are talking about, and you have their attention.

The Sizzling Body

The body following that has a couple of parts to it. After you have their attention in the opening, you want to go right into the body of your presentation. The body of the presentation should contain <u>two</u> <u>things</u>.

First, it should contain the hottest possible "sizzle" available on the candidate.

What is sizzle? Sizzle is an old sales term. It illustrates why you must make a point of reading books on selling! I first heard of it in a highly-recommended book entitled, "*How to Sell Anything to Anybody*" by Joe Girard. Who invented it? Elmer Wheeler, legendary sales trainer, in his classic book, "*Tested Sentences That Sell*" in 1937! Remember in the introduction, I said that to succeed, you must stay on a continual learning curve? Reading books like these will keep you there. "Don't sell the steak; sell the sizzle!" was Elmer Wheeler's landmark phrase. He developed it at his Tested Institute and Word Laboratory to take the question of "what sells?" out of selling. What does that mean?

A sizzle is a raw red flat piece of meat until you throw it on the fire. And then it begins to sizzle and pop, and crack and smells so good. "Sell the sizzle" means to sell what is <u>good</u> about what you have, and not just selling what you <u>have</u>. So the first part of the body needs to contain the hottest sizzle or accomplishments and achievements of the person that you are talking about. That value will give that person on the other end of the line a reason to listen to you .

But the second part of the body after the accomplishments and achievements (sizzle) is the number of <u>facts</u> that help round out the presentation so that the person knows what you are talking about. Obviously education and the number of years of experience will help this person make a decision whether or not they are interested. But that by itself is <u>not</u> enough!

We don't only want facts. We want Sizzle. Without <u>both</u>, you have not done your job and will get poor results.

What is next? This is a sales business, right? Let's talk about the <u>close</u> that is so important to get the attention and the cooperation of the person you are talking to.

The Close

We talked about the opening and what the body contained. But what should the close contain?

The close should contain a <u>benefit</u> statement for the company which would tell them why you feel this person has <u>value</u> that they can bring to the company. Then make a statement. This statement must call for a <u>direct</u> <u>response</u> from the person you are talking to.

Sometimes we are direct with a statement like, "I felt certain that you would be interested in talking with this person".

This is an obvious close, but might lose the conversational flow we want to maintain. A value or benefit statement maintains that flow, and also allows you to close by asking if this particular candidate could be of value to the company.

Ask this person if he had thought about adding someone like that to his staff, or if they would be interested in discussing with this person the possibility of joining their staff. They have to give you a response to that, but you avoid the trap of coming across abruptly.

PULLING IT ALL TOGETHER

Let's talk about how we might market an industrial engineer who has made his particular company money by redesigning plant layout, and has done some time and motion studies and efficiency reports. We are going to give the company an opening, and a benefit statement. Then we are going to close them.

That script might sound something like this, "Hello, Bill. My name is Larry Nobles, and I am a technical recruiter with The Reality Group here in Tulsa, Oklahoma. The reason I called you today was that I just recently recruited an industrial engineer. Now I talk to industrial engineers all the time, but this one in particular stood head-and-shoulders above all the engineers that I have talked to. Specifically, this individual has just made his last company five million dollars through his expertise in industrial engineering! He redesigned their plant layout, and has done some efficiency reports which is going to improve their revenue drastically. He has 5 years experience, with a BSIE out of Georgia Tech, and is currently available for the right opportunity. I felt he could really be of benefit to your company and your industrial engineering staff with those kinds of monetary talents. I was wondering if you would be interested in having a discussion with this particular candidate about joining your staff. What are your thoughts?"

Now this person must respond to me as to whether or not he has any interest. Of course, there are various responses that he might actually say, and we'll discuss them in the next chapter.

The Overlooked Key

At the end of your presentation, I want you to do one thing. It is two words, and it is called "shut up!" Once again, where does this critical concept come from? A Legendary classical sales trainer named J. Douglas Edwards, who wrote a book with Tom Hopkins entitled, *"How to Master the Art of Selling!"*. Recommended reading.

The single biggest problem we have as salespeople is we can't quit talking long enough to let our prospect give us a response. We hate silence. Those pauses drive us a little bit nuts and soon as we get to that, "I wondered if you would be interested in talking to this person about joining your staff".....pause.... "and also, well, I thought maybe he would" ... and here we come rolling back in.

You can lose sales by jabbering over inanities that we don't need to be talking about. Shut up! Wait for that person to respond. You just made a solid presentation to them! This potential client may be thinking about how to respond to you, or thinking where this person might fit into their situation. Don't interrupt, and wait for their response.

RECAP

Let's talk about what we just said. We opened and told him who we were. We covered who we were with, what we were doing, and who we had. Then we went into a body in which we told this person that this particular candidate was better than any we had found. We told them "why", because we added the sizzle, or the accomplishments or achievements of that particular individual. We rounded it out with facts, so they would know the level of person we are talking about. In the close, we added a <u>benefit</u> statement that said, "If you hire this person he will bring value or benefit to your corporation." Then we made a close that directly solicited a <u>response</u>, "yes" or "no", or "maybe", from the hiring official. It was not too directed. It was not so vague that we did not get into the business discussion that we wanted.

That is the kind of good, smooth marketing call that most people are going to respond to favorably, and that will help you to achieve great success, when combined with the proper selection, good selling skills, and appropriate numbers.

MARKETING: POST-PRESENTATION

9

*T*here is much more to a Marketing Call than simply selecting the right candidate, making the right presentation, and having the right objectives.

No matter how well you accomplish all of this, you'll encounter varying comments, options, and objections. How should you respond?

Moreover, who do you call? When should you call? How many calls does it take? How do you stay focused?

Let's address these and other issues to enable you to maximize your results from the critical initial client contact.

COMMON RESPONSES

There are a lot of responses you will hear, though they will repeat themselves after awhile. Let's go over the most frequent, and talk about some of the things you can say that might help you with your sales approach after you have made your presentation.

No Needs

Obviously many people will respond to you that, "That sounds good, but I just don't have any needs". Well, in our business it is difficult to place people when there are no openings. Hopefully you have a great candidate. If the person doesn't have any needs, however, it is not easy to create one in corporate America.

Can it be done? Absolutely, or at least in a significant percentage of circumstances! Mastering the specific techniques to do so will increase your production <u>substantially</u>. But frankly, it requires a high level of sales skills to be successful at it. It is not the place to start. Once you have a solid foundation down, then is the time for serious "Rebuttals".

The best ones for this objection may be found on Steve Finkel's video series specifically addressing overcoming objections and closing entitled "*Book More Business!: The Second Edition*". Make sure it is the <u>second</u> edition, as the updated version contains much additional material. I've seen phenomenal financial results from his eight industry-specific answers to this common objection. But is that the place to concentrate if your foundational sales skills in this business are not excellent as yet? I don't believe so.

It is a lot easier if they say, "Well, I really don't have any needs right now. Thanks a lot", to go <u>directly</u> into some questions about your market information regarding their needs. Alternatively, go into a trial interview if he or she has no openings, but wishes they did.

Trial Interview

Sometimes they will say, "Boy, that person sounds good! When I am looking for someone like that, I can never seem to find them". Then you might go into a trial interview. Just say, "Why don't we put you two together on the telephone and let you talk? Let the two of you get to know each other. You never know when something is going to happen in your firm that would cause you to have an opening for this person. If you and the candidate hit it off and you really see value, you might go to your management and get an approval to bring them in for a possible hire. This (title of candidate) is certainly exceptional."

This is a good low-key easy-to-use technique which frequently gets good results.

If a trial interview does not result, you should go on to obtain market information. Like, "How is your company doing? Are you hiring?" And so on. Those kinds of questions will allow you to accomplish the <u>rest</u> of your objectives, which are client development and advertising. Stay tuned for more on those subjects later.

Resume?

Another way they come at you is, "send me a resume". Oh, what a killer! Many people interpret this as a positive response. It excites inexperienced recruiters. However, it is frequently the worst answer you can get. Why? Because you send them a resume and guess what? They never return the phone calls!

"Send me a resume" in our business is what I call "throwing the doggy a bone". It's the best way to get you off the telephone and get them out of a sales situation without saying no. It sounded like they had agreed, didn't it?

Of course, sometimes they do want that person. So when they say "send me a resume", react very enthusiastically and say, "Great! What position are you going to be considering him for?" And you are right into taking your search assignment.

However, if the person says, "Well, I am not going to be considering him for any position". Then say, "I am confused. I am sorry, but why would you want to waste time looking at a resume?" <u>Force</u> this person to say either, "I have an opening that I am considering them for" or " I don't have an opening, and I don't need the resume".

You only need to send resumes when a company has a <u>seriousness</u> about interviewing and hiring. And guess what a lot of these people are doing? They are absolutely taking most of us for all they can by collecting resumes. They get a good databank at our expense, and may call them later and hire them without our knowledge. This is especially true if you are dealing with Personnel/HR. There are trainers of HR people, many of whom came from our industry, who <u>teach</u> them to do so!

<u>Don't</u> <u>buckle</u> <u>under</u> to the "send me a resume" response. React enthusiastically with "what opening"? Then go right into taking an order. Try to set an interview after you take that order rather than mailing a resume.

No Search Firms Allowed?

We also have some that say, "I don't use agencies".

The biggest errors that are made by responding to that particular statement is that we start rattling off all the great reasons why our industry is wonderful, and all the things we can do for a good client. You just <u>know</u> this person has a particular problem that somewhere, some how, some way you can solve, and they have decided not to use search firms because something has happened. But there is only one reason to them that they do not use us, and here we are with seventeen reasons why they should use our firm.

Well, that is <u>not</u> going to help you. The first word out of your mouth when they say, "I don't use agencies" should be the word, "Why?" Be surprised! <u>Everybody</u> in corporate America today utilizes our services because of the value we bring to those corporations. So when they say, "I don't use recruiting firms", say, "I am surprised! Why not?"

Listen intently, and find out what the problem really is. Then you have a chance to overcome the specific objection.

Previous Problems?

When you get objections, many times it is because of a problem they have had with another company in the past. They tried that firm, and they did not get a quality candidate — or they hired somebody that did not stay.

I had one individual who did not want to use us because the last person only stayed six months and left, and they had paid a big fee. I had to educate that person that it is not the recruiter's responsibility to retain their employees once that person is on board. We are paid to find the person they are going to hire. We get paid for search. We get paid for interviewing, for checking references, for evaluating and presenting candidates for them to consider to hire. Once they hire and the candidate is on board, that is it, other than such guarantee as your firm may provide. It is their human resources department and manager's responsibility to make sure that person is well-oriented, well-trained and is retained.

Once he understood the difference and quit connecting us with that particular candidate, then he saw it really was not a problem, and he still needed the service. I was able to go ahead and do business with the person. Educating a prospect will sometimes develop the prospect into a client.

Tough Prospects?

Actually, I get excited about the "no's". I love it when they say they don't use agencies. Why? Because I love the battle, and the enjoyment of talking to them about how I can be of value to them.

Some of my best clients were people who never wanted to use me in the first place. If you are skilled and tenacious, you will see the same thing. Once you convince them to utilize your services, if you provide that top service, you will have them forever! It is like a converted smoker, or religion. If you have provided a top level service to a "convert", you have a true long-term client.

A Major Client

I will give you an example. I had a man in accounting back in my early days right in my hometown that had a 30,000 dollar opening. Now the fee on was only nine thousand dollars, but this guy said he doesn't use recruiters and would never pay nine grand to hire an accountant. I tried to tell him why he should, but he would not listen.

Some of my exchange partners called me, and asked, "Do you have this accounting order with this company?" I replied that I had tried to get it, but had not been successful. "Well," they said. "He ran an ad in our paper." They faxed me the ad. I took out my ruler and measured it, called the papers for prices, and found that the size ad he put in the newspapers cost him fifteen hundred dollars each. He had put them in five major cities, the one I was in and four surrounding. Then he would have relocation expenses.

So I called him and said, "Wait a minute. I do not understand your attitude. You will not pay me nine thousand when I have the candidate sitting right here in Tulsa and ready to go to work, qualified for your position. Yet you spent almost that much on advertising in other cities. And you don't even have a candidate. Even if you have a candidate, you will have to spend money to bring him in and to interview him. You will have to spend money to relocate him. So you are saying to me, I am not worth nine thousand dollars but you went out and spent nearly that in advertising up-front, with no guarantee of results!"

Well, he did not like the fact that I called him on it, and he got angry and hung up. I thought, "Oh, well. That is that". At least I had given the man the knowledge he needed to make an intelligent economic decision about the way he did business.

Those types of problems sometimes have a real silver lining to them. If you will take the time to discuss with these people the advantages of using our business, you will find some very good clients by doing so. If there is an opening and they are just not giving it to you, be sure to call back in a few weeks. See chapters on desk organizing and planning.

"Corporate Policy"?

When you get the "I don't use recruiting firms" or "I don't pay fees" response, then ask why. One of the occasional answers that I have found is that it is "corporate policy". What a great cop-out for the person you are dealing with! It's "corporate policy" means that "you don't need to talk to me, because I can't do anything about it".

One of the great responses to that is, "Who makes corporate policy?" They start to stumble and stutter and ask what do you mean? "Well," I generally reply, "if you don't make corporate policy and you can't use me or pay my fee because of it, then I need to talk to the person who made that policy. Because that is a decision that is economically not correct for your company."

You will find out one of two things. Possibly there really is not any such corporate policy, and you were hearing an excuse to keep from having to talk to you about it. Alternatively, you will find out who does make corporate policy. You can call that person and get them squared away and do business with them. But you don't need to be speaking with someone who does not make that decision or does not have the power to reverse that decision.

I had one low-level guy who told me this, and I asked, "Who makes corporate policy?" He replied, "Well, uh, the Vice President has made that corporate policy." And I said, "Fantastic! Well, then, I will talk to him about it." And he said, "You can't call him." And I said, "Why not? Doesn't he have a phone?" I don't have to have anyone's permission to call anybody about corporate dealings and about being a consultant to that corporation. Neither do you. And it scared this person to death that I might call his Vice President, and discuss corporate policy with that individual.

Don't give up! Survey after survey in corporate sales has showed that it is the fifth call that gets the business! Keep beating on those people's doors until you determine there is no reason to be on it any more. Once you have changed their mind and cracked the account, you will get very good business from them.

THE BUYING SIGN

You will receive another response frequently, but surprisingly, many do not recognize it. We call it the "Buy Sign". That means they have asked you a question about your candidate. Now how do we handle that? You would think a "Buy Sign" of a simple question about our candidate would be easy. But for many, it is not.

Our problem is that we always answer that question, and then sit there pensively on the edge of our chair waiting for them to say something. Guess what they do? They ask another question. And that is not what you want.

For instance, you make a presentation and the prospective client says, "Larry, is that a local candidate?" "Yes sir. This candidate is right here in town." Did you hear that silence? There is nowhere to go with that kind of answer. And so he will ask another question. He will say, "Well, if she is here in town, then how much money is she making?" "Well, this candidate is only fifty thousand dollars right now, and I think that is quite reasonable for her experience level." Here we have the silence again.

When we have a "Buy Sign", answer the question as positively as possible and then <u>close</u> for <u>the</u> <u>interview</u>. If the person is asking you questions, he or she is at least curious and will be interested in what you are talking about.

Remember this about our business or about any sales situation. ***He who asks the questions controls the conversation.*** If you are allowing clients to ask all the questions, then you are allowing them to control the direction of this sales presentation and where it is ultimately headed. But if <u>you</u> ask the questions, then you control that situation. Respond as positively as possible, and then ask a closing question about whether they want to see this person.

A Better Response

For instance, he asks, "Larry, how much is this person making right now?" "Well, she is only making fifty thousand, and for her experience level, that is quite reasonable. Is there a time where I can set her up to talk to you about your particular situation? Uh, she has Thursdays and Fridays set for interviews. I could get her over to you since she is local on Thursday afternoon. What does your schedule look like?"

Go right for the close, and begin to ask questions that require this person to make yes or no decisions about what you are presenting. If you just answer the question and then never say anything, you constantly allow him to ask one question after another. Guess what? If you allow them to ask enough questions, they will soon find an answer they <u>don't</u> like, and the interview will never happen!

When you get a "Buy Sign" remember to answer it as positively as possible, and then close for an interview.

THE MOST FAVORABLE RESPONSE

Of course, what you hear every once in a while is, "I would like to see that person. That sounds like somebody I would really be interested in." Well, gee whiz. Don't drop the ball now!

Many new consultants will respond "Good. This is a great candidate and I will get the resume right over to you." The hiring authority did not say <u>any-thing</u> about resumes. Don't be hung up on paperwork . If needed, the candidate can carry the resume with him.

<u>Immediately</u> set a date and a time for that to happen. Go right for the jugular and say, "When can we set this up? Give me a couple of available dates and times that you will be open, and I will call the candidate and get it set for you."

A Partial Search

After you have the date and time arranged, then take a search assignment. One of the critical factors that causes us to miss placements is when we setting interviews initiated by a marketing call, but have not obtained the information we need to get from the company. You <u>need</u> this information, both to prepare candidates and to close them. If we cannot prepare them for an interview, they will not look good and will not get an offer. Even if they get an offer, we have no information on how to close. Make sure when somebody says "I want to see that person", you get all the information you need to do your entire job properly!

At this point, you don't really need to take a full search assignment. There are lots of questions that are not necessary at this particular stage. We can fill them out later if we are going to continue to do searches for other people.

What do we need right now, given that we were marketing a candidate? We need the duties. We need to know the background that they are really looking for, so we can compare and see if other candidates might be qualified. We need to know the "Key to The Hire" and what do they really want. Those are mandatory, so we can prepare our candidate to look as good as possible in there. We need to know things that help us with this interview much more then taking a full search assignment. These topics will be covered in depth in later chapters.

If you can take a full search at this point, by all means do so. But if you have a hiring official that is strapped for time, then get the "need" information to prepare and close the candidate. You can call back and complete the rest of the order at a later date.

OTHER OBJECTIVES

Another answer that you are going to get is, "Let me tell you what I do need". Or they will give you a hint which is, "Well, I don't really need that kind of person". <u>Listen</u> for those kinds of statements so you can go into an order. Many times you might call and present a great candidate and while they may have an opening, you have not asked for it. <u>Always</u> <u>ask</u> <u>for</u> <u>openings</u>.

Remember, our first objective is to try to get this person a send-out. But our second objective is try to get some other opening that we can work on within that company. So when the person says, "I really don't need that type of person, Larry", then my initial question is, "Oh, what kind of person <u>do</u> you need?"

If they say, "I don't need anyone at all", I generally ask a value statement about their company and their needs. For example I might say, "Let me ask you this question. What candidate can I bring to you that will be of value to you? When you are looking, what is the background that is hardest for you to find?" I don't mind saying that I added that question after reading Steve Finkel's book "<u>*Breakthrough*</u>!", which I strongly recommend.

When they answer that question, it tells me who to market to them in the future. "Larry, I can never find enough of this type of candidate or enough of this type of engineer". <u>I</u> <u>make</u> <u>that</u> <u>notation</u> and I put that in the file so I can retrieve that information. When I do have that hard-to-find person, I will know to call that company.

Find out if it is <u>current</u> or <u>future</u>. "Well, I need someone like this, but I need to get an approval. If you have someone like this, then call me". There is a lot of "future business" that goes on in marketing. Be alert for it. Put it down in a "tickle file" and call back on a certain time or date to obtain your new assignment.

If they do say, "That is not the kind of person I need. What I am looking for is a mechanical engineer", then say, "Fantastic! Is that the actual title you are trying to fill, or would it be Senior Mechanical Engineer?" As soon as you get them to answer that question, you are right into that search and you can continue to ask questions.

<u>Don't</u> say to them, "Would you like for me to do a search for you?" Those words are a little much for a new hiring official whom you just called. Say to them, "What is the job title? Or is that the job title? Is it a mechanical engineer? Is that a staff engineer, or would that be a senior level?" "Well, that would be a senior level." "OK. How many years experience would you want me to find you to bring you a Senior? What do you consider a senior?" They say, "Well, Larry, that would probably be above five years".

Get right into questioning! Take them right through the order, sell the fee, get a search assignment and start working on it if it has the quality you seek. But start <u>tomorrow</u>. Finish your <u>plan</u> today!

Realistic Time Constraints

In most instances, you do not have the time to ask <u>all</u> the questions you might like. Certainly if they are easy-going and feel like they have the time, you can. But you can hear on the phone when somebody is rushed or under pressure.

So what you want to do when you get down to Market Information, Client Development and Advertising (your last three objectives) is to have the top two or three questions, and ask those. If it feels good, you can go forward with other questions. If you sense that time is of the essence in this particular call, then get some key questions answered, and call them back and complete your objectives later. It might take you four to five phone calls to a company before you get enough questions answered to tell you whether or not you are going to make a client out of them.

Let's assume we just made a presentation and the prospective client gave us a response that they don't need that candidate. We ask them if they have any needs, and they said no. Where do we go from there?

MARKET INFORMATION

You now go into market information, questions relating to the company, the market, and the industry. A question might be "Tell me, how are you doing this year? Is your company expanding?" Or, "Have you contracted a little? How are you doing?" And they will tell you. Or "How big is your staff?

How many people do you have on staff in this engineering function? How is the industry doing right now?" Get market information that tells you where this company stands. You might even ask this person, "How do you think your company ranks in your industry?" Ask them their own opinion of their company. Then ask one last one, "What company do you respect the most?"

As you begin to get this information, you find out who is who in that particular industry, and you can begin to work with them.

CLIENT DEVELOPMENT INFORMATION

What kind of questions do we need to ask? You want to ask questions pertaining to placement and your business relationship with that hiring official. Questions like, "Do you use outside sources? Do you pay fees?" Or, "Do have a recruiter that you rely on for all of your placements? I would like to have a chance to do business with your firm."

Here is a great question that has really rocked some officials, "The reason for my call is I want to be the consultant that you rely on when you look for top people. How do you go about making that decision? What can I do to become that recruiter?" It is an interesting question, and you will have some fun with the answers.

For advertising, obviously, the last thing is, "My name is ____ . I am with the _____", and <u>leave</u> <u>your</u> <u>phone</u> <u>number</u>.

Then your call is thorough and you have met all of your obectives. Send a follow-up letter and a card, so they can keep it on file. You will be able to do a lot of business with a lot of companies. People <u>will</u> call you back. Don't forget to send your card! Your small brochure! In the mail! Written! Don't just say "Here's our website!" Don't get their e-mail and send spam!

By achieving your five objectives, <u>every</u> <u>call</u> <u>is</u> <u>made</u> <u>to</u> <u>be</u> <u>important</u>. Each call deserves your best effort. By doing so over time, you will obtain the results you seek for.

GETTING THROUGH

Let me give you some tips on this critical topic after we have initially completed our first few calls to a potential client that might help you. Then we'll discuss the same topic <u>before</u> we have completed a few calls.

First, be sure that you know the secretary of the person with whom you are dealing. I know that does not sound like much, but so many secretaries are treated like pieces of office furniture. They are lied to frequently; some try to go around them, and won't give them their name. Believe me, once you get the "gate-keeper" on your side, then the gate swings wide open. Talk to them like real people and get to know their names. Record their first name on your card or computer or whatever tracking system that you use. The next time that you call the hiring official and the secretary answers the phone, say, "Hi Marsha. How was your weekend? This is Larry Nobles over at the Reality Group." A little small talk up-front where she actually feels like she is being treated like a person and a professional will yield dividends.

Whatever works for your firm is fine. But let me tell you about a recent experience of mine with a secretary.

She inquired as they sometimes do, "Larry, can I ask what you are calling about?" I said, "Yes. I am a corporate recruiter and here is what I am calling about." She replied, "Thanks so much for telling me." I said, "What do you mean?" She said, "Well, no one else will give me that kind of information. Then I get my boss on the phone and he gets mad at me because they are recruiters that I put through. I am happy, Larry, that you called. He does not have any needs right now but believe me, because you were honest with me (don't say I gave you this information), there are two openings at our other plant. Here are the phone numbers and here is the person you need to contact so you might get some business."

Here was a first-time telephone call to a secretary who had been battered by so many that I truly got some business out of an affiliate plant from the lead that she gave me! Why? Because I treated her professionally and honestly. I am proud of what I do. If I am going to be screened out by the hiring official and secretary after I tell them that I am a headhunter, then I don't want to deal with them anyway. It would in any case have been a very difficult time getting their attitude turned around in order to deal with me.

On the other hand, my viewpoint may not be right for everyone, so I'll recommend a terrific alternative. In fact, 156 of them! A book every office in our industry should have is *"I'll Get Back To You: 156 Ways To Get People To Return Your Calls"* by Robert L. Shook and Eric Yaverbaum. If it matters, ISBN #0-07-057721-8. This book literally does contain what the title promises. Warning! Many of these suggestions are not appropriate in a business context, but many are. There is not a person in our industry who will not benefit markedly from this. Gatekeepers, fax, e-mail, it's all here with suggestions from the best sales stars and top corporate executives around. Highly recommended!

This book — alas — is, for some unaccountable reason, out of print. It is in the process of being re-issued as of this writing, and should again be available soon. However, one of the merits of the internet is the ease of finding used or out-of-print books if you know precisely what you are seeking. Don't just settle for Amazon.com. Try E-Bay, or Half.com. Rummage around at www.bookfinder.com, www.bookarea.com or www.allbookstores.com. Go to www.abebooks.com or www.alibris.com. Look around. It will be worth your time to do so.

This is one of the areas where "getting through is getting through", and techniques developed for <u>business</u> telephone selling will generally translate well into our industry. There is no real reason to develop industry-specific techniques in this area, and any you may hear have almost certainly been taken verbatim from one or more of these books. I have indicated my viewpoint. However, if you would like to try other ideas, just start reading on business-to-business telephone selling, "telesales", "teleselling", or telephone sales. See what works best for you. Something will! The Shook/Yaverbaum book is the place to start.

MAINTAINING FOCUS

Some people focus on the overall number of calls to be made. They can fall into a problem in marketing by making those calls by rote. What do I mean "by rote"?

Most of us have two objectives when we make a marketing call. We are either going to present our services to a company, or present a candidate to a company in hopes that they will do some business with us. But after about the fifth call in a row, we are not getting any business, there are no openings out there, and there is no one who wants to see our candidate. We start to lose that enthusiasm. Without the love or excitement of the hunt, our results diminish.

There are a number of ways you can use your thought processes to get the results that you want. I remember when I was new in the business and I was marketing. When I would start my thirty-call program, I found when I did my statistics that <u>all</u> of my results came in the first fifteen calls! The last fifteen calls I was not getting anything! And I wondered why that was? Why was I getting so many results out of my first fifteen?

Evaluation

I tape recorded myself, and I listened to it. I said, "If I was on the other side of the line, how would this guy sound to me? If he called me, how would I respond?" I guarantee you that it is a great way of learning. If you are having trouble, tape yourself and listen objectively.   Or have someone else listen to help you pick out areas that are hurting you in your presentation. I listened to myself. And that is what I heard.

In the first five calls, my enthusiasm was evident. Here was a man who believed in his candidate and in his services. After I got through a third of my program, however, I was starting to slow down a little.

By call number fifteen, I was slowed down considerably and when I got to call number twenty, I was a 45 record on a 33 speed. By the time I got to call twenty-five, I was almost calling and saying, "Hey, I have a good candidate. You don't want to speak to him, do you? I didn't think so. Goodbye", and I was moving on.

That's why I wasn't getting any results in the last fifteen calls. Because they were terrible! Not only was I not getting results, but they were doing damage to myself and my reputation in the marketplace by making sloppy calls.

But is marketing necessary? Absolutely. Marketing is the guts of this business. Marketing gets you everything that you need to make money. But how to keep up your enthusiasm after multiple "no's"?

Why even make thirty calls if you are going to make only fifteen of them with any kind of seriousness and enthusiasm?

THE GROUP OF FIVE

Remember what we said earlier in the book; if your phone is on the hook, you can not make money! Likewise, if your phone is off the hook, but you are unenthusiastic, you will tend not to make money. How do you get better results out of the last fifteen calls? How do you double that effort, maintain enthusiasm and therefore greatly increase your results?

I did it by breaking up my calls into <u>groups</u> <u>of</u> <u>five</u>. I would set down thirty calls, and I would break them up into six groups. Then I would make five calls without hanging up. One right after another. I would be as enthusiastic, cheerful and results-oriented as possible. I would sell hard, and I would close hard. I would continue to ask questions, get information needed to reach objectives, and then go on to the next one.

But after five calls, I would hang up. I would take a break. When I say take a break, that does not mean a smoke break or a coffee break. That means go on to do other things. Call candidates. Make a call to a specific client. Do <u>other</u> jobs for awhile. Then come back in a few minutes, recharged and ready to go with the next five-call program.

By using that kind of program consistently with that one change, I was able to <u>double</u> the results that I got from my marketing program! Try it. You'll get <u>twice</u> the interviews, search assignments and qualified clients...just by concentrating on The Group of Five!

FAIL MORE TO SUCCEED MORE

If you want to be more successful, up your failures! What does this mean? There is a ratio of failure-to-success in every sales effort, regardless of what you are selling. I don't care how many times you make a thirty-call program, you are going to get X percent of "no's" out of that program. You are going to have to learn to live with it and accept it. In fact, you should look forward to it. On the tenth no, I may not have a yes yet, but guess what I've got — ten no's out of the way. Great, here comes the next call. It might be my yes!

Do you want an extended dissertation on this concept? You should. Try reading *"How I Raised Myself from Failure to Success in Selling"* by sales legend Frank Bettger. Get a good sales education to really enjoy and prosper in our business!

You can't control which call gives you your results, but you must understand the ratio of failure-to-success is a constant, at least on a short-term basis. If you want to be more successful, up your failures. What does that mean? <u>Fail</u> <u>more</u> <u>times</u> <u>and</u> <u>you</u> <u>will</u> <u>succeed</u> <u>more</u> <u>times</u>. That is what we are saying when we say if thirty calls is not getting it done, let's do forty. Let's do fifty! Or let's do a hundred-call blitz, and see how many searches or interviews we can pick up from that!

Does that mean skill doesn't matter? <u>Of</u> <u>course</u> <u>it</u> <u>does</u>! You must always strive to improve your selling skills. Don't buy that "this is a numbers business" foolishness. But fail more, and you will succeed more!

WHEN TO CALL

Does time of the day matter? Yes! Marketing is an exciting time in calling companies, but I want the most response from the person on the other end of the line. What I like to do is market in the morning, and recruit in the afternoon. Why? I like to market in the morning because I like to be one of the first recruiters that calls. By 11 A.M. in the morning, he may not be too receptive. I may be saying the greatest thing with the most enthusiasm and having the best candidate, but guess what? He or she may be not listening to what I say. Moreover, survey after survey has shown that most sales in business are made before noon! Yours will be too. That is why you must <u>use</u> those morning hours.

Try to make your client calls first thing in the morning. Get to your potential clients before the rest of the world does. Get to them when they have had their coffee. Get to them before they have been distracted doing business. If you wait until later, they will be snowed under with various pressures, meetings, deadlines etc.

I like to recruit in the <u>afternoon</u> for the same reason. That person has had a lot of calls, and they have had every problem in the world that morning. The boss may have been critical of them as well. They are upset and they are tired. If I ask about Reasons For Leaving, they are likely to tell me!

HOW MANY CALLS?

How many calls should you make? I don't know. Every market is different. What you have to determine is how many search assignments you need on a weekly basis to reach your goals. Then you simply plan enough marketing calls to get there.

Top producers don't plan a call list, and then try to see what happens from that list. They <u>plan</u> results that they want, and then plan enough calls to make that happen! Don't say, "I am going to make thirty marketing calls; I wonder what that will get for me." It is better to think, "I want at least one search assignment today". How many calls will it take to get that? Then make that kind of a plan.

If your call ratio is fifty-to-one, you must make fifty attempts to get one order. If your call ratio is twenty-to-one, twenty attempts will be needed to get one order. Then all you have to do is to plan the number of calls that result in the amount of search assignments that you need. It will help you to understand how to plan your day. Use the "Group of Five" concept to stay highly enthusiastic, make results-oriented calls, and you will get where you need to be.

Declining Ratios

A good indicator that you are losing enthusiasm or not making good solid marketing calls is when your ratios go up significantly. Let's say you have been working on a twenty-to-one ratio and you are now on a forty-to-one ratio on attempts-to-search assignments. (If you focus on attempts-to-interview ratio, it could be the specific candidate.) Remember that "attempt" does not mean "presentation". You may get through only 50% of the time.

That might mean two things. It might mean your marketplace has gone down considerably, and there is not as much out there as there used to be. However, I suggest that may also <u>not</u> be the problem; it is a good excuse. Your enthusiasm, concentration, and ability to make a good call is frequently the real problem in this situation. Set aside a solid hour in the morning to make your marketing calls. Remember that the average call is planned for two-and-a-half minutes, and you can do a quick twenty-four to thirty good marketing calls in an hour. I plan a thirty call list.

Some people like to start at number one and just burn it. They go solid for about an hour. They have their secretaries hold their calls and they make all of those calls as quickly, enthusiastically, and as results-oriented as possible to get what they want out of them. Others prefer my "Group of Five" technique.

MARKETING, NOT SALES

Marketing is more than just getting search assignments. If you <u>only</u> focus on searches, it is sales, not marketing. Getting information that causes you to react to the company is marketing. What is the basic difference between marketing and sales in any corporation? Salesmen sell the product. Marketing people decide where and what that market is, and how to get that product to that particular market. You must do <u>both</u>.

Let's look at marketing as a concept. Marketing has within it a concept that is true of every corporation. It should be true of ours. When we market our services or a candidate, we are trying to identify companies that we can do business with. We want to do <u>market</u> <u>identification</u> and <u>client</u> <u>identification</u>. Whenever you market, there will be companies that you do not want to do business with. And there are companies that you want to specifically try to pursue until they do business with you.

Market identification means your goal is not to thrash around out there in companies, and only look for searches. You need to also determine when you are marketing exactly what is going on within that group of companies or that industry that you are calling.

Working A Local Market

For instance, let's say you specialize in office support in a local market. If you have a bookkeeper in a real estate firm, what you want to do is call every real estate firm in the city that day.

First, that is where you'll find a hiring authority who will most likely want to interview your person, because they already come from a similar company. But also it tells you what is going on in real estate in your local market. Is it a viable industry that is hiring a lot of people? Is it not viable? Is it dead? Have they been having layoffs? How is business? This will tell you where to put your future endeavors and future efforts when you are trying to market. It is called market identification.

Identify a National Market

For those who work a national or regional market, you have a little bit more of a problem. Why? Because you may have a more difficult time identifying those companies.

This is self-evidently an area where the internet will be of <u>some</u> help to you. But if that's <u>all</u> you do, you wil lose out on a great deal of business.

There are directories that will help you to understand why you must go beyond electronic to be able to come up with the companies you are looking for. Some directories are segmented by various types of companies by size, and location. Dunn and Bradstreet has a book called *The Million Dollar Directory*. Within that directory they list every corporation that has in excess of a million dollar in sales in the US. They list them alphabetically in one section. In the next section of the book, they list geographically. If you are trying to find all of the million dollar plus companies in Omaha, Nebraska, you can go down to Nebraska, then to Omaha. All of them are there, regardless of what kind of company they are.

But there is another way of grouping companies, rather than just alphabetically or geographically. And that is called "SIC codes". Every company in the US has been given a Standard Industrial Classification code. That is what SIC stands for. That code tells you what kind of company they are and allows you by using that code to group similar types of companies for your market identification.

There are other directories that will help you. The Thomas Register is a directory in which they list manufacturing firms by product, and it is also available in the library. If you work a partially local market, your own Chamber of Commerce produces local and regional books of firms available within that area and classifies them and categorizes them for your use.

There are publishing houses for your industry as well. If you research the publishing companies, you may find a directory that is specifically suited to your specialty or the companies that you are trying to attract. If you don't know of any or can't seem to find them, ask your candidates!

Why Research?

In general, your odds are best when you keep candidates and search assignments within the same type company. So if we have a top performer in a rubber company, we want to move them to another rubber company. Why? Because that person would be easily hired and they have the skills that permit immediate accomplishment of the job that needs to be done. The company would see more value in hiring that person than anybody from chemicals or some other unlike company.

Why Market Identification?

When we are doing market identification, we are trying to determine which companies within that market we want to work with, and which companies we do not want to work with.

Frequently, we get turndowns which are avoidable due to poor market identification. Why? Because what we are doing is taking people out of top companies and trying to move them down to the weak, poorly-managed, low-morale, failing or unstable companies. It does not work that way.

Market identification is the systematic narrowing of our focus to a limited number of high-morale, well-managed, stable, profitable, expanding companies. We want to work hard to make those people our clients. It is so much easier to take someone out of a poorly-managed, unstable company and give them a great opportunity with the number-one company of that industry than it is to do the reverse. So we not only do market identification when we call these potential candidates, but we do potential client identification.

We must have both kinds of companies to be able to do our jobs, companies in which we place people and companies from which we get people. Because we can't mix those two, Client and Market identification becomes critical to our success. Believe me, top producers know all of the good companies and who to work with, and have many of them as clients.

Difficult Companies? Good!

Here is a law you can live by that will really help when you are judging companies. Sometimes you are working with a company, and there is a difficulty in placing people within that company. The company does not respond well, and they don't take or return your phone calls. They want to cut your fees, and you are having problems getting them to cooperate. They have a bit of an attitude about our business and our call and what we are trying to do. You cannot coach them to improve interaction to yield a better quality of candidate.

There is a reason those companies react that way when you call them. As the rule, any time there is a difficulty in placing people with a company, there is an opposite and equal ease of recruiting people from that company. They are frequently a poorly-managed company with low morale and they are not doing well. You will find out that people there want to leave.

Difficulty Recruiting From?

Now the other side of the fence works also. Sometimes you find a company and you talk to their people, and no one seems to want to move; they are all happy. When you have a difficulty in recruiting people from that company, you have an equal and opposite ease of placing top-quality people with that company.

In your first pass in marketing, you need to go through your list of prospects once. Find out which companies are the top companies, which ones tend to be expanding and have good reputations with high morale. You want to put those people into a client development program and beat on their door consistently. We'll cover this in the latter chapters of this book. Marketing as a concept means you must go through a marketplace, and identify companies to develop and companies to never call again. You need both kinds of companies.

Every day you should have those particular objectives in finding those companies. Of course you don't call the same company every day. But certainly monthly or bi-monthly, you need to be in contact with the head of the department in which you are trying to place people. Follow up consistently until you get to know that person. Talk to them about candidates, your service etc., until you begin to get orders from them. Then fill those orders and develop them as a client.

The previously-mentioned "Group of Five" will keep you sounding fresh. Good luck and good hunting. Get out there and make some great calls! By doing so, combined with the other topics we'll cover here, you <u>will</u> achieve your goals!

RECRUITING: FINDING THE BEST

10

*W*hat is the "most fun" portion of our business? Putting aside "cashing the check", what do executive search consultants enjoy most? To me, it has always been recruiting. Why? Because it enables us to be the corporate equivalent of the Fairy Godmother. There sits the candidate — perhaps talented, but perhaps limited at his current firm in terms of upward mobility and income, slightly bored due to a luck of challenge. And then...the phone rings! It's us! And with our magic wand, we reach out and touch the candidate, and transform his life!

All right. Maybe it isn't quite like that. But close. Sometimes very close.

Do they know that we are the corporate equivalent of Fairy Godmothers? Not always. It depends on what flaws they see in their current position. If they see no flaws, what then? Well, it depends on how flawless their position really is. Frequently, it is far less so than they pretend. Generally, we ask questions to detect hidden problems, or to motivate the potential candidate to disclose difficulties they had previously not considered or faced.

Can you motivate people with better opportunities? Yes. Absolutely. There are a number of sophisticated sales techniques for doing so. But even after doing so, you must create in their minds a <u>reason</u> for leaving their company, or the end result may be that they won't move. There are a lot of people that don't realize their career is not moving properly until they talk to us. Our knowledge and understanding of their industry enables us to talk to people about their careers, where they are headed, and what they want to do in life. Then with our skills, we can identify or create concern or unhappiness in them, and show them how to improve their lives.

The Fairy Godmother in Action

Let me give you an example that might allow you to see how it works. Recently I spoke to a young engineer who was in process control in a small plant. He had been there for almost four years, and he was getting pretty good as far as his experience level was concerned. But that small plant had two problems. One, they did not have very many controls or very many advanced controls, because they did not run a lot of complex units. Two, they had a very small control system that most other companies had outgrown a long time ago. If this man stayed there another three years and became a six-or-seven year person at that small plant and control system, he might <u>never</u> be able to move out of it. Why not? Because corporations would be able to find other people for the same amount of money or less that had the right experience on the right control system and in the right size plant.

So I talked with this young man. He was not unhappy and he liked his boss. He liked his job. He wasn't getting paid particularly well, but did not know that, because he didn't have any other exposure. I discussed with him his needs and his future. He got to realize the truth of what I was saying.

By discussing it with him, we created an unhappiness and identified a career problem. We were presenting a bigger company in a better control system at a higher income. However, had we not helped this engineer see that he did not have this where he was, he would not have moved in the end.

Ultimately, we moved him into a much improved and more satisfying career. But did he realize that he needed one when we first spoke? No. Were our services extremely beneficial to him and his family? Yes! Did he do an outstanding job for the client, who paid the fee happily? Yes, indeed.

Emotional Trauma

It is absolutely a true statement that more people hurt themselves in their careers by staying put than ever do by moving to the wrong situation. That is why we do them a major favor when we identify or create concerns about their present position. If we don't, the end result may be that these people will just stay put, and their careers and lives will thus be stunted.

One of the things you must understand is how emotional a career decision is. With very few exceptions, the single biggest high-stress decision in a person's life is a job change. The top five stress factors in a person's life are: A death of a spouse. A death of a family member. Divorce. Job change. Relocation. In most of these areas, there is no choice. But the last two are optional.

When you say to somebody, "Why do you want to look at this?", they will say, "Well, because you said it had this specific type of opportunity." That information is not enough. You must clarify in the candidate's mind that he or she does not have that kind of opportunity at the present position. As we discuss those situations you begin to create the unhappiness, identify the career problem, and make a serious "I want to leave" candidate.

OBTAINING CANDIDATES FOR CLIENTS

Critical as it is, recruiting is only one of the ways we find candidates. We constantly talk about recruiting. Why? Because there is a specific technique that helps us enormously in producing the amount and quality of inventory that we need, and which many in our industry do not do well. But is it the only way? No.

Should this be your first step? Again, no. There are other ways of finding candidates. In fact, let's put recruiting in perspective. What are the five ways of finding a candidate in the order of importance?

One: Your *current candidates*: When you get an order, you first look and see what current candidates are on or in your desk that you can refer.

Two: *Other candidates within the office*: there may be candidates other consultants in your office have in their desks, and you just don't know about them.

Three: *Going to the file* and pulling out old candidates and requalifying them. As we briefly mentioned under "dead file", if you do this, you have emergency phone numbers where you can trace these people and find them. You are talking to people with a known background and they know you. There is a relationship there, because you (or someone at your firm) have talked to them before. You can either re-recruit them for the situation that you have available, or you can get referrals from them. Your odds of a recruit lead are high because they know who you are, and you have dealt with them in the past.

<u>Four</u>: Your ***exchange partners'*** current candidates: these are people who work in other firms with whom you speak on the phone who may supply a candidate for your current search. "Split business" has merit, though it should <u>not</u> be a good recruiter's first step. Be selective here. Don't overdo this. A good recruiter can find a <u>lot</u> of candidates on his own for half of the fee, which is what it will cost you if you have someone else provide the candidate!

<u>Five</u>: Is ***real recruiting***.

Recruiting is fun and it is important. I enjoy hunting out the right person for my client, and finding them the precise individual that will make them or save them a lot of money, and benefit the candidate as well. However, let's not overlook the first four ways to finding a candidate as well as recruiting .

REAL RECRUITING

Surprisingly, many in our industry are reluctant to utilize this extraordinarily effective methodology, or have simply never been taught. Yet, the best recruiters <u>consistently</u> outperform non-recruiters on our industry! It is easier, of course, to play games on the internet, competing with your clients' HR department for the <u>same</u> candidates. Internet trainers long ago realized your clients would pay far more than your firm for information about hustling up candidates on the internet. If that is what you think "recruiting" is, you'd best resign yourself to mediocrity. The <u>only</u> way to realize maximum income and insulate yourself against the internet is to learn to recruit properly! By doing so, you'll obtain a far better quality of candidates <u>not</u> <u>available</u> <u>in</u> <u>any</u> <u>other</u> <u>way</u>.

Getting Through

But how do you get through to the proper person?

Usually, you can reach the person directly that you want to speak to. That is particularly true if somebody that you call has a singular function within the company. Even though we don't know who that person is, if we know the title and there is only one title like that, then we can recruit at ease because we know we can reach the person.

If there are multiple people in a given position, ask them to put you through, or just ask to be put through to the department. I have had people say, "Well, we have twenty chemical engineers. Which one would you like to speak to?" I would simply say, "Well, I am not sure. I need to speak to the one that handles the lube unit. Can you tell me who that is?" "Well, gee, no. Down here at the front desk, I don't have that kind of information." "Fine. Why don't you put me through to the department and I will ask them?" The secretary of the department comes on, and I talk to her about which of their chemical engineers handles the lube unit. If asked, I say I am a consultant to their industry and there are some questions I would like to ask. They generally identify that person and put me through.

I have had people say, "What is the call in reference to?" Rather than making up something, I simply say, "I am a consultant in Tulsa, Oklahoma. I represent a client that needs me to find a very specific type of engineer for them and I need some direction and some help. I was told that this particular person might be able to give me some direction, and that was why I was trying to get to them." Every time I do that, I get put right through.

You might want to talk with your manager about the techniques you use when you are going into a company when you do not have a name, but you are trying to talk to somebody within that particular area. I prefer the up-front professional "this is who I am and this is what I am doing", approach. If these people want to respond they can, and if they don't respond, that is fine too.

See previously-mentioned "Getting Through" in "Marketing" chapter for other ideas.

GETTING NAMES

One of the things that can help you with this sometimes frustrating areas of our business is to have names. It is so much easier to call up and say, "I need to speak to Jeff Jones, please", than it is to call and try to find out who he is.

If you don't know the name, you can use an in-direct source. Well, what is an in-direct source? Think about who might know this person. Then you go ask that person for the name of a potential recruit.

For example, one of the recruiters in my office works sales. He was looking for a frozen food salesman. I suggested he go down to the supermarket, go to the person in the little glass in the middle of the market, ask for the manager, and say, "Hello, I shop here all the time. But I am also a recruiter, and I am looking for a food salesman. May I ask you for your professional opinion? Who are the top three salesmen that call on you to sell you your goods and services?" He got the names of the top three salesmen, got their cards and and phone numbers. He then called them. That is called an In-direct Identification.

How does this In-direct Candidate Identification work in our office? We sometimes have files that can help us a lot. Let's say we are looking for a programmer who needs to have application experience running banking applications. In our files, who might know that person who is not a pro-grammer?

You might go to your banking files. Let's say you have a loan officer in there who has wanted you to help them. They know the names of the programmers that work in their bank; all you have to do is call them up and say, "I need to speak to your programmer that works there." And they will give you the information that you need. Sometimes just brain-storming is effective. You might know someone whose mother-in-law works at a bank. We can ask specifically who this person is and who we can talk to, and we can develop names. It is easier to go to a company and ask for a particular person then it is to try to dig out a name of the person at the front desk. So use an in-direct method to research names.

I will tell you that resource material is the best way from keeping from doing a lot of research calls.

Lists

When recruiting, not all people are going to respond to us. Like marketing, we have to make a number of calls to get the amount of recruits we need. If we are making a number of calls that only get us names, we are doubling the number of calls we need to do to get the amount of inventory (candidates) we want. One of the ways of cutting those calls in half (or reducing them great-ly) is to get and use resource material. Unlike directories that tell us about certain types of companies or certain industries, we need research that will tell us about certain kinds of people.

Now where can we get these? There are lots of lists available as a list of peo-ple, and you can get them from list renters.

Alternatively, joining an association that has those people that we deal with has merit. For instance, you might join the chemical engineer society if you place chemical engineers. When you do that, many of these associations have membership rosters of engineers all over the United States. With your entry fee, you get that association book.

Trade journals and magazines carry names of people. If you are working in a specific area, subscribe to the trade journal or magazine of that area. Every week or month it will come rolling into your office with new names of people who have done things or been promoted, who works where, and so forth.

Set up a name retrieval system that keeps these names and phone numbers handy, or at least names and locations where you can find the information. You can retain contacts. For instance, every time that you go through a list of companies you turn up certain names in the companies, even if you did not talk to them. You need to have a retrieval system in which you can place those people's names.

Three-by-five cards will work, as will computers. File it so you will know how to call them later. Sit down and brain-storm with the people in your office or your boss. When I recruit, I don't have to make a ton of phone calls just finding names. Why not? Because I have continued to work my niche correctly.

The most extensive and creative body of information on "Identifying Candidates" is contained in Steve Finkel's video series "The Art of Recruiting". Volume III is two 45-minute modules specifically addressing this topic in great detail. This series is utterly mandatory for those who wish to maximize skills at recruiting.

There is also complete coverage in detail of the proper techniques of Direct Recruiting. While most effective, this methodology does require a higher level of selling skills. For that reason, you will probably find it easier to start with Indirect Recruiting, which is what we will address.

THE THREE TYPES OF RECRUITING

Broadly, there are actually three types of recruiting calls.

Direct Recruiting is calling and directly presenting the opportunity to the candidate with the clear intention of recruiting him. To be done properly, it is a sophisticated fairly complex methodology requiring a number of nuances to head off objections before they occur. However, some objections will of course occur, and it will require rebuttals involving subtle skills in selling to deal with them. These are not effectively explained when presented in a written format.

Voice inflections, correct pace, emphasis and intonations as well as precise verbiage are far more important in good Direct Recruiting. As such, it is not really appropriate for presenting in a book or training manual. It is <u>highly</u> effective when done properly.

Indirect Recruiting, by comparison, does not require the demonstration that can be easily accomplished in a video format. This is essentially presenting an opportunity on a basis of "Who do you know that might be interested?" This presentation frequently yields a volunteering of themselves as a potential candidate, of course, but there are other purposes to be achieved. These, as well as the manner of presentation, <u>are</u> appropriate to this book, and will be covered in-depth.

Thirdly, we have a "background inquiry call". This is not a recruiting call in actuality, as it rarely yields immediate results. However, it is a low-key way of making contact and may lead to a genuine recruiting presentation in the future. It is certainly the least likely to yield instant results, as it requires no particular selling skills, but is utilized by some people. Again, it is presented here.

BACKGROUND INQUIRY CALL

Let's talk about a background inquiry call. This does not refer to presenting an opportunity and asking them who they know. Rather, you are going to start talking specifically about their background. One of the benefits is that people love to talk about themselves, and many will be more then happy to answer your questions.

Let us take an example. You have a name of Jeff Jones and you know that Jeff is the programmer in the bank. You call up Jeff and simply start off with what little you know and start to ask questions.

So it goes something like, "Jeff, this is Larry Nobles over at the Reality Group. Uh, you are a programmer at First National. Is that correct?" "Well, yes, it is." "Well, how long have you been with First National, Jeff?" "Well, I have been here a couple of years." "Who were you with before First National?" "I only have two years experience. Actually I was in college before I came to First National." "What college did you go to?" "Well I went to OSU and I got my degree in ...." and here we go and we find a lot about this particular individual.

As we begin to find out about this person, it is obvious that questions will be asked of us. We introduce ourselves, indicating that we are a recruiter, we work in their specialty, and that we would like to be able to handle their career changes when they feel it would be necessary. Ask them if they have thought about a new opportunity or career change. They will say, "Yes I am looking, or "No, I am not".

Now here is the critical question on the Background Inquiry Call. Without this, all you are getting if you call somebody who says "No, I am happy" is that you know a little bit about somebody and you have got some information on the three-by-five card or computer file.

Permission to Call Back

One of the things you can do is similar to what we did in marketing. Your response should be, "Well, I know everyone generally enjoys improving their particular situation in their career, and I am sure you are like that also. Even though you are happy now and you say you are not interested in making a move, what kind of opportunity or company or what kind of challenge might I call you about that would change your mind? What would you be looking for that would cause you to say, 'Hmm...Even though I am happy now, if that came along, I would certainly be ready to act?'"

So you now know what kind of opportunities to call that particular person about, and you know he or she will probably respond to you. It is setting up future recruits, based on what they might tell you that they might look at or how they may want to improve themselves.

This technique may work for you. It is far the weakest of the "Recruiting" techniques and generally requires a specific type of personality to be effective. It was promoted for a while a number of years ago, but is not generally suitable. Some people with a specific personality have found it useful, but it really cannot be generally recommended. It is not terribly sales-oriented or effective, but is easy to learn.

INDIRECT RECRUITING

Indirect Recruiting is opportunity-based, and a different ball game entirely. We are not going to directly inquire about this person's background. Rather, we are going to initially present an opportunity that sounds very good. However, your "opener" will be indirect, thus the name. We are going to construct a presentation designed to yield a response of, "Gee, that sounds so good I would like to look at that."

The <u>disadvantage</u> of the indirect presentation is that you don't know much about the person you are talking to generally, and you have to presume that it fits them. The <u>advantage</u> of the opportunity is that because you are talking about something of value, you give these people a reason to talk to you. Because you are doing so, they tend to <u>want</u> to open a business conversation with you or talk to you about the opportunity.

Sometimes if we get them excited enough, they become candidates with us on other opportunities besides the one we are on now. They may also be willing to refer friends or other people to us on this specific opportunity. The presentation we construct tells them two things. It tells them we know a good opportunity when we see one. And it tells them we have the clientele available for them to make a career change that might help them in the future.

Call Objectives

Let's talk first about the objectives of the Indirect Recruiting call. When you recruit, you have four objectives.

<u>One</u>: We want to get a specific candidate to fill the specific opening that we are currently trying to fill.

<u>Two</u>: We are going to try to get excess candidates that don't fit the opening that we are trying to fill, but will fit other openings. One of the single biggest missed steps in recruiting is we develop a way of getting the single candidate, but we don't pay attention to how to get excess candidates. In this book, you are going to learn how to do that.

The <u>third</u> objective: To get referrals from these people about other professionals who might be qualified whom we can call to discuss our particular opportunity.

And the <u>fourth</u>: We want to make industry contacts.

Every time you make an industry contact just as in marketing, you need to get to know the person. You need to make a file on them. You need to send them a card if they are in a hiring capacity. And you need to get your name out there, so people can call you.

Now let us talk about building that particular Indirect Recruiting call, so it is as effective as possible.

RECRUITING: BUILDING THE PRESENTATION

11

*B*uilding the right presentation is critical to get the results we are looking for. Many who use the indirect method have been taught to go out and make a presentation, and to ask the person who they might recommend to us. There is much more to it. While not as sophisticated in terms of salesmanship as Direct Recruiting, there is still far more complexity to the Indirect call than you might expect.

First of all, we have to ask ourselves what we are asking these people to do. Most of the time we have a very short presentation. Let's assume that presentation is excellent, and contains some good sizzle about the company or job we are talking about. We ask these people who they know whom they can recommend.

Now think about it just for a second. We have been talking to someone for thirty seconds or maybe a minute. And we are asking them to do is give us the names of their friends, so that some headhunter can call them and get them to change jobs. We need to be a little bit better at it than that. Put yourself in the prospective recruit's shoes. Suppose a salesman calls you up and says, "I know you don't want to buy, but if you'd give me the names of your three closest friends, I can call them and try and sell them." Do you give them the names? Probably not. You don't know how your friends are going to react.

The <u>same</u> things are happening to these people when we call up and talk to them about a great position and then say, "Who do you know?" They are reluctant to start firing off a bunch of names. Only a logically constructed presentation founded on solid sales principles will get the right sort of reaction.

Why <u>aren't</u> we getting those objectives met in a call of this nature? Mainly it is because we are presenting what we are <u>looking</u> for, rather then what we have to <u>offer</u>. As long as we present what we are looking for, we will encounter two problems that make it very difficult to get people to respond to us.

First, when we talk about what we are looking for, there is no enticement there. There is no excitement. There is no <u>reason</u> for this person to co-operate with us. Secondly, it allows them to screen out qualified candidates. So we end up, even if they are co-operative, getting no names.

TWO DIFFERENT CALLS

Let me see if I can clarify the difference by giving you a couple of examples and see which one you would respond to, or might give me names for. In the first presentation, I am going to tell you what I am looking for. And in the second, I am going to tell you what I have to offer.

A Standard Presentation

So it goes like this.

"Hello Bill, my name is Larry Nobles and I am a recruiter with The Reality Group in Tulsa, Oklahoma. By the way, do you have a minute to chat with me or did I catch you at a bad time? Oh, well, good. Well, one of the reasons I called is I am working on behalf of a client company of mine to find them a project engineer that can come on board to handle a large project for them. Now I am probably looking for a project engineer that has some very good chemical background, including some larger capital projects. Prefer them to have a Master's degree or maybe a Bachelor's, but they would prefer the Master's.

Probably somebody out of a large plant because some smaller plants don't have the large capital projects that I would be looking for. I was wondering who you might know that I could talk to as far as project engineering is concerned. Do you know of anybody that might be interested in a new project position?"

Now did that particular call entice you? Did it excite you? Did it get you to say, "Oh boy, what this person has is for me. I've got to go and look at that!"? There was nothing in there like that. I gave you no reason to respond to me. I gave you no reason to say, "would I want that position?" I did not even tell you what the position was.

Secondly, do you remember what I said I was seeking? Preferably someone with a Masters. Perhaps this is somebody who knows a good project engineer who is thinking about moving, or thinks they may be interested in hearing about a new situation. But the potential referral only has a Bachelors. What is the thought process of the person? "Mmm, well, I guess I won't refer that person to this recruiter."

The <u>more</u> information you give the person on the candidate you are seeking, the <u>greater</u> the chance that this person will screen everyone out that they know. It is quite possible that they will find something wrong with each individual that they may consider, and not refer them to you at all. The more specific you are, the more they will screen out. Thus, we don't get that lead, even though they may have been co-operative.

The other factor that can kill your situation is that there is no excitement or reason to respond. When you hear people in our industry saying "this is a numbers game", you can now see why they believe that. They forget that it is a <u>sales</u> game. Even if those people are willing to respond, they screen out the people they know because of the boring inadequate information that you gave with this presentation. Then the "numbers game" believers are surprised when they continually hear, "Gee, I don't know anyone like that."

Let's go back and re-construct that presentation. Let's put in nothing about what we are looking for except project engineer. But everything we have to <u>offer</u>.

A Better Way

Let's try this.

"Hello Bill, my name is Larry Nobles. I am a technical recruiter with The Reality Group. Have I caught you at a bad time or do you have a minute to spend with me? Fine, I am glad you do.

A top client of mine has asked us to find them a project engineer to come in and handle capital projects for them. Now this particular project is going to include a revamp of one of the units in the plant. Based upon the successful completion of that project, this person would then be promoted to Project Manager. At that point they will release the contract people they have on hand to help with the project, and this person will start to hire and build his own project staff in this plant. My client is one of the top Fortune 500 companies, and this is one of their larger and most technically competent plants. This particular individual is going to be able to move up the ladder both in this plant, and if need be, on to corporate in the near future. I am looking for a project engineer who may not have that kind of advantage in his current organization, or may not have that fast a track into management. I was wondering, who do you know that you think would deserve a move up like that?"

Now, what did I say I wanted? The only thing I told them was a project engineer, with no education mentioned, so they can't screen anybody out. What did I have to offer? I offered challenge in that I had large projects to be managed. I offered opportunity in that as soon as they completed that project, they were going to be able to move up to management and building their own staff. Beyond that they could move up even further in this plant because it was larger, or into the corporate headquarters.

I gave the candidate every reason in the world to respond. In his mind, he is saying, "Gee, that is a good one. There are not many project engineers who walk into a job opportunity that has that kind of opportunity, challenge and future to it." So we have given them a reason to say, "Me. I would like that look at that." Or if they don't <u>want</u> to say, "Me", they really want to think of somebody, because they know a lot of project engineers that do not have this opportunity where they are.

I did build in a mild close at the end of that sizzle that I have given on the company. What did I say? I said I am looking for someone <u>who</u> <u>probably</u> <u>does</u> <u>not</u> <u>have</u> <u>that</u> <u>opportunity</u> <u>where</u> <u>they</u> <u>are</u>. Suppose this particular person I am talking to has talked to his boss about his future and was told, "There isn't much here. Our company is not moving forward and we are not getting any bigger. There won't be anything here for you." Or even if there is some future, does it measure up to this? If there is any dissatisfaction in his present situation, we have a candidate! We click in these people's minds that what we are looking for is somebody that wants to improve themselves, who doesn't have the opportunity in front of them that I am currently offering. That will help them think of certain types of people.

I have a potential candidate challenged and excited. He will probably want to either volunteer himself or his friends. And I have not given him any information that will allow him to screen out anyone.

NO SCREENING OUT

Why don't I want these people screened out? Do I want them referring people to me that don't fit my opening? Absolutely! When I go through my recruiting scenario, my objective is to get as many candidates from this recruiting call as possible. It may be a specific candidate on this order, or a candidate that is over-qualified or under-qualified for this order. I can utilize them on other searches. I want to produce as many project engineers as possible.

An Exception

The only time I don't want to do that is when I am recruiting outside of my normal specialty. For instance, if I am looking for a left-handed widget designer and this is the only left-handed widget designer I will ever place in my life, then I don't want people who are not qualified. I don't want a lot of excess candidates that I have to interview and put on file, because I am not going to do anything with them.

But in the normal world of recruiting and achieving our objectives, we want all the candidates to respond positively. In that way, we have as large a data base as we can to make the interviews and placement necessary for us to reach our goal. You can entice people to co-operate and respond by saying what you have to <u>offer</u>, rather than what you are <u>looking for</u>.

SCRIPT WRITING

When you use the script that we are going to work with, I want you to be sure to write these out, and have them in front of you. Of course, though we say the same thing over and over again, we don't want to sound like we are reading anything. It just takes a little out-loud practice before doing the script "for real".

This script has an opening, a body and a close to it. We want to break this opening and ask a question before we get to the actual presentation that we are going to make. Again, the opening is who you are and who you are with, proceeding to what you are doing, and what is it is that you are looking for. Then you are going to ask the question if the person is free to talk.

So it would go something like this, "Hello Bill, I am Larry Nobles and I am a technical recruiter with The Reality Group here in Tulsa Oklahoma. I have been put on an assignment by a top Fortune 500 client of mine to find a project engineer for one of their top spots. By the way, did I catch you at a bad time, or would another time be better for us to talk?"

Now why do I ask that question? Why don't I just go on with the presentation and close when I am talking to these people? Well, two reasons. One, remember that this person may be in a bad spot. He may be in a room full of people in which he can't respond to you. He may be sitting in his boss' office when he takes the call because somebody paged him. So you want to give them an easy out if they want to talk to you, and a chance to get back together when they can talk privately.

Second, it is an indication that we want to talk to <u>them</u>. Remember when we get the end, we are going to say "Who do you know?" Some prospective candidates don't have what it takes to say "Me". They are afraid that you are going to put them down and say, "No, fool! If I wanted you, I would have asked for you." You need to give them some indication that it is OK to say "me". Why else would we be worried if they were available to talk, if we were not talking about them?

So it is a hint. It is a way of saying we are talking about you. The opening is who you are, what you are, who you are with, and what you are looking for. Then ask that question before you move on to the body of your presentation.

The Body Sizzles

Now the body of the presentation contains the hottest sizzle possible about your current opening. When we start to create recruiting presentations, we have two kinds of sizzle that we need to deal with. We need to deal with company sizzle, and we need to deal with job sizzle. Both of them are important to the candidate. You have both things that you have to present in the body.

Because this is a less complex call than Direct Recruiting, you have less time to explain about the opportunity. Direct Recruiting allows you to really discuss the merits and value to them in far more detail. That's one of a number of reasons why results are much improved once you have mastered it. In Indirect Recruiting, we must be more concise, as our initial opening is asking for referrals. But sizzle is still possible, though to a lesser degree.

The Close

Now let's go on to the close. Besides enticing them with our presentation in the close, we add the tag line about the person that we might be looking for. Who <u>are</u> we seeking? We are looking for that person who does not have this or can not obtain this in his present position. This sort of tag line makes people think about themselves or other people in those situations. Then we ask a direct question to get them to refer someone to us that they might think is good in that arena.

Two things about the close. The close starts with the word "Who". It does <u>not</u> start with the word "Do", and "Do you know anyone?" It starts with the word "Who". "Who do you know?" So remember that little key to make like an owl, and go "Who" when you start that close or that question about getting other people.

Be sure not to use the word "interested". You are not asking for people are interested in changing jobs. These people don't know whether people are interested in changing jobs. As soon as you say, "Who do you know that is interested in changing?", they don't know. It screens everybody out almost automatically!

There are a number of ways of asking this question. I use the question earlier, "Who do you think deserves an opportunity like this?" I asked for somebody specifically that is excellent, but is not getting ahead. That is one way of phrasing it.

Alternatively, "In your opinion, who is the best project engineer that you have ever worked with?" Here I asked for no recommendation whatsoever, except for them to rate somebody. That is an effective close, because you are not asking them to judge anything about interest.

Note that throughout the script, the opening, body, and close, we describe what you are looking for without screening people out. The candidate has a pretty good idea of what you are looking for, though you have not said a word about years of experience or degrees or an exceptionally specific background. He or she is liable to respond to you by giving you the names of the people that can help you find who you are looking for, or they can give you the names of people who actually will respond to you. You have given him a <u>reason</u> to do so.

As in marketing, when we finish our script, remember two words. What is it? That's right. J. Douglas Edwards' classic sales technique: "Shut up". You've got to give this person a chance to think; remember, the next one who talks loses.

Now that we have got the script in hand and we have the close, let us go on to talk about some of the responses that we are going to get, and possible answers to those responses to help you maximize results from this critical portion of our business.

RECRUITING: RESPONSES AND REBUTTALS

12

*R*esponses that somebody might give to an Indirect Recruiting presentation are numerous. How you respond will significantly affect your results from this important methodology. Let's go over some of them and talk about what do we do when we receive certain responses to the presentation that we just made.

NOT LOOKING

Obviously, one of the most common is, "I don't know anyone who is looking for a job." As mentioned previously, that could be precipitated by us if we use the word "interested" in our close. Every time you say to someone, "tell me somebody who might be interested" or "Who do you know that might be interested in this situation?", you limit dramatically the people they can give to you. Even if you do not say that, they still may give you this response because they <u>think</u> that is what you are interested in.

One effective rebuttal that I have seen used when someone says, "I don't know anyone that is looking for a job" is, "Great! My company is looking for that top talent who is probably not out on the street looking for a job. We are looking for somebody who is great in project engineering, not somebody great at looking for jobs. So who do you know who is great at project engineering, and is <u>not</u> looking for a job?" This can be quite effective.

I like to say, "Well, I understand that you don't know anyone that is looking. But there are a lot of your friends or acquaintances who are looking that you don't know about. Let us face it, people who are looking for jobs don't just walk up and down the corporate halls with a sandwich board saying they are looking for a new job. It just doesn't happen that way. A lot of people know they are looking, but for confidentiality reasons simply do not spread it around. I understand that you don't know anyone that is looking for a job.

That is not what I'm concerned about. What I am concerned about is finding the best project engineer that I can find, whoever that may be.

If they are interested, that is fine. If not, they will probably refer to me a good project engineer. I will go from person to person until I finally find that right individual who wants to move up in the world. So based on that, let me ask you this same question in a different way. Who do you know that you think quite highly of in project engineering, whether or not that person is looking for a job?"

What I have done is go back and said, "You don't know that they are looking, but I don't care if they are looking. All I want to know is if they are good. Then I'll present the situation to them and let them respond to it."

Asking For Help

Asking for help is a powerful sales tool. So is the enticement of doing a friend a favor. The following manner of asking combines both.

"OK, do this. Refer somebody to me that you think might <u>know</u> a good project engineer. I just go from person to person. I might talk to fifty to a hundred people before I finally find that engineer that is right for this position. Somebody out there is going to get a great favor done for them. They will get a great career, a super move, better salary and a move up in the world. You know, I don't know any bigger favor for a friend or acquaintance than to improve their life. I just want to talk to someone that might know somebody. I don't care if they are the right engineer or not.

Who do you know about whom you would say if there is one person that knows project engineering, it is this guy? He probably won't be interested, but he may know who is. I am just kind of at my wit's end as to who to call. I was hoping you could give me some leadership in that direction. So who do you know that just knows engineering?"

You will get more referrals by <u>defusing</u> the idea that they need to give you somebody that is right for the job. That is your best choice, but as a secondary step, focus them on somebody that may not be right for the job but might know other people.

<u>Continue</u> to get names of people. If you are at the end of your name calling list, you can continue to produce other referrals. Call enough people, and you

will find the person you want for this specific opportunity. In doing so, you'll come up with candidates who are right for other positions as well.

I'LL HAVE MY FRIEND CALL YOU

How about the one, "I will call a couple of friends and see if they are interested, and if they are, I will have them call you. What is your telephone number?" Now, I always leave my number so people can get back to me, because I <u>have</u> had people call me and say, "I have talked to so-and-so who said he had talked to you. I want to look at your opportunity." But mainly, they never make the phone call.

Again, you will want to try and defuse the thought that they should call these people. Let <u>me</u> call them. Personally, if I cannot eliminate that idea, I am going to continue to talk to this person until they make that phone call.

So here is how it would go. I'd say, "George, you know, I appreciate that. I think that is a great attitude on your part that you would be willing to help friends gain some information that might dramatically change their life. I can't think of a better favor you could do for anyone than to give them the opportunity to increase their lot in life. Let me say this, a lot of people tell me I know some friends and they have them call, and George, guess what — no one ever calls. Why do you think that is?"

I start to make George think about why that would happen. And he generally says, "Well, I guess because they are not interested." And I say, "Well, no. It is not because they are not interested. It is because they do not have enough information to know whether or not they are interested. Off this short presentation that I just gave you, this little amount of <u>information</u>, you can't possibly answer the questions they have to determine if they want to seriously pursue this situation. You really can't help these people by just giving them this information and my phone number. The way to do it is give me their phone number and let them call me. That way they can ask me the questions."

If you don't get the right response, but the person is cooperative, stay on this! You are only looking for a referral. Try this, "George, you don't need to be doing my job. I don't think you should be put in the position of calling other people with the thought of giving them recruiting information. Let me do that. I am the professional at doing it. So if you want to help these people, let me have their names and numbers, and I will give them a call."

"The Art of Recruiting" video series has many extremely effective techniques for obtaining referrals that are best suited to Direct Recruiting. But the line of "I'll keep your name in strict confidence", while drawn from a Direct Recruiting methodology, can be combined with the above approach to increase results with some people.

No Names?

What if he still says, "I understand what you are talking about. But I am not the the type of person who gives out my friends' names"? I get very enthusiastic and say, "Well, fine. Listen, I really appreciate your help. Tell you what, George. It is 2 o'clock now, and I will call you back around three. Let me know what they said so in case they have any questions, I can answer them. I'll speak with you soon. Goodbye."

Now why am I am I doing this? Because the number one reason that they will never call is because these people never make the phone call! Now 3 o'clock rolls around, and his phone rings. And he is thinking, "Oh goodness. It is probably Larry. He probably wants to know what those people said. And I have not even called them yet." I continue to call back until he makes those phone call, or gives me the names.

Generally one of the two things will happen. Yes, it does get frustrating, and they will at times just flat lie to you and say, "I made the calls and no one is interested and forget it." But you have a greater chance that those contacts are going to be made. More likely, though, the first time you call back, you'll hear a big sigh…. and you'll get the names of some excellent potential candidates!

BUYING SIGN

There is also, as in marketing, a person who asks a question about the job. We call that a Buy sign. If they ask a question about the opportunity, then answer it as positively as possible. Then close to see if they are interested for themselves.

Mirror Response Close

You close by using a mirror response. A mirror response means you ask back the very thing that was asked of you. That is why it is called the Mirror Response Close.

Let me give you an example. Someone says, "Larry, how much does this position pay?" That is a Buy Sign. Answer it generally, not specifically. "Well, George, my company is open at this time. Obviously, it depends on how much experience I bring them. They are certainly going to pay more for 10 years experience than 5 years. Now my company will certainly encourage someone financially to get them to make the move. Let me ask you, George, is financial opportunity important in your next career change? Is that what you are looking for, a financial move up?"

What have I done? I have answered it positively. I have left it open. I have not killed myself with money. And I have asked the person if they <u>want</u> to be recruited.

Money?

Do not tell them how much money is being offered. Yes, I know some people use money as an enticement. Unless you have a tremendous bag full of money to offer them, don't. As soon as you answer the question, "How much money is being offered?", you'll kill yourself one of two ways.

That person may be making as much or more money than you are offering. They may want to respond. But as soon as they hear that it is 60,000, and they are already making 60,000, they <u>don't</u> respond. So you lose all of the candidates that might have responded <u>and</u> you lose all of the referrals they might have given you, because the money is too low.

Alternatively, the money might be too high. Yes, too high! If you say your client company will pay 60,000 and the guy you are talking to is qualified and making 40,000, he is going to run home and may say to his wife, "Guess what? A recruiter called me today and offered me a job for 60,000!" He is all excited and he goes and tells all of his family and friends. He goes to the interview, and he gets offered 46,000. And he turns it down, because now he must tell these people why he only got 46,000. He is depressed about the offer instead of being enthusiastic about it. You have killed yourself.

Answer the question as positively as possible without revealing information that would lead to the salary. Then close to find out if this person is serious about moving.

Where is it Located?

How about where is it located?

"Well, this job is located north of you a short distance. It would mean a relocation from your current position. But it would not be so far that you could not drive back and see friends or anything you might want to. Let me ask, George, is location important to you if you make a career change?"

Again, I am utilizing a "Mirror Response Close" to see if he wants to be recruited. Some will say, "Oh, no I was just curious. I am really not looking." That is fine. At least it gives me the chance to close when that buy sign comes around. He may be asking for a friend. Go to referrals.

Be especially careful not to give information that would allow him to identify the client. See the following topic for explanation.

Who Is The Company?

If they say, "Who is the company?", a lot of us crumble and say, "Well, I am not suppose to tell you, but it is GE."

If you make this mistake, it will cost you fees! Now you have put it out on the marketplace as to who is it. I have verified that I have lost placements because somebody told someone in the lunchroom, and that person went directly to the company, and got the job. I am sitting out there as the direct cause of the placement, but no money in my pocket and no way to retrieve it! Don't let this happen to you!

If they ask, "Who is the company?", here is a useful response.

"Obviously George, I am hired for my confidentiality. One of the reason companies use people like me is because we can scour the countryside for the best possible candidate <u>without</u> their name getting out all over the world that they are looking. Let me ask George, is the company's name important to you at this time?" I am mirroring back exactly what he asked me. Why is he asking? Find out whether or not these people are ready to move.

MAXIMIZING REFERRALS

Another possibility (honest!) is <u>they</u> <u>might</u> give <u>us</u> <u>referrals</u>. They might give us the names of two candidates that they think would be qualified. Suppose he says, "Well, you can call John Jones and Betty Smith. Those are two engineers I know that I think are pretty good."

I remember when I started recruiting, it was so much fun to get names via referrals that I <u>consistently</u> made a basic mistake.

The trap is that many of us get so excited about getting a name after all of these negatives that <u>all</u> we get is the name, the telephone number, and nothing else! It happened to me, too.

The first time I got two people's names, I said, "Thanks a lot. I really appreciate your co-operation". Then I hung up and I didn't have their phone numbers or where they worked or any way of getting to them. Embarrassed, I called back the person for their numbers. And he said, "Yeah, I thought you might be calling back, because you didn't know where they were", and he gave me their names and numbers. We had a good chuckle over it.

If someone is willing to give you a referral, then they are willing to tell you what they know about that person. So my question after he says, "Call Betty Smith and John Jones" is, "George, in your professional opinion, who would you rate the highest? Betty or John?" "Oh, I think Betty is." I'd say, "Well, why?" "Well, she has got six years of experience, whereas John only has got three. "Hmmm", I say. "What about talent? What does Betty do?" And I start getting information about Betty.

Ask, "How do you think she will respond to my call? Why do you say that?" A lot of times these people refer me to those who they know are looking, and it helps me to know that. Don't call up and play these indirect games hoping they will volunteer themselves. If I find out someone is qualified and looking, I go at them totally differently from Indirect Recruiting.

I now have information on John and Betty that tells me who they are, how experienced they are, what they have done, what their education is, how they might respond to me, and why. Based on that knowledge, I change my approach when I call them.

RECRUITING A REFERRED CANDIDATE

If you have been referred to this candidate, the presentation changes.

The first thing I do is to verify the information that I have on them. "Hello Betty, I am Larry Nobles. I am a technical recruiter with The Reality Group in Tulsa, Oklahoma. You have been with Mobil for two years since you moved from Texaco. Is that correct?" She says, "Well, yes, Larry." "And you are out of Arkansas University, is that correct?" She said, "Well yeah. How do you know that?" And I said, "Would that be around 1984?" She said, "Yes, I did graduate in '84."

What is happening to Betty right now? I bet she is saying to herself, "Who is this guy? How does he know all this about me?" In fact, frequently an actively-looking candidate will ask, "How do you know all this information about me?" I simply say, "It is my profession to know this about you." And then we go right on. This is a situation in which it raises the person's interest when you know this. And they will respond and talk to you better.

After you verify that this information is correct, then make your presentation. Rather than closing with, "Who do you know?", however, the close should be, "Does this sound interesting enough for you to want to talk to about it further?" It is a very soft close. Just ask them if we can talk about it.

Remember, gaining the information from the referral about the person gives you a strong edge. Once you gain that information, go to the prospective candidate, qualify them that the information is correct and make your presentation on how good the opportunity it is. Then use a soft close. You are going to get a lot of recruits who respond to you in that manner.

Over-qualified Referral

If the prospective candidate is obviously over-qualified, tell them you know that they are not qualified. Then give them your presentation, and ask them to refer someone they know. One of the ways that I do it is by <u>complimenting them</u> on their position in industry. Then they have to live up to that billing.

It goes something like, "Bill, I know that you are too qualified for what I am looking for. I understand that. But I am looking for this type of position. Let me tell you about it." And I give him the greatest company sizzle. "Since you are the guru of project engineering in this arena, tell me who do you recommend? Who do you think are the best two or three engineers you have ever dealt with?"

I have rarely failed to get names like that because they have to live up to their billing. I had one guy get out a directory and start thumbing through it. He could not think of anyone, but he had to live up to his billing and try to find someone that I could call. When they are over-qualified, stroke them with some compliments about them being knowledgable and people knowing them, and you will get some names.

A FAVORABLE RESPONSE

Another way that people respond is exactly what you want when you make your presentation. They might answer, "Well, I may be interested." Say, "Well, great!", and act a little surprised. "Fine. I did not know that you would be interested. But of course, I would be happy to talk to you about this situation. I tell you what, I don't know your background very well. Let me ask you a few questions and that will help us along."

A Concise Qualifier

At this point too many of us jump into an interview. We are in the middle of a thirty-call recruiting program that we want to get through, but we spend forty-five minutes talking to someone who ends up not qualified for our position!

In the interests of <u>completing</u> your Daily Plan and this specific search, ask them five questions. Don't get distracted with the wrong candidate! Completing your Daily Plan means you recruit <u>fully</u> only <u>right</u> candidates during prime phone time! Based on those five questions, I make a decision whether or not to go on into the interview.

The Five Questions

And the five questions are:

<u>One</u>, What is your current job title?

<u>Two</u>, How many total years experience do you have in doing this? Not with this company, total years of experience industry-wide.

<u>Three</u>, What is your current salary structure? How much are you earning?

<u>Four</u>, what is your education?

And then the <u>fifth</u> question is an open question that changes depending on the specific search on which you are recruiting. It is a qualifying question that tells you whether or not this is the right type person you want to fully recruit right now.

A Non-Qualified Example

For instance, suppose I am looking for a quality control engineer. We have to use a little technical jargon here to make this example work. I need about five years experience in a metals company that does non-destructive testing, such as x-ray.

So I would say, "What is your job title?" And he would say, "I am a quality control analyst." And that is what I want. And I say, "How many years have you been doing this?" He responds, "I have been doing it for six years." Sounds good so far. And I say, "What is your education?" He says, "I am an engineer by current education." I ask, "What is your current salary?" And he says, "About $65,000."

Now all of those are great. Narrow it with a question pertaining to this opportunity. Up to this point I look good, but then comes the killer question. "What kind of testing do you do in your quality control?" And he says, "I am an expert in destructive testing." And I ask, "Do you have any experience in x-ray or non-destructive?" And he says, "No, all six years has been spent in this lab, and all we do is destructive testing." Well, he is not my man. He was great to that point. But the qualifying question knocked him out. That question will obviously change, depending upon how best to qualify the candidate I am talking to, based on the individual search.

Do I still want him? Absolutely! I am a specialist in quality control people, and I want him as a candidate. So after those five questions, I will say, "Well good. I really enjoyed talking to you. Why don't I call tonight or tomorrow night while you are at home. You need to get back to work and I do too, but we will go over some ideas about this opportunity, where you are headed, and so forth."

Why did I get off the phone after asking those five questions? So I can go onto my other recruiting calls, and <u>complete</u> my project! I don't want to waste time interviewing a quality control person that doesn't fit my assignment, because I need to find one who does. But I don't want to lose this person. I want to move him into being an excess candidate. So that night when I interview, I "find out" that he doesn't fit. And I will tell him very honestly that the position that we talked about is not right for him.

I never say, "You are not right for the position." Say, "The position is not right for you. You obviously have a great career path, but this one requires someone with in-depth experience in non-destructive testing. I would hinder your career if I put you in there and your performance did not measure up because you don't have the right kind of specific experience. So let me tell you what we need to do. Let me go out and look for the same type situation that we just described, but in the destructive testing area. When I do, I will call you and we will go have a look at it. How would that be?" And he will say, "All right".

What I have done is convert a recruit into a candidate that I can use any time, and on other opportunities. I take the recruit and move him over to a candidate. That is the way you go about converting the candidates.

TIGHTENING UP THE "SHOPPERS"

One last point on the candidate's interview. Remember, they are shoppers until we determine why they want to leave.

They must describe their Reason For Leaving. If they cannot, then the 24-hour close comes in. When I get someone that cannot describe for me his reason for leaving, I say, "Why did you respond to me? Why should you leave your present company and go to work for the one I described?"

If they can't describe that, tell them that they shouldn't be moving forward on an interview. What I say is, "Do you know what you should do? You should sit down with your family and tell them that you got a call from a recruiter with a great opportunity. But you need to determine whether you should leave your present firm before you go out there and interview. Then call me tomorrow, 24 hours from now, and tell me you are ready to look, and are serious about leaving. Or, tell me that you are not serious about making a change."

Using that technique, you can separate the tire kickers from the real candidates. You can refer those individuals that are serious about leaving to your clients, and you can make and close the placements. If they can't describe a valid reason for leaving and say why they should get out of where they are, they are not a serious candidate. Using your techniques, you can create unhappiness. If not, you can use the 24-hour close to help them get serious, so they are more commited before they start interviewing.

Does this mean that you should not be overcoming the objections of the "Reluctant Recruit"? Not at all. In fact, when you progress to Direct Recruiting, you can and <u>must</u>! It is one of the very reasons the sophisticated sales techniques involved in this advanced methodology are so effective in recruiting many high-quality candidates. But it takes good overall sales skills and good training to support this.

However, even there, identifying candidate concerns is mandatory, and there are a number of ways of doing so appropriately.

You will find, however, that eliminating "shoppers" is a critical element at <u>any</u> level of recruiting.

A FINAL CLOSE

You now have the techniques that are necessary for you to go out in the recruiting marketplace and talk to people by means of Indirect Recruiting. As you gain more experience, confidence, and improve your selling skills, you will find Direct Recruiting has great merit. I have mentioned the best source to learn it correctly. But again, many people stay with Indirect and do very well.

One last point about people. No matter who you talk to or how they respond to you, how many names they give you or what they do, always remember they are important. Say to them, "Before I leave you, let me ask you a question. What is your situation like?"

Show some interest in those people! Many of them will say, "Well, I am interested but not in that type of opportunity." Then they will tell you the kind of company they are interested in, and you can go right ahead and recruit them.

Always ask specifically about each individual, and show interest in them. I guarantee you that your level of candidates produced by recruiting will go up.

Real recruiting is how you "deliver the goods" for your clients. It is much of the value we provide. Without mastering these skills you are doomed to become a boring and bored "paper-shuffler" or "net nerd", hoping to get candidates to a client before their own HR staff, advertisement, or job posting yields the same candidate. With good recruiting skills, you can be a top professional, a highly-regarded and highly-paid Executive Search Consultant!

Good luck and good hunting. It is fun out there! Put a smile on your face. Call people and offer them great positions in the world.

Combined with the right skills, some practice and some study, you are going to be a success in recruiting. And once you learn it well, you will be successful forever!

CANDIDATE ANALYSIS: THE OTHER SIDE OF MATCHING

13

*A*s we talked about earlier, we should view ourselves as industry problem solvers. People move because they have problems. Likewise, managers hire specific individuals to solve problems. If we can find out what those are and we can supply the right talent or opportunity, then we have done a great job in recruiting and a great service to both.

Clients enjoy hearing about top candidates. Top candidates enjoy hearing about top opportunities. But to "put the deal together", it takes more than enjoyment. It takes hard knowledge. Where do we get it? Our candidates' initial interviews with us and our analysis is a major source of that needed information.

INTERVIEWING CANDIDATES

The interviewing area has some very specific objectives we must understand. When I find placement problems, my first step is to evaluate candidate pre-screening.

Some consultants have a lot of candidates and searches, but are unable to put them together as far as setting interviews. Some are able to put them together and set up interviews, but nothing ever seems to come quite into focus, and no placements occur. Why is this?

Frequently, a consultant has come to me and said, "I have a closing problem" or "I am at the end of the placement, but I am having problems with it." When I start asking them about that placement, in many instances, they don't know the answers to basic mandatory questions.

Those difficulties can very frequently be traced back to something not asked in the initial candidate interview we conduct.

Why is it critical to interview a candidate properly? Because every step of the way, it could cost us the placement if we don't have the vital information it should provide. And it can cost our client their chance of hiring top talent.

Sometimes we interview people that come into our office; other times it is done on the phone. Regardless, the specific objectives are the same. Those specific areas must be covered in depth.

OBJECTIVES OF A CANDIDATE INTERVIEW

What are we trying to accomplish when we interview a candidate? Too many times, all we ask is a few questions. We believe we have a "feel" as to how serious they are, or whether they are any good or not. We send them out, or put them in the file until something comes along. But have we done a good enough job of initial screening and evaluation to really know what we have? Frequently, no. So first of all, let us understand our objectives.

Technical Information

The first step is to understand the candidate technically, so we can identify the right position and opportunity. Candidates have <u>professional</u> reasons for job change and professional values that they are looking for. They have criteria they use to judge this; if they don't, then you certainly need to help them set those parameters down. Understand the candidate technically and know what they are, what they do, what their goals and objectives are. Only by doing so can you can identify the right position and opportunity for this person.

When you <u>do not</u> identify the right position or opportunity for this person, many times we call that either a "turn down" or "lack of interest in the candidate". Frequently, these problems start right here. If we did not do our job in understanding what makes this person tick and what choices they will make professionally, we don't know which opportunity they will accept. Then we simply start to shop them around to see if anything happens to strike their fancy, hoping they will happen to fall in love with something. Only after we have understood the candidate can we identify that right job or opportunity for them.

You must also develop the information necessary to sell the candidate's talent in the marketplace. One of the reasons that specialists are more effective than generalists is because they know what separates a good candidate from a poor one in their particular specialty. It is hard sometimes for people to explain to you how good they are. You, therefore, must ask the right questions. If you cannot <u>differentiate</u> between candidates, you are only selling a commodity.

As you work your area of specialization, become an expert, so you can ask those questions of your candidates that tell you whether you have a great, good or not-so-talented candidate. You can thus adjust to those companies and positions where you send this person. Remember there is a good solid company out there looking for that good solid candidate. All positions do not require super-stars. That is what I mean by matching goals, skills, abilities etc., to the right job.

Develop the information necessary to sell the candidate, understand their worth, and <u>why</u> and <u>where</u> they are good specifically. Only then can you explain it to your client.

Co-operation

It is also mandatory to <u>gain the co-operation of the candidate</u>. By doing so, you can manage the interview process, close the placement, and frequently see long-term benefits post-placement.

We are the advisors and the knowledgeable consultants. However, the company is the one that makes the decision on the offer and actually decides on what to extend. The candidate is the one that decides whether to accept that position. For us to affect the completion of the search to the maximum degree possible, we must have the co-operation of the people involved.

The way to get co-operation is to be <u>sincerely interested</u> in the candidate. We may talk to ten or fifteen different candidates per day. Soon they can become just paper, or data on a computer screen. Under the circumstances, the tendency is to just talk to them as if they are just another cog in the machinery that makes our big wheel turn. We can't do that. This is a real person with real fears and problems to be solved in the marketplace, with a family that will be affected by the decision that they are making. You will gain co-operation from your candidates when they feel that you are trying to do something <u>for</u> them rather than something to them. Be interested in the people and understand where they are coming from. You can't put your value system or the way you make decisions on the candidate. You must find out how <u>they</u> do so, and then make the appropriate adjustments to best control the outcome.

Analyzing the Cautious Candidate

Let me give you an example of gaining co-operation. I had a candidate one time who was a highly analytical engineer working in Research and Development. He had called me and was fearful because his company was in a take-over situation. He was not sure what to do, or how his job was going to be affected.

When I looked further into his background, I saw he had been through two layoffs and another take-over in his eight years in the company, and had not yet left. Highly analytical people tend to be fairly conservative in their career moves. So long as he was not being kicked out of the company, he might not have what it would take to make the move. What should I do?

I did not say, "Oh yes. Let me have your resume, and let me start shopping you around to see if I can find something for you." Rather, I started gaining his co-operation. I began by seriously asking him, "Let me ask you how you make decisions? How adventurous are you? To me, it sounds like you are a highly analytical person. Since you have stayed eight years in a company that has struggled for a long time, that tells me change is difficult for you. In fact, you probably have not changed your hair style in quite a number of years. Would you agree with me that change is difficult?" And he said, "Oh yes. I really don't like it. I have a very set routine that I enjoy." We had a long talk about his ability and what he might be up against emotionally if he were to go out in the marketplace and start interviewing.

I also saw this person as having a very significant chance of being counter-offered. He was very important to the company. The odds were great that they would fight to keep him if he said he was about to go to another company. Even though he sent me his resume, he and I agreed that he would not interview until he came to me committed to leaving. That was a while ago and he is still with that company.

Was I wrong to help this person see that staying put is really what he was going to do? Did I lose a placement? No! He has since referred candidates to me resulting in three fees, and keeps me informed of openings at his current firm regularly. He still refers people to me. Why? Because he saw that I was trying to do something for him rather than to him.

It is true that there are three objectives. We must understand the candidate technically, so we can identify the right job. We must develop the information that is necessary to sell that candidate's talents to the marketplace. But let us not forget that <u>three</u> is to gain the co-operation of the candidate, so we can manage the interview process. If they will co-operate, trust us, and do what we ask them to do, we have a good chance of closing the placement....to everyone's benefit.

CANDIDATE INFORMATION

What information should you have about a candidate? What questions will help you get it, and why do you need it?

First we need basic candidate information. This refers to the candidate's name and address, and three telephone numbers. Yes three telephone numbers. We need a home telephone number. We need a work telephone number to reach them if we need to contact them during the day about setting an interview. And we need an emergency phone number.

Emergency Phone Number

An emergency phone number must be <u>other</u> than their current home number and their work number. Why? Because they may move away. When you try to find them and you pull them out a year later and call their home, it's disconnected. You call their work, and nobody knows where they've gone. What then?

If you have an emergency phone number, you can call and trace them, and find them where they are. That should be the number of a family member who is quite stable in their address and phone number that will always know their whereabouts. A mother or father. A brother or sister. A very good friend. Or whomever might be able to give you contact information.

Is this appropriate for a recruited candidate who is not actively looking to make a change? Probably not. Ask. But for an open-to-opportunity cooperative candidate or one who contacts you (and there will be many such people), it will make you a great deal of extra income.

There is nothing worse than having a recruiting assignment and no one to call, unless it is pulling 95 people out of that file, 94 of which you can not find. It is a simple a waste of time. Don't let it happen to you!

Educational History

After we have obtained the basic information, we need to know the education of the person. It will become very important in various searches with mandatory or preferred types of education or degrees. If your field is one of these, this will be critical.

Know the degree. Get the letters, like BS, BA, MS, MBA or PHd. There is a reason for that. Use the letters to see if that matches their major. Ask the degree, the major, the institution, the year of graduation, and the GPA. I say degrees and majors, because, as an example, if someone says they have a BA in chemistry, something is wrong. Chemistry is a science, not an art. You may have uncovered someone that is fudging on what they have actually accomplished in college. There are people out there who claim they have degrees that they do not have. When you try to find the institution, it is burned down and no longer exists and there is no record.

It is your job to verify some of this information for your clients. This is especially true if you have "net nerd" tendencies and are getting candidates off the internet.

Make sure you get the year of graduation; many will list the degree that they have worked on, but if there is no year of graduation, they may not have graduated.

Grade point average is important; many companies measure the learning ability of the candidate based on that GPA, even if it is many years old. Remember to get a GPA, and out of what? A 3.5 out of a 4.0 is a good grade point. A 3.5 out of a 5.0 can sometimes be considered an average grade point.

Also ask about professional certifications. Find out if your candidate is certified as a Professional Engineer, or is a CPA if they happen to be in accounting. Find out about the certifications that they hold.

It may seem silly to get college information on a seasoned professional, but you never know what a client will consider important. A client who himself had a high GPA may well over-stress this in hiring decisions. Obviously, however, the less experienced the candidate, the more critical this will be.

WORK HISTORY

After you have basic contact information and educational history, we need to find out about current company. Who are they working for? Get the dates they are working for that company and their current position title. Always get the month as well as the year of the dates worked for previous firms. Even a small gap as two months at least may indicate that this person was terminated from that company prior to getting their new position, and you will want to know why.

Again, especially if you pull candidates off the internet, be suspicious. A genuinely recruited candidate is usually legitimate. However, The Olsten Center for Workforce Strategies did an extensive survey of HR managers, who indicated that 40% of candidates obtained from the internet had blatant falsehoods in their resumes. A major study by the prestigious Boston Consulting Group yielded similar results. Be alert under these circumstances! You will lose a client if fabrications of this nature later come to light.

Income

Find out about salaries, bonuses, and the last and next increase. The salary should be a W2.

When you have someone that gives you a larger income than you think may be realistic, give them an easy out and say, "You know, that is odd. None of my other candidates at your level in this industry is making anywhere near that. I probably did not make myself clear. I want to make sure that I have only your salary.

Please don't add any bonuses to be paid the following year or benefits, which you probably did. All I am looking for is your W2 total. We may have to provide that W2 to a client if they are concerned about your salary level." When you say that, they realize that you are on to them, and you have given them an easy out, so they can say, "Oh, yes. I did include a lot of stuff. Here is my real W2!" Also find out if they have a bonus and what it was.

Why do we want last increase, next increase and dates of last and anticipated increases? The amount and date of the last increase is important because it gives an indication of unhappiness in salary if they have not had an increase in two years. Also, they will probably be looking for more money if they have been at the same level for a long time. However, if their last increase was last month, and they just jumped from $50,000 to $55,000, you won't have to get them a great deal over $55,000 to make them happy, if it is the right opportunity.

What you do not need is for the company to be about to make an offer, and the candidate says, "Oh, by the way. I just got an increase and I am now earning more." Then we have to go back to the company and try to get money to match that. Be careful about the increases and when they came. Be sure to cover this with the candidate.

DUTIES

When you are asking about duties, don't let them just rattle on about what they do.

Ask for the top three duties that they perform in the order of their importance. It is highly critical to know this when you are matching the duties relevent to a specific search assignment. If their number-three duty was only done 10% of the time, is the company's number-one duty going to match? If you send them over there, the company will say, "He is really light in this area." What happened was that you had identified a duty that was a minor part of the candidate's current job, but a major part of your client's job.

Find out about their supervisor and title. See if it is possible to check with that person. Obviously, it will not be if they are still employed there. If that is the case, don't ask about checking references at this time. But if they have left, then certainly you want to check references and perhaps openings.

REASON FOR LEAVING, AGAIN.....

As mentioned previously, when you are interviewing a candidate, be sure to get the Reason For Leaving. The reason for leaving must be specific and professional. If you leave it in the general sense, you could get yourself into trouble.

It is not enough for you to know what the reason for leaving is; the candidate must know. Nail him or her down and then get a commitment, as we'll discuss shortly.

If the candidate should see the same problem at your client as exists at his or her present firm, we call that a "turndown". If the candidate identifies that problem exists <u>after</u> they accept the offer, then we call that a "fall-off". Neither has to happen. Here is how to avoid it.

What Kind of Reason?

What do we mean when we say the Reason For Leaving must be <u>specific</u> and <u>professional</u>? And what is meant by "general" terms? What general terms do you hear? You hear words like "opportunity" or "I need a better challenge". Why can't we deal with those? Because we don't know what they mean.

I had a person who wanted a challenge. I said, "OK. I have a failing oil company in Tulsa that I would like you to work for. They have a challenge for you." Well, he got the offer, and he turned it down. And I said, "I thought you wanted a challenge." He said, "Yes, Larry, I do. But I don't want <u>that</u> much of a challenge!"

The problem is that a <u>general</u> topic can be molded to anything that person wants to make of it, and we don't know exactly what to get them. So we have to say, "Specifically, what is the problem?"

Specificity Example

A candidate once said to me, "Larry I have no opportunity." He had been an accountant out of a big 6 public accounting firm (as we called them at the time), who had been an internal auditor. He had left them because he did not like the travel and he did not like internal auditing. He went into an accounting manager's job in a local corporation, and now said he did not have any "opportunity".

Well, that is a general term, and what was needed were specifics. So I asked, "Why don't you think you have any opportunity?" And he said, "Because I have only have one avenue of promotion. That is to a controller, and there are no other avenues for me to move up." And I asked, "Well, why don't you want to be controller?" He replied, "We just lost our controller. Three accounting managers were looked at for the position, and another one got the job. Larry, I agree that the other person should have the job. He's got six years at the company, I've got two and he is very good. But I am dead-ended, and I am going nowhere for another three to five years." I understood specifically his reason for leaving. He had no opportunity and could not move up.

Gaining Commitment

The Reason For Leaving must be reinforced. The best way to do this is gaining a "Commitment and Agreement" technique with the candidate. By doing so, you will emphasize the problem, and clarify the solution.

Here is an example utilized in the above situation.

"Let me see if I can recap what you have told me and see if I am on target. You said to me you have no way of moving up. That is reason enough for you to leave, which I agree with. What I need to find you is another corporation in which I can put you at your current level. But it should either give you the opportunity for more than one area in which you can be promoted, or a time-frame for promotion, even if it is in one area. Would you agree that is what we are looking for?" The reply should be, "Yes. That is exactly what I am looking for."

Now here comes the commitment question: "If I find that for you, are you willing to quit your present position and accept my company's job?" You should hear, "Yes". I don't want any other answer on that commitment. "Maybe" is not enough! If we have identified the true problem, he must proceed once it is solved. If I say, "If I provide it, will you commit to leaving?", I want a "Yes!". Especially if you plan on marketing this person, you must have a serious candidate who has made a decision to leave if you find him what he wants.

I took this particular candidate that we've discussed over to a client of mine. As mentioned, he was currently an accounting manager, and did not want to go back to being an internal auditor, which is what he had been with his Big 6 public accounting firm. I got him a job with a company that would put him in nine different departments for a period of two months per department. At the end of that time, he would get promoted in one of those departments. He said to me, "Larry, I can be in treasury. I could be in financial analysis, I could be in tax." I said, "Yes. Depending the department you do well in and the one where you and the manager hit it off, you will get promoted in that department."

As soon as he got the offer, he said, "I'll take it!" He didn't say, "Are there benefits" or "I don't know." He said, "I'll take it!" Why? Because I had solved the reason he was leaving his current company. Guess what the title of the job was? You are right — Internal Auditor, the same position he did not like at his original accounting firm! But he took that because, as he said, "I can stand that for eighteen months to get promoted and get where I want to go in my career."

Candidate Closing Power

Understand that RFL - Reason For Leaving - equals <u>candidate</u> <u>closing</u> <u>power</u>. Whenever the person starts to get nervous about leaving, nervous about changing, nervous about making that big career move in his life, you can go back and say, "Didn't you tell me? Didn't we talk about this problem?" "Yes, that is what I want out of life. I've got to get the guts up enough to go and do it." Reason For Leaving is very effective <u>candidate</u> <u>closing</u> <u>power</u> when combined with good selling skills.

Professional RFL

Now, not only must it be <u>specific</u>. It must also be <u>professional</u>. That means there must be something wrong with the professional area. Personal reasons kill placements, they don't make them! Yes, a lot of people will say, "I want to move because I have this specific personal problem." Well, people do change every now and then for personal problems. Sometimes they'll change locations and companies because of family or other reasons. But in general, if the personal problem can be solved without a job change, your deal is history!

A Warning.....

If a person is making his first job change, he is likely to turn it down because he has never done it before and it is scary. In fact, if he has been at the company longer than seven years, he probably will not leave on his own. He will have to be forced out <u>or</u> something dramatic will have had to happen to cause him to leave, or he would have done so by now. The average candidate only stays with a company about three-and-a-half years in today's market. If he has been there seven years or longer, there is a reason he is staying put for so long. Be very careful about working with this kind of candidate.

A Personal RFL Error....

I once got a call from an engineer out of the Dakotas who said, "My wife wants us to move home to Texas." We knew he was going home to Texas; she wore the pants, so to speak. But we said, "You are with a multi-national company. They have a plant in Texas. Why don't you just transfer?" He said, "I have already talked to them, and they will not transfer me. They say I am making too much money for the Texas plant, and they say I have no career at that plant. So I have to leave. I have talked to my boss, and I have talked to my boss' boss. I have talked to personnel and I have talked to HR in corporate. The only place I can go is Chicago. I've talked to my wife to see if we can move to Chicago. She said, 'Watch my lips; Texas!' So I have no chance or choice, but to move and leave for Texas."

Is that professional or personal? It is <u>personal</u>. It has nothing to do with his professional life. In his professional life, he was happy. He had been there for eleven years. He loved it, and had never made a job change. Now we should have seen this coming like a freight train. He had never made a move. And he is telling us he is going to pick up, move to Texas, and quit his company.

Well, we knew it was a serious situation, so we did get him an interview in Texas with a top client. He flew there repeatedly. He accepted the offer. He had a house hunting trip. But two days before reporting to work, our client called us and said, "Did you know that your engineer backed out?" We said, "No!" Then we called him and said, "What is going on?" He said, "My company called me, and asked why I was leaving. I reminded them that I had said six months ago and for the last six months, I have to move to Texas. And they said to me, 'We have a plant in Texas'!"

We went over all the counter-offer procedures. We went over anything we could think of. We told him he was dead-ended, and he wouldn't get a promotion. We told him that he did not have the right type of experience for that specific plant, with which we were familiar. We told him he was earning too much money, and that he would not see any raises for a couple of years. It did not matter. His <u>personal</u> <u>problem</u> of moving to Texas had been resolved, and no matter the damage he was doing to himself by accepting a counter-offer with a bad plant and no upward mobility, he was not going to leave that company. Why not? Because when that personal reason can be resolved without a job change, your deal is history.

THE 24-HOUR TIGHTENING TECHNIQUE

So what is the answer? When people tell you about the personal reason, you should use a 24-hour Tightening Technique on them that helps get past that. Let me explain what that is.

I had a candidate call one of my recruiters and say he wanted to leave this particular area to get better education for his children. Now is that personal or professional? It is personal.

We said, "What professional reasons do you have for leaving your company?" He had none. He liked his company, and didn't want to leave them. We told him plainly that we didn't think he would leave. And he said, "What are you talking about?" We said, "What happens when you get that offer, and you really have to face walking into your favorite company and resigning? We don't think you will do it." He said, "Well, it will be hard." I said, "Here is what you need to do; go home with your wife and sit down and say, 'my recruiter has identified that I have a personal problem with leaving my company, and not a professional one. We need to make a commitment to our family that this is a large enough problem to leave and go to another school system. I am going to stop a good career path and a happy employment with a great company to do that. If I am not determined on this, in the eleventh hour, I will probably back out. What am I going to do?'"

He called us the next day and said, "You are right. Our children are quite young, and another two years in this school system is not going to be detrimental to them. I am not serious; you are right, and I am not going to look."

It may seem that by doing this, you are losing candidates. I don't believe you are losing candidates at all. I believe you are <u>identifying</u> <u>tire</u> <u>kickers</u> who after the eleventh hour and after two months worth of work on your part will back out.

In this situation, we didn't have a serious candidate. There was <u>no</u> chance that this young man would have accepted an offer. It would have resulted in a turndown. Instead, we filled the position with someone who accepted, and the candidate has referred others to us, resulting in multiple fees.

Does this mean, especially if you progress to Direct Recruiting, that you should not overcome objections and recruit the "reluctant candidate"? Of course not! You can increase production dramatically if you have the sales skills to support this methodology. But when you do, don't forget to identify the candidate's professional concerns. Otherwise, there may be trouble ahead.

PREVIOUS EMPLOYMENT

It is easy to overlook previous companies that the candidate has worked for. We center so much on current employment that we sometimes don't pay attention to the two previous companies. You need to go back about 10 years in a person's background because all of that information is relevant. Past ten years, you don't need to find out as much, as a general rule. But ten years is still recent information, and you should get it.

By doing so, you get indications of things you should check out on your candidate. Let's say that in the last three companies covering twelve years, he has always been a project engineer and did not show much progression. He may not be talented enough to go beyond that level, or may not <u>want</u> the management area and may be rising strictly up the technical ladder. There are a lot of things that can be inferred about that. It leads us to ask certain questions that help us know what is going on with this candidate.

In the previous companies, check position titles, dates there, and duties so you can analyze career progression. As an example, suppose the candidate started as a project engineer. In his second job, he left as project leader and now he is currently project manager of a company. You have somebody who has either been at the right place at the right time, or has a pretty good set of qualifications and talents because of the rise through the companies that he has been with in the past. A client will want to know this!

ACCOMPLISHMENTS AND ACHIEVEMENTS

As we've discussed, when you are interviewing the candidate, a critical point is accomplishments and achievements. That gives us the necessary information to market this person and get companies interested in them. It is also the thing that will <u>close</u> placements with the client, because it will make that candidate look better then all of the other prospective employees walking in there and getting interviews. As covered previously, there is a clear hierarchy of achievements. Review the section closely when you re-read this book.

Match right, maximize your results — and win!

MUTUAL COMMITMENT

A frequently overlooked positive is gaining a commitment from your candidates that they are going to reward you for the hard work that you put in.

I have no problem telling some candidates that this is a free professional service to them that could literally change their lives and family fortunes dramatically for the future! I am willing to spend my time and money on their behalf.

However, I require something in return, and that is co-operation. I require honesty and total honor in telling me what they are looking for, and their evaluations of what I have presented to them. I need to be kept informed on what they are looking at, other interviews they have, and when they are about to accept an offer.

Once this is understood, a few days from acceptance, I will be able to gauge the timing of the situations I am dealing with for them. You don't want to set three interviews, and then find out at the last moment that they just accepted an offer and are no longer on the market. You must be kept informed what is happening with them.

I also ask them to refer others to me. Part of their payment and help to me is providing me with other top candidates, so I can help with their careers. As they refer those people, I can get them to refer other people to me; the list goes on, and it helps me to constantly build a stable of qualified people and a list of names.

THE "DO NOT CONTACT" LIST

Don't forget to get the "do not contact" list, the names of companies that the candidate has already interviewed with that you do not need to be contacting. You don't want to interfere with anything that they have currently going. A "do not contact list" is a list of possible placements for you, <u>if</u> they have already been ruled out of that situation. If they tell you that they interviewed with XYZ company and it did not work out, you should pick up the phone, call XYZ company, and see if you can place someone there. Don't start giving your own candidates competition when they are still in contention. But it does help as a source to develop other possible placements if they are not.

Surprisingly, interviewing candidates and getting full appropriate information, while obvious, is rarely done well. Even experienced people will lose fees due to short-cutting this step, and not know why. Frequently, problems start right here.

Do it right <u>every</u> <u>time</u>, and the warmth of a completed search will be yours far more often!

AVOIDING CANDIDATE PROBLEMS

14

*M*atching the candidate to the client is critical. Nevertheless, there are all sorts of traps and problems that can cause you to lose the fee after you have done so. Many of these deal with non-business related aspects of selecting candidates. Most can be eliminated by up-front knowledge of the problem.

Candidates are not just business people. They have personal quirks, wants, and needs which can make or break deals. In other instances, business circumstances not related to direct income can affect the placement.

"Deal-breakers" – problems that pop up at the eleventh hour — can cause you great difficulty. Here are some areas that must be considered if you are to truly maximize your income.

CONTACT INFO

Of course, you'll get home and work numbers. But sometimes that isn't enough. Once you set up an interview, also find out where the spouse is as far as phone number.

Sometimes when you can not find the person you are looking for, you want to call the spouse to make sure you get information to that person. Know when and where you can reach them. Rather than going days without finding someone you need to reach quickly, you have a way to contact the candidate. It is a bit premature to obtain this at your initial conversation. When an interview is actually set, however, it is a different story.

LOCATION, RE-LOCATION AND LEASES

Find out if they own or rent their particular dwelling. If they rent, see if they have any particular problems with breaking the lease or moving. Even if there is only a commute, renters may choose to move.

I also like to know about locations they might consider. Even if you recruit the candidate for a specific opportunity, broaden out the locational possibilities. Ask some questions. You already know where they went to school, so you know one area that is probably acceptable. Where they currently live is certainly acceptable. Then find out about his or her family homes. Where is he from? Where does the main family reside? What areas of the country?

By doing so, you have that personal draw as well as professional if we find them the opportunity in the area. Find out that and now you know about different locations that would be top priority for them to get to. Ask about other geographical preferences or other areas that they would be willing to move to. Where would they <u>not</u> relocate to, regardless of the opportunity?

Be sure you qualify them solidly in this area. Too many times you will talk to people that would "not live in a certain city for anything" and the next time that you call them, they are gone. You trace them, and they <u>are</u> living in that particular place! Be careful that you are not just asking questions about thoughts and ideas, but serious decisions that they will make based on the opportunity. You don't want to pass over an opportunity for someone.

A great question here to help you determine the <u>real</u> importance of re-location or commute is to ask them the four criteria they would use in evaluating the acceptance of a new job. Then ask them to rank them in order of significance.

If a person puts location as the number one criteria of evaluating a new job, then you know they are much more location-conscious than they are career-conscious. The person who puts "a career step" first, meaning the opportunity to get a greater challenge and to be able to move up the corporate ladder, and does not even list location is clearly a career-oriented person. They will probably make the decision that is best for their career and the family will go along. It gives you a great set of criteria to use in evaluating those new opportunities.

COUNTER-OFFER PREPARATION

Also be sure to ask at this point their idea about a counter offer. If you refer to it as a "Buy back" when initially discussing this, most people ask what is meant by that. That's your opening.

Say to them that they are going to go to their company and resign. Then the company says, "Hey, where are you going? We can't lose you. Why are you doing this? We want you so badly that we are willing to offer you the same money and opportunity that you are getting from the new company." Even though the person was unhappy, that always feels good. There is nothing better in the world than to be told that you are wanted.

When you talk to them about the counter-offer, project them forward; give them a "for instance". Let's say this happens and they walk in, and the company says "Don't go. We will give you this. What would you do?" When they answer, then ask them why or why not? Don't just accept the fact, "Oh, I will never do that." I have had people say that, and then turn around and do it. That is because I did not ask the question, "Why not?". Help them determine <u>why</u> accepting a counter-offer is wrong for them.

We have figures that show it is disastrous to people's career when they accept counter-offers. There have been articles written in the Wall Street Journal and similar publications about the problems associated with it. The majority of people — some surveys indicate as many as 80% — that accept counter-offers are gone within the next six months.

Why is that so? It is mainly because ***the counter-offer never resolves the reason why the person was unhappy to begin with***. Tell the candidate that many people were at a certain income, unhappy with the company and their own personal growth, not getting more experience in the job, and just treading water. They then decided, "Well, for me to get ahead in the world, I have to get out of here." So they go out, get a good offer and are ready to go. Then they walk into their present company and quit. And their company says, "We can't do without you", and matches the dollars. It makes the person get their head turned, and they think "what a good deal! I was unhappy, but now I am happy." But if the Reason for Leaving remains, the counter offer is meaningless.

"Now", I tell people, "all you have is a 'richer' problem. Instead of earning a <u>reasonable</u> income, the accepted counter-offer puts you higher. For you to leave, a new firm will have to offer an <u>unreasonable</u> income. And you are not worth that. So what they have done is hem you into a position that you cannot leave unless you are willing to take a cut or move laterally. And you are still going to be unhappy because all of a sudden you are going to turn around and say, Wait a minute! I am making more money, but I have the same problem."

Talk to them right now and get their heads set correctly on the counter-offer, or you are going to have difficulty in the end. If you wait till it happens to talk about it, you are going to be in trouble.

Presuming that you're going to work with this candidate now (as opposed to putting him in the files for later resurrection), I believe in covering this in the initial candidate interview. Others may disagree. But you will find that addressing this before the counter-offer is extended is mandatory.

FAMILY DISCUSSIONS

Make sure the candidate has discussed a job change or re-location with his or her family! You will be surprised how many have not done so. Or they may have said, "I am thinking about it", but the family does not know how serious this is. If you spend time finding this person some interviews, you risk having professional egg on your face by putting him in front of clients when he won't accept an offer. You should know if the family is aware and supportive before you make that time investment.

I had one individual where I dialed the home number in error and the wife answered the phone. I said, "How do you do? I am Larry Nobles. I wanted to call your husband; obviously, I have dialed the wrong number. I need to dial him at work." She said, "Oh yes, he is at work now." And I asked, "What do you think about this wonderful opportunity he is looking at, because I think he is going to get an offer?" She responded, "What opportunity?" And I said to myself, "Oops! I got problems." Guess what? I explained the really excellent opportunity, and she said, "Well, if that is out of town, then he can forget about it. We are not going anywhere!" I had not done a good job in qualifying about the family.

Family is important. They are part of the decision. Kids will have to be moved to another school. The spouse may have to change jobs. They may lose friends or see them less frequently. They will have to change homes. There can be a lot of problems associated with that. It is almost a rule that if you are going to relocate someone, then you should always find a way of speaking with the spouse. It is not always possible. But it is always wise. Be sure to discuss with the candidate about problems they might have, or issues with family.

A consultant with my firm almost lost one placement, and the candidate would not tell him why. All he would say was he couldn't take that job. Finally we got it out of him. They were a member of a very narrow religious sect, and couldn't find a church in that town. Well, that's fine. We could deal with that once we knew what the problem was. We called the headquarters of his religious group and found a church twenty miles away. He accepted the offer the next morning. Why didn't the candidate think of doing this? Who knows? Solving problems of this nature is our job.

That situation caused me to build in the following family qualifying question.

"For instance, are there any personal difficulties, such as church or real estate problems, that would keep you from accepting an offer that you really want?"

Find these things out now, so you don't go through a lot of thrashing around without ever being able identify the problem and solve it.

HOBBY QUESTIONS

Ask about any leisure activities or hobbies. Now why in the world would we ask that? Why do we care what they do with their spare time? Because many people do not live to work. They work to live. To these people, their hobbies are important, and they will not give them up to take some job, no matter how excellent it may be.

I had a candidate who one of my top clients in Tulsa really wanted. However, he lived in the Colorado Rockies, and was a back packer. He did it every weekend, and it was the great love of his life. He would not come to Oklahoma, because he did not think that we would have anything like a backpacking club.

We contacted the President of the Oklahoma Backpacking Club. We had the President call him and discuss how active they were, and the many times they went out to the Ozarks over the weekends. The candidate accepted the offer the next morning .

To some people, the things they do for fun are important enough to jeopardize a career or job, so they can continue in their hobbies. Find out, and do some research.

BONUS OR VESTING PERIODS

Ask about any bonus or vesting periods. Do not leave this out! When we get to the offer, they may think they can't leave because they are going to lose out on a vesting program which will mean an amount of money to them. We want to <u>know</u> about that.

You will frequently be able to talk to some people about how small that vestment really is. Sometimes it will be less then a thousand dollars. Are they going to wait three or four months in a dead-end job, and pass on the best opportunity they have seen over that kind of money? If you don't find out and address this problem, some will. Talk to the candidate about those situations up front, or you end up doing all the work for nothing.

INSURANCE QUESTIONS

Are there any insurance carrier needs? Sometimes there are health needs in the family and if they switch insurance carriers, it is a major problem. This can be significant at all income levels. Many have some clauses that would not protect the family and when they find out, they simply cannot leave.

You may have to limit that candidate to a larger company that has so many employees that there are no pre-existing condition clauses in the insurance. The person can take the job and their family could be immediately covered, regardless of the health problems that existed before.

CHILDREN

Discuss attitudes, ages, and the needs of the children.

Problems of special education or hospital needs are obvious. But sometimes you find the family with kids in high school. Ask. If a senior has to be taken out of school, it may be a problem. The parents may want them to graduate from the school they have been going to for the entire high school years. Find out about the family needs now. Perhaps the candidate can move and live apart for a few months until graduation. Or they may move quickly for the entire senior year.

The solution to these problems will need to be identified and figured out.

Getting the critical information mentioned above will help you to gain the cooperation of the candidate. It will also help you to put them in the right position, and avoid problems at the end.

Placements are made by the skill of the consultant. Obtaining the right information in advance is a good example of this truth.

WRITING SEARCHES: CRITICAL KEY

15

*W*hat are the most important facets of our business to master in order for you to maximize your success? That is a very complex question. In 1975, an industry trainer named Phil Ross came out with an audio cassette series entitled, *"The 28 Steps to the Placement Process"*. According to Mr. Ross, there were 28 steps; dropping the ball in <u>any</u> of these areas can cause you to lose the placement and the fee.

Nevertheless, I'd say the top three are as follows: first, organizational skills, which includes a good written Daily Planner. Without that, you are flailing around. Your skills in other areas will serve little purpose if you are just plain not effective. With these skills, you will out-produce many who may exceed your talents.

Secondly, I'd say your ability to identify and recruit candidates is critical. That's what they <u>pay</u> us for. If you can find quality candidates <u>not</u> available through the internet or ads and <u>not</u> actively looking to make a change, *you will prosper in this business*. If you can't, you'll just be trying to get the same candidates to clients as everyone else.

Thirdly, however, is taking a complete search assignment so as to enable you to select properly. Despite the fact that all that is required is to fill out the Search Assignment form completely, it is surprising how rarely this is done. It may be that your firm does not have a form with the appropriate questions. Or perhaps you are asking, but are not getting full information to enable you to evaluate the search properly. Many in our business settle for incomplete information. It is an expensive flaw.

Consider that if you are the best alive in this business but you have selected the search incorrectly, nothing will happen. You will get poor results <u>regardless</u> of your other skills. If you have candidates, the potential client will be reluctant to interview. Either client or candidate will be reluctant to proceed past the first interview. If you get an offer, it may be a poor one, and your acceptance ratio will not be high. What a mess!

Taking a thorough search and evaluating it properly is <u>critical</u> to your success — and easy to do.

Let's take a look at this mandatory portion of our business.

In writing search assignments, as in interviewing candidates, we have a certain set of objectives that we need to reach.

OBJECTIVES OF A SEARCH ASSIGNMENT

The first objective to taking a search is to understand the order technically, so we can <u>recognize</u> the <u>right</u> <u>candidate.</u>

One of the most serious problems that we have is taking generic descriptions. A generic description is always phrased in number of years and doing a certain job in a certain industry. You can recognize those assignments easily. Unfortunately, they do not tell us <u>which</u> candidate to refer. It tells us that there is a job opening, and that's all.

Because we usually work on contingency, we know we have the right to drop an order or toss in the upper right hand drawer and walk away. Thus, we tend to get sloppy. Frequently, we do not take information specifically enough to make a valid decision as to whether or not these are serious search assignments.

Taking old-style "job orders" and developing <u>search</u> <u>assignments</u> are two different skills. You must learn to avoid writing "job orders". To me, that is no different than reading an ad in the newspaper or job board.

It has happened to me, too. There is a job opening, and the company told me about it. But there was not much serious motivation on their part, it was kind of a ho-hum attitude between both of us, and I took the specifications down. Rather than having a search assignment, I know where there is a job opening. Can you fill something like that? Not unless you get lucky. And probably not even then. Don't try.

There is a significant difference between that and a genuine search. Be serious about each and every order that you take.

As you are taking the <u>full</u> information, start <u>developing</u> your client. Talk to them about starting a relationship with you, not just filling an opening for them. Don't just take ho-hum information and put that order in another file, one of many on which you might refer a candidate if someone comes along. If you do, you may be missing a lot of good relationships and business. Only after we have understood their <u>specific</u> needs technically do we know which candidate to refer. Rather than taking a generic order, take a technically-specific order so you can identify the <u>right</u> candidate.

Sales Strengths

Our secondary objective is to develop the information necessary to sell the opportunity. When we discussed the candidate interview, we learned that candidates have certain problems. Only certain companies or positions will fill those needs. Those are the ones that we want to be able to send them on! Otherwise, turndowns and an unwillingness to proceed to a second interview will be the result.

When we develop information necessary to sell the opportunity, we are also developing information about the opportunity at the company and what is good about it. What areas would interest the candidate to come and work for them? Once we find that out, we will not only be able to know which candidate to refer, but we will be able to sell that opportunity to that candidate. By doing so properly, we get their interest level high enough to bring about a completed search and an accompanying fee.

Co-operation

It is also imperative to gain the co-operation of the hiring official, so we can manage the recruitment process and close the placement. Too many times we have not sold our value to the hiring official. They do not see us in a consultative mode and don't take advice from us.

How many times have we taken an order, presented candidates and referred resumes (perhaps mistakenly), and had a potential client not even return the phone call? They saw no value. Even if they do return the phone call, they may or may not see the people or co-operate with us. We did not do a good enough job in explaining how we are going to go about referring people to them and working with them to <u>their</u> benefit!

When you are talking to companies and obtaining searches, it is incumbent upon you to develop those areas of co-operation. Companies must <u>want</u> to listen to you, want to see your people and want to hear from you. You do that by raising their interest level and gaining their co-operation in the initial part of taking the search.

WRITING SEARCH ASSIGNMENTS

If this is a top search assignment, we are going to spend hours and hours of our day trying to find people that will fill the bill for our client company. Only the right questions and complete answers will allow you to choose.

What information do you need to do so?

Company Information

Obviously we want the name, the address, and the phone. But we also want to get the size of the company, and we want to get that in both their revenues and number of employees.

The mistake I see made many times is that we only get the overall company's sales and employees. If we are dealing with a multi-billion dollar company that has 22 plants nationwide, their name is quite famous in the marketplace. What we need to know, however, is where this person is going to work and the size of that particular area or plant, because that is what they are going to be interested in.

If the position is in the sales division of a large company, for example, there may only be three people in the entire branch in that city. The candidate may expect to show up and see some gargantuan place. There may be two people there and an empty chair, and he is there to fill the third one. Make sure you get the figures of sales and employees where this particular job resides.

Product or Service

Find out the product or the service that these people provide. What kind of business are they in?

I see a substantial number of orders come through my office from exchange partners for "Acme Engineering" or some general name like that, with <u>no</u> indication as to what kind of company that they are. Do they manufacture and work with metals? Are they an environmental company and work with gases? Do they provide a service, and work with no products whatsoever? What is that service, and to whom do they sell it? Are they a research and lab service?

If you don't know what they do, you will not be able to sell it to the candidate. More importantly, when you are looking for a candidate for a metals company, what is the obvious candidate you want to refer? Sure, someone with metal experience. Make certain you get a very <u>specific</u> and complete readout of the product or service that they provide. <u>Don't</u> accept a general statement.

Related Companies

Under company information also, make certain you obtain the names of the parent and the subsidiaries. There is nothing worse than referring a candidate to his own company because you did not know that those two companies belong to each other! Sometimes a parent has a different name than the company you are working with. Some of the subsidiaries under this company have different names, and do not seem link at all.

If you take a person out of one company and refer them to another company, guess what? You may have just referred them to their own parent. Not only could they have a problem; you could be in great trouble if that person were to lose their job over your referring them to their own company. Parent, other divisions and subsidiaries are a must.

Source Companies

Some info I like to get, since I may be thinking of recruiting on this, is their top competitors. I like to say, "Who are your competitors out there that you respect? If you could choose some companies from which you want to hire a candidate, who would those companies be?" You are now getting the hiring official to give you the company name so you can research and source. Find out his ideas about where the candidate could come from. This could help you tremendously because when you bring someone from a competitor you <u>know</u> he respects, you have another selling point in order to set an interview.

JOB DESCRIPTION

After we get the company information, we are going to ask them about the job description. What is this new employee going to be <u>doing</u> at that plant? Again, the problem is that we get generic desciptions. This does not help to qualify the candidate in order to know which one to send them.

Under job description, get the exact title, what they call this person. Some people are "title conscious" and many companies call certain types of people different things in other companies. Find exactly what they are going to call this particular title, including the word "senior" or "staff", or anything that might set it apart from a generic title.

Duties

When you get to the duties of the job description, ask the hiring official to describe the three top duties in order of importance to that company. You will find sometimes many companies have trouble doing this. Why? Well, you made them think.

Remember we are consultants. We are the ones that help companies think through what they are doing. When you say, "Give me the top three duties, in order of importance to you", you'll get a little bit of a pause, and the person has to start thinking what do they really want this person to do for this company. This help you enormously to screen and sell candidates to that company.

Ask for other duties also. You want to make sure that you have all the duties. Some may be of less importance, but a candidate with experience in those particular duties could be significant.

Sometimes you have to help a client by giving them examples. What about this kind of experience or that? What about someone with these kind of talents? If you had two different candidates with particular talents, which one would you pick? Help the hiring official work through the thought process of the specific background that will help them hire the right person.

Key To The Hire

Within duties, there resides one specific thing that will make or save this company more than any other. And I call that the "Key to the Hire".

My image of it is that this company has a lock on this job, and I am looking for the candidate that has the key that will open that lock. That is why I call it the "Key to the Hire". I want to say, "What is it within these duties that is <u>most</u> important for you?"

A good question to ask is, "Once they get into the swing of things, what are the first things that they will be working on?" Identify various projects or things that they will have to know soon. Look for people with accomplishments and achievements in that particular area. Companies are going to be enthusiastic about seeing those people! All of a sudden, talk about resumes and interviewing times, etc. drop by the wayside. Why? Because you have the candidate, not a candidate!

The "Key to the Hire" is what tells you that. Develop a part of your order that separates this. It will help you not only to determine which candidate is best, but will help you sell that candidate's talents to the company.

Staff Numbers

Also find out the number of people to supervise if it is a supervisory position. Not only should you ask about the number to supervise, but what kind of people. If they are going to supervise six, are these six technicians or support staff? Or are they six other professionals? There is a real difference in the level of responsibility, depending on who will be going to supervise as well as how many.

If there is no supervision, find out the size of the staff they will be working with. This is sometimes critical when considering upward mobility. Suppose you are putting them in a staff of twenty-six engineers with whom they are going to have to eventually compete for the top position. That particular job may not look quite as attractive to an upwardly-mobile engineer as another with a smaller staff. It will help you in describing or painting images or pictures of the job to the person you are talking to. They must <u>visualize</u> themselves in that position.

Double check the location of the job. You could be obtaining an order from corporate headquarters, but the job is three states away. Make sure you understand where the job is located and the amount of travel involved, so you can describe that to your candidate.

Reporting Relationship

Find out who this person reports to. We certainly want the name, so we can prepare this person for when they go to the interview as to who will be their immediate supervisor. When they interview with that person, it may be a little different from interviewing with more peripheral people. They must know who that person is prior to the interview.

It is also important to know the title of the person, because who they report to is seen as a step up even though the job title may be the same. A Lead Engineer reporting to an Engineering Manager, for example, is different from a Lead Engineer that reports to a Vice-President of Engineering. One is a higher-level job than the other one. Titles vary by industry; get specifics.

Education

Companies will claim "educational requirements". Make sure that you understand whether the education is mandatory, or only preferred. Many companies may be willing to accept experience over education. Ask if it is mandatory, or if a non-degreed individual who has come up through the ranks and has very good experience is acceptable.

Ask for the primary education that they are looking for as well as alternatives that work also. For example, sometimes they want a chemical engineer, but a chemist will do.

Disqualifiers

Ask for disqualifiers. The way we ask is say, "What areas of a person's background would disqualify them before I bring them to you?" They might say, "If they are non-degreed, certainly that would disqualify them." Fine, but are there other areas?

We are looking for the black-and-white areas that will allow us to screen out people, and not refer someone to them that will not work in the first place. Make sure of the disqualifiers. Has the client thought through them? Are they just preferences or a true "I will not hire this type of person"?

PERSONAL QUALITIES

As you send more candidates to a client, you will more clearly identify "chemistry". Initially, you must ask.

Ask for the type of person you are looking for. Are we looking for someone who is a team player who works well with a group? Or are we looking for somebody that stands alone, is assertive, and can stand up on his own two feet when people are coming to him with questions, various projects, and demands?

Try to get an indication that will help you find the kind of person that is sought.

SELLING THE SEARCH

There are two kinds of selling points with which you must be concerned. One has to do with the job, and one has to do with the company. We call this "sizzle", as mentioned previously. Job sizzle would be the opportunity. Company sizzle would be stability or growth. Both areas needs to be paid attention to. Ask your company hiring official to help you with that.

Remember you have sales skills and can make many opportunities positive. Just as all people are not stars, neither are all positions. But most have good qualities.

For example, suppose you ask what would interest a candidate and hear, "I don't know if they are going to be interested or not. This is kind of a dead-end job. We are a small company and there is not going to be any upward mobility here. We get a lot of great work to be done, we are a good company, and we have a lot of fun. But I don't know if there is any real opportunity."

Should you actively recruit on this? No. But remember there is a job for everyone, and there is a candidate for every opening. In that instance, we want to start asking about the good portions of the <u>job</u>, and forget about the <u>opportunity</u>. We are not looking for a ladder climber that has to be promoted in two years or they are going to be unhappy. We start talking about how long the company has been in business and the size, the family atmosphere and company picnics that seem like family.

Those are things that <u>are</u> important to some candidates. Some candidates could not care less about it and it is not what they are looking for. Fine. As stated, we would not recruit on this. That's where your "excess inventory" may come in.

Find the selling points of the position. Candidates are different. Combining positives of the position with a candidate's Reason for Leaving is the key to acceptance and a fee.

BENEFITS

Ask about benefits or vacation policy. Sometimes when people move from small to large companies, the increase in benefits could be significant and positive. Sometimes newer companies in the market are giving extended vacations to people that have extended time in their history. For instance, a person with ten years experience, even though they are just joining the new company today, gets three weeks vacation. That kind of vacation policy is very much "sizzle" for someone who is concerned with losing the vacation he has accumulated, or who is more motivated by hobbies or family.

Are these important to a candidate concerned with upward career mobility? Usually not. Are they critical in some placements? Yes.

HIRING PROCEDURE

The exact hiring procedure is an area frequently overlooked by many. The problem is that when we talk about hiring procedure, we don't have a <u>statement</u> on the way we are going to work. Rather, we end up asking the hiring official, "Well, let's see. When I find a candidate, how do you want to work this? Can I call you or send you a resume?"

What are they going to say? "Send me a resume", of course. They are trapped in the area of just reading resumes to see how good someone is.

The problem with resumes are that they are not a very good measure of a person's talents. Some of the worst people can make some of the greatest-looking resumes. Some of your brightest individuals just aren't very good at putting together a good resume. You have to help hiring officials understand that is not the way to identify top talent and choose which one needs to be interviewed.

Avoiding the Resume` Trap

You can get around the resume trap by telling them how you are going to handle the situation.

Companies who are going to pay you a lot of money expect you to know your job, feel comfortable, and say, "This is how we are going to handle this." Some of us are reticent to make statements, because we are afraid of a backlash from the hiring official. Well, I have found it to be just the reverse. If you are assertive in your knowledge of your business, and say, "This is how we are going to handle this", most times you get an OK from people. I seldom get a problem from my presentation.

Tell them <u>how</u> we are going to refer candidates to them. I would say, "I think I have an idea of the candidate that you are looking for now that we have discussed the job description. Let me tell you how I am going to handle this. I am going to go out in the industry, and I am going to talk to a lot of my industry contacts based on the specifications that you have given me. They will refer me to some of the top people in this area. I will make contact with these professionals and talk to them about this particular situation. I will screen them down to the best one or two. When I have done that and have a commitment from those candidates that they are ready for an interview, I will call you and give you a review of their background. Presuming you agree at that time that they are the kind of candidate for your situation, we will set up a time to get you together."

In general, I have most people say, "All right. That sounds good." I never said a word about a resume.

But what if the person comes back and says, "Well, yes, I hear what you are saying, but I want a resume"? I say, "I will get you the resume. I know it is a vital part for the interview. What I will do is present these people to you and we will talk in-depth about their background. Ask me whatever questions you need answered to determine whether you are interested in a meeting with them. Once you have all your answers, we will decide on a time for an interview, unless you feel they are not qualified.

In general, when I have screened many people down to just one or two, they will be on target and you will want to see them. As soon as you decide that you would like to see them, I will put their resume together, and you will have it for your face-to-face meeting."

I am not saying to not send resumes. Resumes may even help when my hiring official is going to interview. They hurt us when you allow a decision on an interview based <u>solely</u> on the resume, and not through your information or knowledge of the candidate.

Develop a presentation that tells the hiring official how it is <u>going</u> to be handled rather than <u>asking</u> them. We are not trying to keep resumes out of the hands of hiring officials. We are only trying to keep them from making the decision to interview off the resume. Focus on a discussion with the consultant (you) that is handling that candidate.

Telephone Pre-Screen?

For those of us who work a regional or national market, frequently the candidate has to be flown in. There is a lot of expense in doing that, so those people will probably do a telephone interview first.

It is important to know who the pre-screener is. Who is going to make that decision? Will it be the hiring official? Or will it be a human resource clerk making the call who may have very little knowledge about the situation and can not interpret this person's background ? They will be very black-and-white in their approach.

Knowing who is going to do the phone interview will make a difference in how we prepare the candidate for that telephone interview. The objective of the telephone interview is for the candidate to obtain a face-to-face interview. Too many times we do not treat the telephone interview as seriously as we should. Remember that a telephone interview is an interview, not a conversation. It needs to be handled with all the smoothness and professionalism of any face-to-face interview. We will discuss helping the candidate to do so in the next chapter.

Interview Procedure

Another thing we need about the hiring procedure is the time per interview, and the procedure that will take place during that time. Many of us don't ask about the amount of time that the person should expect to spend at that interview.

Sometimes they can last an hour, and they are going to just meet with someone quickly. Sometimes it is an all-day session that includes lunch, plant tour, and several different interviews at the plant. You need to know how much time to tell people to allot. It poses a preventable problem when the candidate is there at noon thinking they have an hour interview. All of a sudden there are two more people to see. Then they have to make a decision of being late back to their work by two hours, or cutting short the interview by not seeing the other people. This is not a position in which you want to put a candidate. Find out how long they will be there for the interview.

Decision-makers

Find out who the decision-maker is and the title of that person. You obviously want to be dealing with the decision maker; it is very tough to be selling a human resource clerk when they have nothing to do with the decision to hire. If you are not talking to the decision-maker, not much is going to come of it.

Find a way to eventually talk to that person. Tell them you will give them the feedback from the candidate. They should want that information, and hopefully will want you to call them with that information. When you do that, you establish contact, and you have a chance to do some selling. It is critical to talk to them about the process of making a decision, and help them though the interview and the decision to make an offer.

TESTING

Find out if there is going to be testing done. Are there psychological tests? Are there behavioral tests, aptitude tests, or anything that the person will have to pass that will tell the client whether to hire this individual?

I personally do not believe psychological testing is a good tool for the final decision. Certainly, such tests have consistently been noteworthily unsuccessful in our industry, and in most others as well. It is only an indicator, and a poor one at that. But some companies use it as a crutch to make the entire decision.

Also you want to know if they give medical and drug screen. Then you want to question your candidates on the likelihood of passing a physical or drug test, so they know it is coming. Obviously these will not be required at a first interview, but let the candidate know they will be eventually. It is surprising how many candidates "choose" not to proceed once they know.

DETERMINING URGENCY

To help in determining urgency, look for both a "target date" and a "trouble date". What is the target date to hire this person? By what date will the client be in trouble if you do not have them on board? These questions will yield solid information to determine urgency.

Get a date. Don't accept the terms ASAP. That does not mean anything, and has different meanings to different people. Find out both dates.

Other Sources

Ask if they are using advertising, scrounging on the internet, or other recruiters. You need to know what your competition is out there. If they are advertising or net scrounging and they find a passable candidate in this way, they will be reluctant to pay your fee to hire someone that you bring them. It is highly unlikely (depending on the quality of the candidate they seek) that they <u>will</u> find a good candidate from ads or the internet. A recent well-researched *Wall Street Journal* article indicated that the four largest job boards <u>combined</u> yielded only 2% of total hires, and most of that is not of the level or quality that would be of interest to you. However, let them fail before you actually recruit heavily on the search.

If they are using other recruiters, find out how many? If they have already given this to four or five other recruiters, I might still refer existing candidates in hopes they will hire mine. But I do not think I would actively recruit.

If they have not given it to any other recruiters and you feel like you can fill this job, then go for an exclusive now. Ask them if you can work on it and get a commitment from them to use you only! If you wipe out the other competition, you have a significant chance in making money. Go for the exclusive!

Current Activity

Also in qualifying, ask what is their current activity? What has been happening on this particular job? If it has been open for three months and they have interviewed people but the position is still open, how serious are they? The critical question here again is why not? If it is not a money problem, you may find out that the hiring official has been turning away the same types of candidates he told you he would hire.

You don't always come into the search on day one. If this is not an existing client, you may come in at the eleventh hour. They may have already done a tremendous amount to try and fill the opening. Sometimes that is good, because they may be in trouble, and there is an urgent need that you can fill. Find out.

COMPENSATION

When you ask about salary, don't ask them about a salary range; ask about a hiring range. Too many times we get a salary range of 50 to 60 and they will not hire more than 55, because they are not willing to go above midpoint. Find out about both the salary range and the hiring range, so you know what level you can work. If their salary range is 50 to 60 and their hiring range is 50 to 55, you may have some candidate earning 60. But you probably don't have a deal, unless the candidate is willing to take cuts or move laterally, or the client will extend the salary range dramatically.

Also ask about any bonuses that might up the income. Ask about their relocation policy. Should the new employee just hire a truck, or will the company buy houses? Do they pay real estate fees? That way you will know if you have a candidate with a problem.

COVERING FEES

Straightforwardly address your fees, but do so at the end of the call. Let me give you an example, "Are you familiar with our fee structure?"

The response will almost certainly be no, if you have not dealt with them before. As an example, here is what I'd say to explain.

"Well, the fee for our services is based on a percentage of the candidate's first year income. The income that you just quoted could be as high as 50,000 dollars. At that level, our fee would be 30% of 50,000 dollars or 15,000 dollars. Is that agreeable with you? Fine. I will send over a letter that confirms our agreement."

You should have a presentation you can say as smoothly and powerfully as I just did for you. When you do that, it will keep the negotiators off your back.

Don't go in and say, "Do you pay fees?" Give them a good solid presentation and you will find a lot of them agreeing with you.

There is much more to obtaining full fees, of course, than making a smooth initial presentation. Many firms will try to offer you less than a full fee. It is easy to just say "no", but that won't usually get you the full fee. Many who claim they pay only discounted fees can be "converted" and will become excellent full-fee repeat clients. However, you'll need intelligent effective multiple rebuttals to do that. Again, sophisticated rebuttals are not conducive to a written format. Your best source for these specific responses is an eight-module video series entitled, *"Book More Business! The Second Edition"* by Steve Finkel. See his website.

By obtaining all the information you need when you are writing a search and clearly presenting your fee, you will be well-positioned to intelligently select and complete the assignment, avoiding many problems along the way. Even if your firm has a good search assignment form (and many do not), there is much more to taking a good search than filling out a form. Time taken to master this step is mandatory to achieving high production.

CANDIDATE PREPARATION

16

One of the key qualities of good selling and good marketing is the ability to represent your product in the best possible light, maximizing the positives and minimizing the negatives. There is a massive difference between a dirty unwashed used car in someone's driveway with a "for sale" sign on it, and the same "pre-owned" car, gleaming and bright in the dealer's showroom!

Our business is no different, at least in our need to apply good salesmanship to our product.

The preceeding analogy is not totally accurate. Why not? Because in the example, the automobiles involved are identical. Good recruiting, however, will absolutely yield a far higher quality of candidate than could be found by the client in any other way. Internet candidates or ad responses, with very rare exceptions embodying total luck, will never compare to the high quality candidate with the precise skills and experience that a true recruiter can bring to the table, any more that a K-mart suit can compare to a hand-made suit tailored specifically to you.

But let us put that irrefutable fact aside for the moment, and assume that your candidate does not have major advantages.

Why would your candidate get hired when there are people walking off the street or the internet that are free, and yours have a sizeable fee attached to them? One of the reasons is your ability to prepare the candidates for what they are going to encounter at the company. You will make them look better, more intelligent, better-prepared by helping them to interview correctly, emphasizing that which is most important to the client. They will simply give a superior impression. The poor people who walk in off the street are interviewing based on the three-line ad in the newspaper or the job board, and are not nearly as able to give information that will help them obtain the offer that they seek.

Let us go over the steps necessary to get a candidate ready, and by doing so, increase your production markedly.

THE RIGHT TIME

When you are preparing a candidate, make sure you are doing it at the right time. When do you prepare a candidate? The biggest mistake is having an interview set on Friday and being so anxious to get the candidate ready that on Tuesday, we make the call and tell them all about it!

That candidate is going to have a lot of things happen to him between Tuesday and Friday. He may even have other interviews. Even if he doesn't, he is going to go to sleep and forget all the sage advice that you gave him to help him along. If at all possible, the best time to do it is twenty-four hours prior to the meeting. That gives them a little time to think about it and practice, and do some of the things that you have talked about and gone over. But it is not too early that they may forget a lot about what you went over in order to help them.

RE-SELL

The reality is that when preparing candidates, you may be asking them to do things that may be against their natural inclinations or thoughts. In order to gain their co-operation and motivate them to really listen, you must get their attention early.

So number one in candidate preparation is to resell the candidate on the opportunity. Explain again why they are going there to interview, and what the company has to offer that solves their concerns about their present firm. Get them excited again about this opportunity! The more excited we get them, the higher their interest level will be, and the more they will pay attention to us and take notes. Thus, the better they will interview when they get there.

PACKAGE THE POSITIVES

Next you must "package the positives" that the candidate brings to the table. What does "package the positives" mean? It means that candidates have certain ideas about how good they are in certain areas, what they can do for the company, or have done in the past. You must be able to pick out of the candidate's background those positives that are going to be most meaningful to your client company, and motivate the candidate to emphasize these areas.

For instance, suppose a candidate has a serious set of accomplishments and achievements in one particular facet of his background, and likes to talk about it a lot. However, the company only utilizes that particular talent in 5% of the position that they are looking for. The client will not have a lot of interest if you do not correct this, and that interview will fail. Think specifically, "what should I have this candidate talk to the company about?"

Go to your Search Assignment and look at "The Key to the Hire". What is it that will cause that client to hire someone and what talent, duty or project that the candidate may bring to the company would make them most attractive? That is what you want to tell them to discuss. Make certain to give the candidate the information that he needs to make him look as talented and good to the company as possible.

The candidate may talk about a different part of his background on a different interview with a different client, because that particular company has a different set of needs. "Package the positives" by telling the candidate what portion of his background to concentrate on in this specific interview.

"Controlling the Flow"

An interview has a certain flow. Hiring authorities have their pattern of questions, but much of the direction is based on the candidate's responses. If I can get the candidate to emphasize the right topics and get the company to ask about the right portions of his background, there is likely to be a happy ending.

This is what we call the "flow of the interview". You control what questions are asked and what answers are given, so that the information exchanged allows the company and the candidate to know each other and evaluate each other. By doing so, you maximize odds of an offer and acceptance.

PACKAGING THE NEGATIVES

Another thing we would like to package is the negatives. Some candidates, while excellent overall, will have problems in the past which pose difficulty in getting hired. If we are good enough interviewers, we have found out what they are. Candidates may have a hard time talking about them. If they are not well prepared, they will stumble and lose the chance for the job at this juncture by not being able to properly explain their negatives. Again, we are speaking of top professionals with problems which are factually of little significance.

Let me give you an example of a negative that was overcome that might help you to clarify this important concept. I had an engineer one time from a small town in Oklahoma who had been with one plant for many years. The plant had closed, and he was now looking for a job. Since he was from a small town, there was no other plant for him to work for. He had been unemployed for four months while he was scouring the country for a new plant. He was not a sophisticated man, and he was having trouble in giving a smooth interview. When he was going into some of the bigger companies, he was not looking as good as he should. He could not explain to these people about his old company closing, and how he felt. This qualified engineer came out in second place with a lot of companies before I saw him.

In fact, when I interviewed him, I asked why he had been unemployed for so many months, and he said, "Well, Larry. I have been looking, but no one has hired me yet." I sure didn't want him to say that to the client! That did not make him look very attractive, and made him look as if something was wrong.

I explained to him that we were going to have to say things in a different way. It would be far more effective to just say what he <u>was</u> looking for, and what he had seen in different companies that he had not liked. I asked him that, and he said, "One of the things I have seen in some companies is that they did not look very stable. I don't want to be jumping around all the time. I have been with the past company for eleven years, and I want to be that long with another one. I don't want to move because when you lose your job, you have to relocate. With my specific background, there is no one else locally to work for."

I had him explain it that way to the company. When the company said, "Why have you been unemployed for four months?", he said, "I have been looking for a home to settle down. I want to find a company that is stable enough that I can stay with from now on. I am a family man and I don't want to move my kids around in different schools. Now you are the kind of company that Larry tells me has some good stability, and that is the kind of company I would like to work for." So here we have taken a person's presentation from a Negative and turned it into a Positive. Now he presents himself as someone who if they hire, will be there forever, and a very positive aspect has been brought forth. Did I get an offer, and an acceptance of an excellent position for this candidate? You bet I did! That is what I mean by packaging the positive and the negatives.

Skeleton In The Closet

Another candidate had been fired for industrial spying, and I had to scrape him off the floor just to get him to talk about it. Here I was trying to find him a job with <u>that</u> on his record! I believed in him, checked his character references, and talked to people that knew him; no one could believe that it had happened. Basically, all he had done was take a technical manual that he thought another company had thrown out when he was working on a joint interest situation to see if he could learn something for his company. He had been out of school for five years with a Masters and had been quickly rising within the company. But he could not talk to me about it and admit it. He thought his life was over, and was embarrassed and ashamed. He could not look anyone in the eye and tell them about it. He had not been employed for a good while as a result.

I talked to him about it and understood that he was a good man with a fine background. His references and accomplishments indicated he was highly-qualified. I helped him to sit up and look someone in the eye and say, "I messed up, but I have learned from my mistake." In doing that, he was able to go to my top client and present his otherwise excellent credentials honestly. In fact, the way I closed the hiring official on this man was, "You know, if you give this masters-degreed, experienced and talented man a chance, he will probably double his efforts to prove that you did not make a mistake. And guess what? Of the three people that you are interviewing, he is the only one of the three that you can be sure will not make the same mistake twice." The hiring official laughed and agreed. They hired him! A couple of years later he was still doing extremely well with the corporation, and very happy to have a job. He was again on the rise. Has he sent me business and referrals as a result? A lot of it!

Most candidates, of course, will not have these handicaps and the rest of this chapter is devoted to them. But some of the best people will have some problems. You must be able to help people admit their errors and move forward with their careers. These are highly- qualified competent people who would do a fine job. But sometimes negatives pose a problem. You must help them package or say things in a certain way. By doing so, you benefit all concerned.

INTERVIEW PROCEDURES

Tell the candidate about the interview procedure as you know it. Tell them who they are going to see, what that person's name is, and to <u>write</u> <u>down</u> what you are telling them. Let them know the level of the person they are talking to.

Coach them on what kind of interviews that this person gives, if you know. As an example: "You are going to meet with Mr. Bob Johnson. He is the HR rep and will talk to you about the benefits.   He will be more interested in giving you information than interviewing, but he will ask about this part of your personality and background because he is known to in the past. Then you are going to go from there to the hiring official, Susie Winthrop, who will be your immediate superior. She is the one you will work for if you get hired for this spot."

Discussion Topics

Find out who are they going to see, and what kind of interview they should be prepared for from that person. Are they going to be talking technical aspects of the position, or what their futures hold? They must be prepared for who they are going to talk to and about what they are going to be discussing. The client can thus also be well-prepared as possible to make an evaluation.

I have had some clients say, "Well, don't talk about what we are going to say. That will ruin the interview." And I say, "Ruin the interview? That is what <u>makes</u> the interview. You don't want a candidate in there worried and upset about what might be asked, and shooting off the top of his head on subjects that he is not prepared to talk about. Your job as an interviewer is to evaluate the worth of candidates as it applies to how well they can do their job. We are not trying to trick a candidate and evaluate how well they react to the trick, or how slick of an interviewer they are. I am sure all of us have hired that slick interviewer who really was not very good in the final analysis of doing the job."

I rarely get further objections to my discussing anticipated topics when I present it that way. And the clients answer my questions about those topics without hesitation.

Is there anything required that the candidates should bring with them such as documents that are needed before a hire can be made? If you specialize in some areas of engineering, the client may want possible work samples. Sometimes that can be sticky. The candidates may be working in an environment in which they don't feel that they can take work samples to another client because they are direct competitors. They may have worked with a Department of Defense Contractor, and everything that they do is classified and makes it impossible to bring samples out.

This is not relevant in most fields, of course. If it is significant in your field, usually you can talk the hiring official out of it if there is a problem for your candidate when they go on the interview.

Make sure they know the names and pronunciations before they go in there. Many of these hiring officials will reach out and shake their hand and say, Mary Mumbling, and the candidate never heard her name. Here they are sitting interviewing with the person that they may go to work for, and don't know her name.

One of the keys to good interviewing is to use the hiring official's name a number of times during the interview. It sets a personal tone and makes the interviewer feel that he already knows the candidate sitting across in the chair. Make sure they know those names before they interview, and are fully prepared for what kind of talks they are going to have.

INTERVIEW TIPS

Be sure to give interview tips and information. Make sure that they know how much time they have to spend there. Don't let them go over during lunch for an interview to find out that they still have to meet with the VP for two hours.

Help protect them from some of the things that might happen. What do I mean by protect them? I like to know everything I can about the interviewing procedure.

For instance, I tell people things simple things like not to talk politics or religion. In fact, I tell people in Oklahoma not to talk about Texas football! It may seem odd, but there are people who have prejudices within the interviewing ranks and if you battle those, the candidate is not going to get selected.

I had one hiring official who about five-four and had a bit of that problem with his height. I sent him a candidate that was six-six! The first thing I told the candidate to do when he got in the room was as quickly as possible, sit down. You don't want to stand over him and say, "Well, hello there, little fellow. How are you?" Be sure to prepare them for the individual quirks in the interview.

Professionals Need Help Too!

I don't care what level you are talking about. If you are sending in a $100,000-a-year controller, don't <u>assume</u> that he interviews professionally! Some candidates will do, wear, and say the dumbest things if you don't coach them. If you are speaking with candidates by telephone, ask what might they be wearing to the interview. Make sure they are dressed professionally.

One of the tips that helps a lot is to suggest that as soon as they get to the interviewing area, go immediately to the restroom and take a once-over. Is the collar turned up or tie crooked? Does the hair need to be straightened? Many things can happen going into the interview that can disrupt appearance. Tell the candidate to get himself squared away before going into the interview for what may be the most important meeting he may have.

Interviewing tips, even the obvious ones, should be given, like make eye contact when speaking to the person. Don't smoke or chew gum. Remind the candidate not to drink at lunch if they happen to go out to lunch. Lunch is an <u>interview</u>, not a casual place to sit back. Even if they are invited to do so, I still say no. It is not professional and there is no place for it. Order something light, like a salad. Don't order the half-pound cheeseburger. There are lots of simple things in interviewing like how to shake hands etc.

Sit down with all of your office, and come up with list of tips that they should go through every time. One of those tips may save you a placement!

IMPROVING PHONE RATIOS

You need to make sure to <u>prepare</u> <u>candidates</u> for the <u>telephone</u> <u>interview</u> just as well as you would prepare them for a face-to-face. They must do well on this telephone interview, or the company will not pay the money to invite them in.

In many instances, I even teach my candidates how to ask for that personal interview. Why? Because I feel with some hiring officials, it is harder for them to turn the candidate down on the phone. A hiring authority will be much more reluctant to say to a candidate, "No, I don't want to bring you in", than to hang up and tell <u>me</u> his feelings later. It is easier for him to let me do the dirty work and go back to the candidate and say they are not going to bring you in.

Teach your candidates to be assertive at the end of the phone interview. How? Have them say, "I really like what I hear about this opportunity. I would love to come and see you about it. I have next week in which I think I can get away. Could you see me on Friday? Is that a possibility?" Remind the candidate that the hiring official will tend to invite more people in who invite themselves. Then tell them to say thank you very much for the call, hang up, and call you to report on how it went.

INSTRUCTIONS

After we give interview tips, we are going to want to give these people a set of instructions.

The first one is to be enthusiastic. As with the telephone interview, get him to either push forward to proceed to a second interview or to go for the offer (depending on the hiring procedure). Even if the candidate has doubts about the situation, tell him that the objective in the first interview is to get to "second interview", and then to get an offer. If they don't get an offer, then everything is academic. I call it "keeping the ball in your court".

If you let these people go in and "ho-hum" the interview, many times they come out and say, "Oh gee, Larry. You were right! That is a great spot. I would love to work there." I call the company and they say, "I am not interested in that man. He interviewed like a knot on a log. If he interviews the way that he works, then I don't have any interest in him." So we have <u>lost</u> the ability "to keep the ball in our court", to keep the decisions in our half of the playing field.

Explain to your candidates the importance of being enthusiastic. Then we can decide yes or no once the offer has been made. It beats being sad when they did not appear interested enough to get the offer.

Make sure in the first interview that they don't talk about anything that <u>they</u> want. The first interview is there to show specifically how they can be of value to the <u>company</u>. Tell them not to ask about pay structure, benefits, or vacations. Tell them no statements like, "I want this". Everything is what they can do <u>for the company</u>, the value they can bring to the employer if they are hired. There will be time enough to get complete information relative to what they want later.

MOTIVATING THE CANDIDATE

How can we help people implement our instructions? As an example, I have told people in the past not to talk money. After they come out of the interview, I ask how it went. Sure enough, they ended up telling the company how much money they wanted! Well, obviously, I did not do a good job in my instructions. I told them what to do. But guess what? I did not tell them why they should do it.

Remember this very vital rule; anytime you want anyone to do what is asked of them, you must make it a value to them. Your motivations are of very limited interest.

How do you set up discussing such things with the candidate? Say to them, "I know that you probably know these things, but as a professional, it is my job to help you through the interviewing process. You must look as good as possible. We want to improve your odds of an offer so it is your choice to proceed, rather that theirs."

Talking Money.....

So how do we make it a value to a candidate to not talk money? Don't just say "don't talk money". Tell them why they should not, and tell them how to get out of it.

Here is what you would want to say. "First of all, if you talk money, only one of three things could possibly happen. You may shoot too high and lose the offer to another candidate because they think they can not afford you. You could shoot too low because you want the job badly, and leave some salary on the table. Or you can hit the nail right on the head, and say exactly what the hiring official is thinking. If the salary is between $50,000 and $60,000 then you have a 10,000 to 1 odds of hitting the nail on the head. There are better odds than that in Las Vegas. So do you want to jeopardize your financial career by answering that question? Of course not."

If The Clients Asks.....

Some clients will directly ask about money on a first interview. Later in this book, we'll discuss how you should "negotiate the offer". For the moment, assume you wish this not to happen. Let me tell you how to get the candidate out of it if the client asks about salary.

The way for the candidate to respond is to say that he is "much more interested in the opportunity and the future at the company. If that is correct, the finances will take care of themselves." Have him say that, and then move on to another topic.

If the client is not satisfied with that and says to the candidate, "I know that you are looking for a great opportunity, but I would like to know what it will take in the new position?", then the candidate should use the "fair offer" statement.

Say, "Well, this is only our first interview and I have not quite thought that far. I was so interested in learning about the company and position that I have not come to that decision yet. You want to know something? I think if you decide that I am the right person for this job, then I am confident that you will give me a fair offer." And leave it at that.

If they finally won't let the candidate out of the room without naming a figure, then simply have him tell them what he is currently earning, and that he would like a reasonable increase above that. That will generally suffice. If it does not, then have him tell them that he would not name a figure until he has some time to think about, and could he have 24 hours to think it over and get back with them? Do anything to get out of that situation without naming a dollar figure. It can only hurt you.

That is how you can tell your candidates not to talk money, and how to make it a value to them, so they will co-operate. By explaining to them <u>how</u> to say it, you will increase your odds of it happening just like that.

PRACTICE

Tell people to go home and get in front of a mirror, and <u>practice</u> their answers.

If they do not, that hiring official looks them in the eye and says, "George, I want you. How much is it going to take for me to get you?" He knows I said not to answer that, and he kind of remembers what I told him to say. When he can't remember completely, he kind of starts to stutter. And he says, "Uh-oh" and he blurts out a figure and blows the deal.

Make sure that you help them through that point, and that they understand. Rather than talking money, vacations, or benefits, tell them that they will learn all of that before they have to make a decision. Again, our objective here is to just look good so that the company will give them an offer, or proceed to a second interview.

OFFER ON THE SPOT

Another important coaching point is not to turn down an offer that may be made on the spot. Some companies assume a person is desperate or impulsive, or worry about the candidate accepting another offer. If they like what they see and they don't want this person to get away, they will blurt out an offer on the spot.

Here again, the client has made a mistake which we must cover up. This can be just as bad as talking money, because that offer may not be acceptable. When someone is given an offer, they believe they are expected to answer. Here they are in the first interview, and suddenly they are asked to join this organization! Under pressure, it is always easier to say no than yes. You must prevent this from happening.

Explain to candidates they should never accept or reject an offer on the spot. The exception, of course, is if they know for a fact that this is the company they want to work for, and the offer is totally acceptable. If it is, they have a right to say yes and get a start date to secure that position for themselves. Allow them to say "Yes", but do not allow them to say "No". Say to them that it is a problem in saying no to a company. If you make a mistake in your answer, you can not go back and put the deal back together again. Tell the candidate, "Even if you don't want the offer that has been offered, thank them, say you are very interested, will think about the offer, and be back to them in a couple of days. That is a very common practice, and what it does is it gets you out of the company with the offer in hand. You are intact and now have control of the situation, and we can clarify any areas of concern later".

If they don't like the offer, go to the company and find out if there is more money to be offered or better vacation, benefits or bonuses. Again, we'll discuss your negotiating and closing the offer later in this book.

In many instances, candidates have mistakenly turned down an offer only to find out that the reason they turned it down did not actually exist. In the stressful conversation we call an interview, however, the reason seemed valid, but was not. Tell the candidate to take the offer and thank them, come to you and talk. Then you will see what you can do about getting any problems corrected.

"THANK YOU"

Tell them also to thank the person at the end of the interview for the time that they took to see them. Tell them to tell the client that they are <u>interested</u> in the job. You must understand that 90% of interviewing candidates never do that.

Hiring officials are people too. If I have two recruiters wanting to go to work for me and one is saying, "I really want to work for your firm", all things being equal, that person will get the job every time. So make sure your candidate shakes that hiring official's hand and says he or she is very interested in going to work for them. Leave the client with as positive a feeling as possible.

MOTIVATING THE FEEDBACK

Then of course, tell the candidate to <u>call</u> <u>you</u> immediately after the interview. How do we make it a value to them to call? By telling them that if the hiring official were to call and say, "What did John think about our company?", and we say we have not heard from John, the hiring official is going to say to himself, "If he is no more interested then that, then I am going on to another candidate."

If they do not call you, keep you up to date, give you the information that you need when that company calls, then tell them you can not truly represent them. Tell the candidate that he can seriously endanger chances of getting the right offer if he doesn't get back to you immediately following the interview. I have even made suggestions as to where is the nearest phone to call me back.

Set a time and location to get back to you.

By properly preparing the candidate for the interview, you will significantly enhance your chances of a second interview, an offer, and an acceptance. There is far more within your control than is generally believed. Don't overlook this, and don't get sloppy when you have experience. That's why you must <u>own</u> this book, <u>underline</u> or <u>highlight</u> it, and <u>review</u> and re-read it regularly. Additional production awaits you!

CLIENT PREPARATION

17

*W*hat is the most ever-looked part of the placement process? For many, it is the company preparation for the interview call.

Everywhere I go, I come across recruiters who seem to think that hiring officials know how to interview. Yet even the busiest official might hire perhaps two or three people a year. Even in a "growth year", adding five people is unusual for them. That is not very often to be skilled at something. You watch more people make more mistakes and do more effective selection and hiring on a weekly basis than the busiest hiring authority you know. After six months in this business, you are truly the expert in this arena. You must accept the fact that even your most professional hirers <u>need</u> your help in your area of expertise.

Help them to know that even if they have done this in the past, you do it every day as a standard of your job. It is what we do. It is who we are. And I don't think you will find a lot of resistance.

The best hiring officials are well aware of our expertise. More and more are becoming sophisticated to the fact that an experienced executive search consultant knows what he is doing. It is very comforting to have a consultant tell the hiring official how to go about making the hire. Moreover, it makes them comfortable in an area where they probably do have concerns, even if unexpressed. All people do not know the best way to go about interviewing and hiring.

Think about it. You are a highly paid professional in what we do. But suppose you walked into a doctor's office and said, "Gee, doc. It hurts right here." And he looks at you and says, "Uh, well, what do you think we ought to do about it?" The first thing you would say to yourself is I am going to find another doctor quick. And you would be out of there in a flash. Yet don't many of us do the same thing? We call up a person who gives us a search assignment, and it says that his company hurts here. And we respond, "Well, what do you want to do about it?" If he knew what to do about it, he would not be using you. They would be doing it on their own.

Example

Lose the idea that hiring officials know how to conduct the interviewing process. Frequently, they do not. I had one high level official who made well over six figures. He was interviewing at the $100, 000 level, and could not determine whether he liked several candidates I sent him. After I debriefed the candidates I found out that in a two-hour meeting, this person asked a maximum of two questions. He was so unsettled and unskilled in the art of interviewing and evaluating people that he literally talked about nothing that would help him to do so the whole time. All he wanted to do was <u>tell</u> them about the job, the company and their history, etc. That is fine, but if he does not ask questions, how can he know who to hire?

Obviously, that hiring official needed assistance! He and I talked about why he could not evaluate the candidates. I explained to him that because all the information was one-way, he was not receiving the information that he needed to make an evaluation and decision. He felt very good about my suggestions. We sat down and made up a list of a dozen questions, the answers to which would be important to know to make a good decision. It was nice to be in on that, because those dozen questions were <u>my</u> questions, and I certainly knew the answers before my candidates ever got there.

Did he decide on and hire one of my candidates after a second meeting? Yes. Did he become a repeat client for me? Indeed he did. Did I help him to become a better interviewer and evaluator of talent? That, too.

Helping the Client

People need lots of help when it comes to interviewing, especially clients. Our job is to operate the recruiting scenario so the hiring official has the greatest odds of selecting and obtaining the person he needs. It is the hiring official that pays you, not the candidate. So your service is rendered to the hiring official.

When you are convincing hiring officials to co-operate with you, explain to them that the greatest problem in the recruiting process is if the top candidate they want on their staff says "no" to an offer. That should never happen. The two of you should put your heads together to make certain that does not occur. By preparing the company, you are giving the client the best odds that the candidate will say yes by raising the interest level of that candidate.

Once we have explained and convinced them that it is in their best interest, we are going to talk to the hiring authority about this particular candidate and how to get the company prepared to do the interview.

IDENTIFY AND RE-SELL

First, we need to make certain that we identify and re-sell the candidate to be interviewed. I have had company representatives writing my directions on the wrong resume. I have had them say the wrong thing to the wrong person in the wrong interview! Obviously, it did not come out too well. Identify which candidate you are talking about, and make sure the client has the paperwork in front of him. Why? Because we want these notes attached to that resume. We are going to use that resume in this preparation to prepare the company for the interview.

Re-sell them on the candidate. Help them to understand again why we are interviewing this candidate. He or she had certain talents, background, duties, education, or qualities that caused the clients to want to interview them in the first place. We must go back over that with the hiring official. Explain to them why they must raise the candidate's interest level, so they will be co-operative. Remember we are trying to make it a value to the client, so they will follow our procedure.

Highlight The Resume

Tell them to highlight areas of the candidate's background to ask about. A hiring official may be seeing two to four candidates on any given position. As they do, those resumes start to float in front of them, and information may even get them mixed up. By the time they get to the interview stage, other interviews may have happened. Moreover, they are sometimes tired and not completely ready to see my candidate. But with the right instructions, you can help to keep that from happening.

Tell them where on the resume they can find critical information. Let's say I have a hiring official whose critical "Key to the Hire" is to find someone with revamping experience on a particular model and the candidate has done three revamps, but not in his present job. It was in his previous job. If the hiring official only asks questions on his present job, that candidate will sound unqualified for the position. The information that the hiring official is looking for resides in his past places of employment.

Suggest to the hiring official that he <u>highlight</u> the previous job. Explain that in that time-frame lies the information that will help him evaluate this candidate correctly.

Scripting the Interview Flow

You should try to control the flow of information between the official and candidate, so that those pieces of information needed to make a judgement get exchanged. Many times people who interview have the necessary background and can do the job fine. However, on the client <u>or</u> candidate side, they don't know how to exchange the information to make a proper evaluation.

The client comes out of those interviews and says, "Well, he looks good, but I'm not sure. There is something there I can not put my finger on." Why not? What is the information needed? What is wrong with this candidate that I did not do to help the official get that information? A lot of times there was not enough client preparation to help them get that necessary information.

The way you help a hiring official later on to close the placement is to explore with certain questions, and start asking them to see if you can not come up with the objection. That is why we want our candidate to know what to talk about, and my hiring official to be able to ask about. Make sure the conversation is directed and the proper areas emphasized by questions. When they come out of the interview with positive or negative feelings, at least we have come to a conclusion. We have not thrown our hands up in the air because we just don't know.

PREPARE FOR CANDIDATE QUIRKS

Make sure you prepare the hiring official for any unusual traits or styles that the candidate may have. Remember when we went over the information in preparing the candidate and told him to look professional, and go on making eye contact and shaking hands? The reason that is that first impression is very difficult to turn around if it is negative. As they say, you only get one chance for a first impression.

If your candidate has an unusual appearance or style of fashion, this could turn the interview in a direction that is not retrievable. It is difficult some-time to overcome an impression by any amount of information. You want to protect your candidates from loss by helping the hiring official know about less-than-positive information that is there in advance. Usually, you can wipe out that negative before it ever occurs.

A Common Problem

Let me give you an example. I had a young engineer who, when I inter-viewed him, I could never get to be silent. He was one of those people who when you ask for the time of day, tells you how to build a watch. I could not convince him that he should answer succinctly. He could not do it. He flunked. He tried so hard when he got nervous or on edge, he started to rat-tle off. So I had to prepare my hiring official. The candidate was very tal-ented, and when he was not under pressure and in a working environment, he was not like that at all.

One of the things I do to help hiring officials is to *assure them that there is no connection between the ability to interview and the ability to perform in their jobs.* They are not hiring this person because he is a poor or good interview-er. They are hiring this person because he is a good candidate for the posi-tion. Prepare for unusual traits by preparing the hiring official to look <u>past</u> something that may injure interviewing performance, and get the correct and needed information to make a decision about <u>professional</u> performance.

I like to be able to enjoy my job, so I asked my hiring official a question. I said, "This particular candidate that is coming to see you…. How long do you plan to interview and talk to him?" He replied, "Oh, maybe an hour-and-a-half or so." I said, "Good. You will get one question. Make it a good one!" And he said, "What are you talking about?" I said, "Man, this guy can talk! The guy will just ramble on. Now how are we are going to make certain to control this, so that the interview can go well and you can tell whether or not he is a good engineer? Do you have any suggestions?" The hiring official was a sensible guy and a long-time client. He replied, "Yes, Larry. Tell him when I am satisfied with the information he has given me, I will put a palm up. That is the universal stop sign to quit talking. I have all the information I need, and need to go on to the next question."

I told him I had a tough time preparing the candidate, and he now knew that he would have to control the conversation so he could get the information necessary. Here is again the closing question I use to wipe out that negative. I say, "Do you think you are a good enough interviewer to see past all this verbiage and really know how good an engineer this person is?" What can they say, "No, I am not a good interviewer"? Of <u>course</u> he is going to say, "Well, sure I can do that. I don't want to hurt the interview if I can attract a top candidate." Did I get an offer and an acceptance? You bet I did!

If you see any unusual traits, styles, verbiage, anything that can be prepared for by the company, you can wipe that out before it gets there. If you do not bring it up, that candidate walks in and interviews unprepared, and then you are going to have a difficult time. That official is going to get a bad first impression. The candidate is going to lose the offer and career that could have been theirs, and the client could lose some exceptional talent for the wrong reason.

INSTRUCTIONS

You must give your hiring official a list of instructions just like we gave our candidate. Remember: We evaluate, and then make recommendations. Learn to do this and it will increase your production! Interviewing of the candidate by the hiring official can be a stressful situation. By giving instructions to the hiring official, you can improve the likelihood of putting a deal together that is going to come out the way you want.

What are the instructions that we want to give, and how do we motivate them? The more effectively you motivate your clients to sell their opportunity, the better the chance of a placement.

Tell your people that to hire top talent, they have to be able to represent the company well. They need to be enthusiastic, and help the person feel welcome. When the person comes out of the interview, their interest level should be at it's peak. Tell the hiring official that this candidate should be as high as a kite when they are finished with the first interview. This person may be interviewing with other companies, unknown to us and the client. We are competing for their top talents, talents that could be worth many thousands or millions of dollars to the corporation. We don't want to lose them.

The biggest sin in this business is allowing the top professional that your client wishes to hire to say "no" to an offer. You need the hiring official's cooperation to help you sell or recruit the candidate.

Talking Money

Tell your hiring official not to discuss money. Tell him not to ask this candidate on the first interview how much money it would take to get them to be interested.

Now hiring officials don't usually get told that. Sometimes they cannot understand the reason this is important. Explain to them that your job is to operate the recruiting scenario so that the odds are the greatest that the candidate will accept the offer. Isn't that the objective of giving an offer? To get it accepted.

What do we have to do if the offer is not accepted? We only have two options: to start the search all over again with no assurances that we will find anyone as good, or to hire a secondary talent because the top talent said no. The reason they should not talk money is not to endanger that process.

How can we make not talking money a value to the hiring official? Well, simple. We don't want them to talk money because it could injure the official's ability to hire the right person. I ask hiring officials, "Have you ever had an offer turned down?" If anyone has hired for a long time, he has had that happen to him.

"Let me tell you", I inform them, "how to protect yourself from that. I want to make sure that if you want the top candidates, that they will say yes to you. One of the ways that you can get into trouble and have a problem in the offer stage is by asking how much money that they want. I want you to think of what position you have put that candidate in when you ask that question. The candidate, immediately in a stressful conversation called the interview, says to himself, 'My goodness. What should be my answer?' And in one minute, he has to make a statement that will ultimately decide the answer to the situation.

Many times, he is going to ask for what he wants — not what he will actually accept, but what he wants. That figure will always be higher than it might be at a later date when we, working on your behalf, determine what he will accept. So when you ask that question, you receive a higher number than you would normally.

Now you are sitting here facing the fact that you want to hire this person and you have one of two choices: you could either come up with what they say they want, or insult the candidate with a low offer. You have injured your chances for them to accept the offer. That is why it is not a good idea to ask anything about money. It hurts you, not the candidate."

Don't talk money. If you can get <u>both</u> of them to not talk money, then you have an excellent chance of controlling that at a later date. See later chapter on "Negotiating the Offer" for specifics.

Offer on the Spot?

Let's talk about another area. Don't allow an offer to be made on the spot. I don't care if the client and candidate fall in love. The time to make offer is after the interview, not during it.

Now why is that so? Don't you want your companies to make offers to your candidates? Well, the problem is the same as talking money with the candidate, and that is they may extend the wrong offer which is unacceptable to the candidate. Now we either have to work on a candidate that is unhappy with the offer, or we have to go back and get more money to make that offer more acceptable.

The only time that companies should make offers on the spot is when the dollar amount has been previously agreed upon before the interview ever happened. Some recruiters are <u>very</u> effective with this technique. A consultant on my staff would tell the company, "This is what it is going to take to hire the candidate. If you can not make that offer, then let us not even interview." He would also say to the candidate that same dollar figure. "This is what the company can offer", he would say. "If you can't accept that number if everything else is right, then don't interview." He would have the money sewn up before the interview concluded! At that point, they have both agreed and there is no negotiation to be done.

"HOT BUTTONS"

Paul Micali, outstanding sales trainer and speaker, is the author of the highly recommended book "*Hot Button Salesmanship*". *"First find your prospect's Hot Button (his most dominant desire) and build your presentation around it"*, he says. In attracting both candidate <u>and</u> client to each other, this statement should be constantly kept in mind.

What you can do for the hiring official is to give them the information necessary to interest your candidate by focusing on the candidate's hot buttons.

Just as the client has a "Key to the Hire", so does the candidate. I pass on to the hiring official the candidate's Reason For Leaving. Why is this candidate open to a change? When I say that, I give that hiring official <u>instructions</u> to feed back to the candidate the areas of the company that matches. Help the hiring official understand how to attract this particular candidate!

In his landmark book *"The Marketing Imagination"*, author Theodore Levitt calls <u>differentiation</u> the foundation of great marketing! That is how you sell, and that is how you coach your clients to sell! "Unique selling differences" create advantages, and those advantages cause the candidate to accept the position with your client. That same principle regarding the candidate causes the client to <u>extend</u> the offer in the first place! And if you have not underlined or highlighted some of this paragraph for later review, you should.

The result of emphasizing this properly is that you are having the hiring official help you to recruit your candidate. You see, you told the candidate why this job was good. By doing so, you got them to go on the interview. Psychologists tell us that people tend to believe something more the second time they hear it than the first time, even if it from the same source. Think how powerful that information is if they hear it the second time from the horse's mouth, the hiring official, rather than you, the agent! Then that candidate tends to believe it even more.

When that individual comes out of the interview and you ask him what he liked about it, they normally say, one two and three. This should reflect the Reason For Leaving. That tells me that the company has done their job, that the hiring official has given information to that candidate in accordance with my coaching, and that the candidate is now quite probably highly enthusiastic about joining the firm.

COACH TO CLOSE BY RE-SELLING

Tell the hiring official that if he takes an hour to interview, he should spend the first fifty minutes asking questions to make certain that he has thoroughly evaluated and has an interest in this candidate. Clearly, that should be the first concern of the client. However, once that has been established, it is time to move to the second phase.

The last ten minutes should be spent in giving that candidate these pieces of information. <u>One</u>: the stability of the company. <u>Two</u>: the promotional opportunity, or whatever it is that the candidate is interested in. Send the candidate on his way with positives ringing in his ears! That way, the candidate will have a very high interest level in that company. That is how you and the hiring official as a team raise the interest level of the candidates so they will accept the offer when made.

CONTROL THE DECISION

The final thing to coach the client about is to tell him to write down some notes during and after the interview on positives and negatives about the candidate. What you will do is debrief the candidate, call the company, and give them the results necessary for the client to make a decision on this candidate.

You don't want the hiring official to decide "yes" on a candidate who does not want to work there. You don't want the official to say "no" regarding a candidate when they may have misunderstood something in the interview. Tell the hiring authority not to make a yes or no decision until you can get back to him with the information on the debriefing of the candidate.

What this does powerfully is to put off the decision of the hiring official until you can reinsert yourself in the sales process. That is the most crucial thing that you can do at this juncture. Then we will debrief the candidate and come back to the company, feed them the information, and make a recommendation on the hire. Remember, consultants evaluate and make recommendations. Based on that interview, we will <u>both</u> put our heads together, and see whether or not we continue with this particular candidate.

Now you have the client thinking right, selling right, and ready to be sold by you. You should review this chapter (and this book) regularly as you get more experience. You will tend to drift away from this critical step. It is easy to become casual, especially with repeat clients over time. Stay focused. This is how you prepare a company to get ready for an interview and keep control. Now let us discuss what happens after the interview has happened. But first.....an interjection! A profitable one ....

EIO – A PROFITABLE INTERJECTION

18

*T*he intended flow of this book is to move smoothly throughout the entire placement process from planning and organizing your desk through the completion of the search, and then into developing the initial client to a solid repeat account embodying exclusives. So far, I believe we have achieved this.

Nevertheless, we don't want to sacrifice greatly increased production for you just to maintain a smooth and glorious flow in this book. So I think we have to interject a chapter and technique that will not apply to all people or firms. However, this methodology will apply to <u>most</u> people, and <u>will</u> generate great results if it is done right. While I would say that it is not suitable for newer people, the facts are that the best first-year production I ever saw (348K!) was achieved primarily through its use. So even if you are new, pay close attention to this chapter. If the way you do business "fits the mold", this can really fly. Managers would also be advised to emphasize this as well, depending on the type of operation you run.

EIO

EIO stands for *Employer In Office*. Briefly, this consists of inviting the client into your office for a series of (usually) 3 to 5 candidate interviews, back-to-back. So successful is this technique that when Management Recruiters emphasized this method and kept records on it for all their offices, it was found that it resulted in one fee 84% of the time and <u>two</u> fees 35% of the time! In an afternoon! And this is with <u>one</u> employer in the office. Later on in this chapter, we'll discuss getting <u>two</u> employers in to really shotgun results.

What is the Scenario?

This is an older technique, left over from a time when most of us worked local markets. It is also a remarkably effective methodology, and I don't want it to be lost. When you see the results, neither will you!

Nevertheless, it is not right for all firms. Generally, it requires either working a local market or at least an opening in the same city as your firm is based. You are going to bring 3 to 5 candidates to your client in your office at one-hour intervals. Without these locational criteria, this will be difficult. What is not required is ornate offices. An "Executive Suite" or a neighboring office in your building will rent you an interview room if you must.

When To Do It

Always, when it fits! Inviting Hiring Managers or even (aak!) HR /Personnel to your office is one of the most effective ways of fast placements. When a client agrees to interview selected candidates in your office, he has made a subconscious commitment to hiring as soon as possible!

Offer this service whenever you can reasonably be assured of having at least three qualified candidates there during a single block of time. Morning/Afternoon will work, but so will an evening or a Saturday morning.

Frequently a client will tell you the need is urgent, and he's available to interview whenever you have a candidate. Make sure you bring this up. Test his seriousness!

Economic Benefits to a Client

Any manager knows how his time is split, divided, unfocused. He must create space in his schedule to interview in his office. An interview here, an interview there, perhaps losing a good candidate because he doesn't have time, and then having to decide between candidates he may have met as much as a week or even two apart! What a mess!

Instead, in an afternoon or a Saturday morning, he can have his critical position almost filled by interviewing three candidates back-to-back! No interruptions, no phone calls, no fellow workers wanting to see him, no unexpected crisis popping up. He can concentrate totally on the interviewing process by using your offices!

It is certainly true that the candidate will want to see the "home office" eventually, but for a series of First Interviews, this is the best way of pre-screening quickly and effectively.

Moreover, because he is actually seeing <u>all</u> candidates right now, he will make a <u>much</u> better comparison than if time and circumstances prevent valid comparisons.

Tell him this. <u>Sell</u> this concept.

Confidentiality

Here's another major benefit to the client under many circumstances.

Interviewing off-site in your offices is confidential and discreet. If a company is hiring to replace a current employee who is just not doing the job, does the manager really want a host of potential candidates trooping through his office at regular intervals? Using <u>your</u> office eliminates the problem.

It also happens that a company may be hiring in one area, and laying off staff in another. Nothing demoralizes a department experiencing shrinkage or harms morale more than seeing day-after-day, people brought in to expand <u>other</u> portions of their firm. Talk about how to start a negative ripple effect of decreasing productivity! And if a good candidate "bumps into" an employee from the department laying off, <u>forget</u> about hiring that person. The employee from the shrinking department will contaminate the potential new hire as quickly as possible.

When you take a search with either of these situations, jump on it with an EIO presentation! A practically guaranteed fee — or maybe two — will be the result.

Interview Control and Debriefing

We'll cover Follow-up After Interview with candidates and client later. Suffice to say that there is no better way to control the interview and the debriefing process that by being there in a "hands on" fashion. Candidate preparation is fresh, and only a few minutes away from the interview. The client will tell you right now what he liked or did not like about each of the candidates.

Everyone will "return your phone call"; they are right there! While the client talks with Candidate B, you will be following up with Candidate A, and then <u>coaching</u> Candidate C! Again, see chapter later on Follow-Up, but this will markedly increase your chances of a fee.

Make sure <u>you</u> (not the client) greet the candidates at your reception room, then escort them to the client's interview room, and make the introductions. Coaching of the first candidate should have been done on the phone before the interview.

Candidate Order

Is there a strategy for the order of setting up interviews? You bet there is.

Let's establish a few things. First of all, these candidates are pre-screened and qualified. <u>Don't</u> throw in an unqualified candidate to make the others "look better". It will reflect badly on you if you do.

Also, let's realize that you could be wrong about which candidate is "best". The client may have his own opinion, and if he wants to hire your last choice, don't argue. If that candidate were not qualified, he wouldn't be there.

However, you will be right more often than you are wrong, and that will increase results if you do it correctly and use the appropriate strategy. You should be able to judge them pretty well and, if not, it will tell you how the client thinks for the next search.

Three Candidates

You have three candidates and you have evaluated them as first choice, second choice, and third. You have three time slots on a morning of 9 A.M., 10 A.M., and 11 A.M. What do you do?

9 A.M. - 2nd Choice
10 A.M. – 1st Choice
11 A.M. - 3rd Choice

Why?

The first candidate is solid. He will present himself well, and the client will be immediately impressed with how his morning is progressing. He'll be optimistic and will think, "Gee, I've got a good possibility right here."

The 10 A.M. candidate will be better! Sandwich him in between the two others. If you don't, the client will have no one to compare him to, and he may be over-looked. Don't put the best first, because the other two candidates may dull the memory of your best candidate. If you put the best last, the client may be tired and getting perfunctory, and may not give as good an interview as earlier. He will also distrust his own judgement, thinking the most recent is the best <u>because</u> he is most recent.

Finally, bring in your last choice to make the others look better, and to absorb what may be a less-than-sparkling interview.

Four or Five Candidates

There is also a preferred order for more than three candidates, and it is as follows:

Four Candidates : 9 A.M. - 3rd Choice
10 A.M. - 2nd Choice
11 A.M. - 1st Choice
12 P.M. - 4th Choice

Five Candidates: 9 A.M. -   3rd Choice
10 A.M. - 2nd Choice
11 A.M. - 1st Choice
12 P.M. -   4th Choice
1 P.M -   5th Choice

Again, you'll note that the reasons for this order stated previously generally apply. Give all coaching information you possess to the earlier candidates. Do <u>not</u> shortcut this process.

However, with every follow-up with candidates in your office, you'll be better able to coach later candidates. Follow-up with the client (speedily) immediately after each meeting, but expect short comments at this time rather than the usual extensive information. After all, he's got another candidate to interview.

If you have the sort of office which works the same area of specialization and all the candidate are not yours, the consultant who has the candidate <u>may</u> have the Follow-Up with his candidate. However, coaching information should be immediately transferred to the consultant who has the client.

Frankly, a better way is for the consultant who has the client to handle everything including candidate debriefs, but office procedure in your firm may differ.

Post - EIO

When all this is over, give the client a break. Don't rush in, and immediately get information. Offer him some coffee, let him go over his notes, take a breath. Then sit down and go over each candidate, one by one. The client should have taken notes, and you should have provided him with a resume or "biographical sketch" on each candidate with relevant positive areas <u>highlighted</u> in advance.

Discuss candidates, establish ranking and get the client to commit to the next step. Again, this will not be any different from what will be covered in the following chapters, except that it will be face-to-face.

Sell This Regularly

The ideal situation for this is working a local market. However, <u>any</u> opportunity in the town where your firm is located is a chance to greatly improve your odds with an EIO Program.

Don't be afraid to promote this <u>regardless</u> of whether you have candidates to present or not. Schedule a <u>block</u> of time for an EIO Program a week to ten days in advance. You will "beat the bushes", and recruit hard to get candidates. You will have the motivation of an almost-certain fee ahead to spur you on! When you get a client in your office, he has emotionally commited to hiring at least one. Your "completed search" ratio will be extremely high.

When to Implement

This should be an important part of your ongoing business. Do you have some experience in our business, and do you do any business in your home city? If yes, you should start considering and planning how to go about doing this <u>immediately</u> upon finishing this book and reviewing your underlining or highlighting. Write up a brief presentation on a 5" x 8" card after discussing with your manager, leave it by your phone, and make it a regular procedure to emphasize this.

However, if you are new, you are better off waiting for six months or so. The reason is that you must first develop the skills to support this. Having some sort of established client base helps a lot, even if it is only six months old. At least you have established a track record of a few completed searches, and the rapport that goes with that. The main point, though, is that you cannot pull candidates off the internet for an EIO program. This is not a good idea under any circumstances. However, with an EIO, the first time a client wants to invite a candidate to the "main office" for a second interview and some HR clerk says, "I could have found you that guy for free", you will lose the whole account. Thus your skill at reactivating old candidates and real recruiting must be solid for an EIO program to be effective.

Double-Team with your Manager

Another advantage to you of an EIO program is that you can get your manager involved. The concept of "double-teaming" – getting your manager or others involved to close the sale – is a proven and highly-effective technique. It is just another reason to get a good classical sales education, and why the best trainers in our industry always have a solid corporate sales background before they get into our business. Outstanding sales author Les Dane, in his book *"Les Dane's Master Sales Guide"*, has several entire chapters on this concept, one addressing utilizing others in your office and another on how the Sales Manager can help you to close sales. Everyone likes to do business "at the top", and the enhanced credibility and prestige of the owner of even a small search firm will be very useful in gaining the commitment of the client.

The key to becoming a top performer in any intellectual field (and sales and our business definitely qualifies) is by serious study and learning. Les Dane's excellent books plus other books and videos mentioned here will be of great help in maximizing your production, as will repeat reading of the one you hold in your hands right now.

How Many?

Strive for one a month as a minimum. This is not an unreasonable number once you have been in business for awhile. Twelve EIO programs per year will almost certainly yield you ten additional fees per year, and it may be more. Occasionally the commitment to hire is so strong and the candidates so qualified that the client will actually extend offers to several candidates. And meanwhile, you'll still be making your initial marketing calls to new clients, and developing your current ones into multiple placements.

Doubling Up

You may also consider the possibility once you set up an EIO program a week or so in advance, of multiplying your results by inviting two client companies to your office to interview the same candidates. Clearly, this is not appropriate when you are working on an "exclusive" arrangement. However, surprisingly few non-exclusive clients object to this if you have more than three candidates.

If the interviews are being held outside of business hours, as on weekends or evenings, you will also find it easy to bring the same candidates back a week later for another client. If your first client does not commit to moving quickly on one candidate and these candidates are in-demand, be creative in your thinking and aggressive in your calling other potential hirers of these people. Most candidates, even those not actively looking, will agree to a meeting with another good client a week later if it is local.

Again, "exclusives" with your first EIO program negate "doubling up".

This is For You

Don't think this is only appropriate for old-style office-support "employment agencies". That is not true. The confidentiality and time-effectiveness involved make this an obvious choice at any level. As an example, think of a sales manager flying into a town where his firm has no current office to interview sales candidates. Where will he interview? In his hotel room? If you promise 3, 4, or 5 qualified candidates in your office for professional interviewing, he will be there. The previously mentioned first-year top producer (348K) who used this almost exclusively worked in Electrical Engineering.

Sell this as a part of your regular service! The benefits of providing confidential interview facilities and the considerable savings of time are appropriate to all firms that seek a person in the same city as your office. You can present three qualified candidates one after the other, so as to make a close and immediate comparison. The client can concentrate without interruptions. You can work more closely with the client and assist in getting the right candidate for the job. And you will find that an experienced President/Manager of your firm will assist you in putting this deal together.

Develop a sales presentation of an EIO program for your firm, and practice it regularly in sales meetings. For almost all desks and firms, it will increase business substantially. And for some, it will be highly productive!

CANDIDATE FOLLOW-UP

19

L et's do a little brief summary here in terms of the candidate.

We have prepared the candidate at this point, coached him and tried to protect him from a number of things that could go wrong. We have helped him to be ready for different questions from the company, and enlisted the company's co-operation in order to maximize interest.

If our instructions were followed, the only reason that this does not turn out is because it is bottom-line not a good match. That is all right; we don't mind losing the placement when we have a situation in which they are just not matched for one another. But to lose placements when there are misunderstandings, miscommunication, or illusions of things that are just not so is unacceptable. And it is within our control.

OBJECTIVES

When we follow-up with the candidate on the interview, we have a couple of objectives here. First in Follow-Up with the Candidate is to find out how she did and what her interest level is at this point. You must try to determine in this call what chance you have of closing the candidate if an offer is forthcoming. That is the first objective.

But there is another objective I want you to start working with: gaining information from the candidate that will <u>help</u> you get an offer from the hiring official when you make the follow-up call to him.

Many otherwise good search consultants, in the company follow-up call, tend to call up and say, "The interview is now over with Betty. What did you think? How did it go?" Thus, we let the client say, "Well, I would (or would not) like to hire her." Then we must identify the specific problem and overcome an objection, summarizing the positives, or give up the sale.

Make no mistake; overcoming objections is an important part of selling. By learning to do so, you can increase production dramatically. But following up with the candidate <u>first</u> will help you to know what you'll encounter before it happens. Moreover, if you position yourself with the client in the way that we will discuss, it will help you until your industry-specific selling skills improve.

You can't get great at everything at once. Overcoming objections on recruiting or marketing are more important <u>initially</u>. Focus on that in the beginning. Then refine your sales skills in other areas later.

So the second objective to the candidate follow-up call is to gain information that will help us make that important call to the company about how it went. Get comfortable with the following technique and you can still be better prepared for the company's response, whatever it is.

THE CANDIDATE FOLLOW-UP CALL

The candidate has finished the interview and is now calling us, according to our instructions. The intent is to give us feedback from the interview. How do we open that call?

Well, I like to open it very broadly-based, because it tells me a number of different things about the candidate, the situation and his attitude. Also, it might point me in some direction where I want to take the initial part of the conversation. So I generally open it and say, "How did it go?" or "What did you think?" We are going to let the candidate rattle on about his thoughts and allow the candidate to make a lot of statements about how he thought it went and what was discussed.

A False Evaluation

All you should be really doing initially is getting general impressions, their concepts of the interview. Don't <u>assume</u> the candidate is right. Many times I have had egotistical candidates tell me how well they did, and how they just dazzled the client. They love him, and they believe they have the job in their hip pocket, and everything is great. And then you went back to the client and say not "How did it go?" but, "Boy, did you just love John? Wasn't he everything that I told you? Didn't he turn out to be more amazing than we thought?" Then you may hear, "NO! Don't send me another one like him." Some of our hiring officials put on a pretty good face, even if they dislike the candidate.

At this time, just try to get the general flavor of the candidate's attitude. When the candidate starts talking about rough spots and hesitancies, you will start to get an understanding as to why this person may not be totally impressed with this position. If the perception is positive, you will get some general statements as to why.

Our Job

Our job is to raise the interest level of the candidate to the top of the bell curve. There may be many reasons why that has not happened at this point. But one of the things that you can project for sure; if this candidate is not just absolutely bowled over by this company, when it comes to the offer stage, that candidate will make high demands about this position. The less their interest level, the greater they are going to want things such as substantially increased salary, vacation, packages for moving. You will have a more difficult time closing them, especially if they are talking with other people and getting rival offers that have looked as good as yours, but the money is better.

This is a good reason to learn true Recruiting; recruited candidates are far less likely to be looking at other opportunities.

YOUR ADVANTAGE

What is the answer, especially if the candidate has other opportunities? You will make placements because as a team, yourself and the hiring official have done such a good job of raising the enthusiasm of the candidate. I have had candidates actually accept an offer which was well below the monetary offer of another company. But the other company and recruiter were not skilled in attracting talent. They did not tell the candidate those things were there for them that they valued and would cause them to move and join them in the future of the company, and the recruiter did not properly motivate and coach the client.

Remember how important transferring information is to raise the level of the candidate. You are listening for it right now at the candidate de-briefing. You must judge if there are holes that you are going to have to patch, or a lot of questions that you are going to have to answer to make sure that this candidate is in line once that offer comes. Let them talk, and get an overview. Then try to pick out and make notes on anything that you want to come back to explore, or take from a general stance to a more specific sense as they are talking.

Once they have generally told you how it went, and they are telling you positive things, make sure to reinforce positive responses. If it is a negative, knowing about them early enables you and your client to overcome them as the interviewing process continues. In most instances, I treat negatives at this point as "Well, I certainly understand that; that is something to be handled or resolved later." I treat positives as an affirmation of "Yes, that is fantastic", and negatives as little mistakes. "Well, so what? We will check it out; those are things that we are going to look for."

Do not disregard the negatives. Even though you may treat them a little lightly with the candidate, certainly don't treat them lightly as a whole, because any single one may cost you this placement. Make sure and jot down anything that you hear that may be a possible problem when we get to the end result.

MAPPING THE FLOW OF THE INTERVIEW

Secondly, after opening with "How did it go?", and testing all of this, you want the candidate to tell you everything that happened to her, from the time she walked in the front door to the end of the interview. Then ask her to describe the first person she talked to.

Isn't the first thing that happened the first person that they talked to? Not really. People can have different ways of interviewing. Different companies can put different procedures in place that can cause you problems if you do not know about them. I recruited a candidate once, and sent him over on a very good assignment. When he got there, the Human Resources clerk came out and told this person to sit in a chair, which was a small elementary school desk. This was a large man, and he was quite uncomfortable. The HR clerk thrust an application under his nose, and told him to fill it out. He was not offered coffee, greeted, or made to feel welcomed. When the clerk came back to process his application, he found it in about a hundred pieces on the floor.

In knowing that, I can get them to change that procedure when I send over a recruited candidate. If not, I can prepare the candidate by telling him that this is a little inconvenience he has to put up with to get his foot in the door. If you don't know about it, it is going to bite you.

When they tell you the interview flow, you will get two early indicators as to how things went. First, you will get an idea from the candidate as to what happened, and how did it compare with what you told him was going to happen. If you told him he was going to see the HR person and the hiring official, and he saw the HR person, hiring official, and the Vice President, does that tell you something? Well, maybe. It could be very positive. If you told him he was going to interview with a hiring official for an hour and a half and it only lasted for fifteen minutes, does that tell you something? Well, maybe. And probably something pretty negative.

Those things give some indications that will help to operate this particular scenario. Also, it helps to prepare your second candidate. When you have two candidates, then you know the procedure. You know the client's methods of interviewing people, and if appropriate can try to change it.

After you have interviewed a number of candidates with one company, you get to know them quite well and you can do a very good job in preparing your future candidates. Your area of preparation comes from the second purpose on your candidate follow-up.

ANTICIPATING CLIENT RESPONSES

Find out from your candidates whether there was any time in the interview that the hiring official seemed happy or unhappy about what was discussed.

I ask my candidate very specifically, "Was there a time in the interview that you felt uncomfortable? Was there a time that the hiring official might have looked over her glasses, or frowned or knotted her brow. Or she may have asked the same question three or four times and never seemed quite satisfied with the given answer. What was being discussed when that occurred?"

Now what am I trying to find out here? How is this going to help? Right. You are now finding out about the objection <u>before</u> the client brings it up. If the candidate can give you the uncomfortable time in the interview, nine times out of ten, that is going to be the objection of the hiring official when we call back.

This allows you to get answers for that objection <u>before</u> you encounter it with the hiring official.

One of the great places to get an answer to the presumed objection is from the candidate. Is the hiring official's concern a valid one? In many instances, I have had them say no. If that is the case, you should have the candidate give you the <u>answers</u> that you need to overcome that objection.

Sometimes the candidate says that the client was right. Fine. But are there off-setting qualities? Get the answer to that based on what they <u>do</u> have. When the client brings up the problems, you can answer it.

OFF-SETTING THE OBJECTION

I also ask pointedly, "Was there a happy time in the interview? Was there a time that the hiring official perked up or smiled, or really seemed impressed?"

Now why am I doing that? I am doing it because if I can not overcome the negative that I have just found out about, then sometimes this positive may be big enough to offset it. If the candidate is short on some particular experience, focus on his experience in this other area. The hiring official usually agrees, and will frequently offer to hire them for that experience and bring them up to speed in the other. If the experience they are light in is not very important to the job, but the great area of their expertise is in that "Key to the Hire" area, you win!

Thus, you can overcome the objection without being able to answer it. It is called <u>off-setting</u> <u>the</u> <u>objection</u>. Instead of answering the objection, I accept the objection.

Your candidate may not be able to describe any time in the interview when he thought the client had any decisive response. But if he does, then we really have a leg up in making the next phone call.

CANDIDATE "HOT BUTTONS", AGAIN

Also, of course, we want to know the feedback from the candidate's side. I say to the candidate, "Tell me this. What did you like best that you saw there?" So what answer am I looking for? I am looking for positives reflecting his original concerns about his current position to come up at this point.

Suppose that the candidate says "The thing that I liked best is <u>this</u>", which was his Reason for Leaving. Then I know not only did I tell him it was there, but the hiring official said it was there. He heard it and believed, and knows this is the company for him.

If they give you another answer other than Reason for Leaving, this does not mean that things went badly. It just means something unknown to both of you popped up that they are in love with. So after you say, "Well, yes. That does sound good! Fantastic, that is great for you! By the way did you find out about....?" Then ask for specifics regarding the Reason For Leaving.

CANDIDATE HESITANCIES

Then the other part of that question is, "Was there anything that you did not like?" But <u>don't</u> ask it that way. I like to say, "Was there anything that bothered you?" Then proceed to <u>qualify</u> that negative. That negative may be significant enough to keep the person from accepting an offer, or may be a small irritant of no real significance. How do you find out?

When they say, "I did not particularly like this" or "this kind of bothered me", I am going to <u>test the strength</u> of that negative and say, "I see. That could be a bit of a negative for you. Maybe it is something that we can handle or find out more about it. But let me ask me overall how you feel about the opportunity? The company is highly enthusiastic about you. You just said that they seemed very happy about you in this particular area. That seems to have solved your reason for leaving and you were happy about that. Would this question you just brought up keep you from accepting a fair offer?" And if they say, "Oh, no. It just bothered me, but that would certainly not stand in my way of being employed there", then you may have put the objection to bed without even answering it. You have tested it's own strength.

Remember that frequently candidates say things because you specifically requested them to say it. It may not hold a lot of water in the final analysis, in terms of whether or not they are going to work there.

IMMEDIATE BENEFIT TO THE CLIENT

Again, we are seeking information to motivate the client to proceed to an offer, and to off-set any objections. The next question can help you with the client company. That question is, "What is the most important thing that you can do for this company in your first ninety days on board?"

You want to know from the candidate's point of view what they see as a possible project that they could do or system that they could implement immediately. Anything that tells you that they can go into this company and do something for them right now will be of <u>great</u> benefit.

The question is looking for a value answer. Companies hire people for one of two reasons; they can make or save the company money. If they cannot do one of those two things, they will not get hired.

So with this particular question, you want to look for an answer in dollars and cents if at all possible.

I had one person that said, "Tell him that I can revamp that piece of equipment for them. That unit does not need to be purchased. A turnaround on that may save them as much as twenty million dollars, and I know how to do it." Wow! That is a <u>very</u> strong value to take to a company when they are considering a hire. If you are telling them that someone can save them twenty million dollars, then it does not worry them much in paying you the twenty thousand dollar fee to hire that person.

This question's intent is to provide you with a value statement that you can then sell to the company that would give them a reason to move forward and hire. Just because the person is qualified for the job does not mean they are necessarily the one that the company selects when they finally make the hire. But <u>immediate</u> <u>value</u> will make a big difference!

Put yourself in the company's position. Suppose you have three candidates that you are looking at. They all seem to have the years of experience that you are looking for, are educated in the proper areas, and have all been doing exactly what you want done in another company. How do you decide which one to hire? You generally decide which one to hire based on which one of those three can do the <u>most</u> important thing that the company wants done. That varies from job to job, and could be affected by this specific company. When this person says to me, "I can do this for the company", I say to myself, "is that my hiring official's Key to the Hire?" If it is, then I am in good shape in selling this company into a hiring mode, because I can show value with this one candidate.

"HOLES" IN FOLLOWING INSTRUCTIONS

Pay close attention to whether the person followed your instructions. The first time we get an indication of whether they had followed our instructions is when they call us back. If they called us immediately, that indicates they are following our instructions. If you had to chase them down and find them, then that is an indication that other instructions may have not been followed. I want to know if there are any holes in my placement that I will have to patch.

Suppose the candidate said, "Larry, he asked me about money and I could not remember what you told me to tell them, so I went ahead and named a figure." I am not going to get crazy with my candidate over that, but I am going to at least explain the damage that he may have done to this process. If you know about the damage, then you can do some of the things that could repair it. You can go in with that knowledge, talk to the hiring official and work the placement in a different manner. So long as you are aware of it, it is not going to jump out and bite you. So go over each set of instructions.

An Example

I had one young candidate say, "Larry, I know you told me to express interest in the position, but it did not seem all that important. All of sudden I found myself out on the sidewalk after the interview, and I had not done that." I said, "Anything gone undone can cost us this job. I want you to pick up the phone and I want you to call that Vice President. I don't want you to try and get an answer out of him, but I do want you to say, 'Sir, one thing bothered me about the interview. I found myself after the interview without having a chance to tell you how interested I am in going to work for your firm. I don't know how much enthusiasm means to you, but hopefully when you make the final decision, you will consider me on that job.' " The kid did not think that it was all that necessary, and I had to do a little bit of selling and nagging to get him to accomplish that task.

Guess what? The HR person called me back. He and the Vice President were sitting in the office at that moment, trying to decide who to hire. It was down to between my candidate and one other. The phone rang, the VP picked it up, heard what was said, looked at the HR guy, and said, "Hire that young man! I really am impressed with his enthusiasm, and I like that."

That is a prime example of how anything in the placement can kill it if you don't protect it. And anything in the placement can make it, if you make sure those things happen that we know to be right in the process. Make sure things are done right ... every time!

TRIAL CLOSE

At this point, I use a trial close and ask the candidate, "Tell me, is there anything that you can see right now that is a problem large enough to keep you from accepting an offer?" I want to know <u>now</u> if there is something that would keep them from accepting a fair offer. Once you know, you can begin to work on it and try to overcome it and correct it. If everything is all right, I want to know what they would consider a fair offer to be? I am only looking for a general idea of the figure.

At this point we should have enough information from the candidate to go to our client to give the debriefing, and get the best possible result!

Let's do so.

CLIENT FOLLOW-UP

20

*D*epending on how things have gone thus far, this may be our first crisis up to this point. If all has gone well, the flow of this placement may have appeared to be fairly easy. We have obtained and selected the candidate and client, and got them together. We collected appropriate information, and got them all prepared. Now this call is the call where we find out what is going to happen. Depending upon on how we handle this call, we can affect the placement process significantly.

Do not take this call for granted. If you call up the hiring official, and say, "Well, how did it go?" And they say, "Oh, I don't know. We did not think too much of him", and then you <u>quit</u>, you lose. We are here to try to make placements happen. We are here to represent the client and the candidate, and to motivate them to do what is in their best interests.

Do you believe that the candidate can do the job, has what it takes, and has good references? Then it is incumbent upon you to <u>use</u> your skills and utilize those areas of knowledge in order to help that person get employed with your client. By accomplishing this, you will solve the client's problem and assist the career of that manager. Help the hiring official make a hiring decision!

Let's talk about going to the company and see if we can help them make a decision upon this particular candidate.

ANTICIPATE THE OBJECTION

If you have the information that we just outlined in the candidate follow-up call, you now have the information that tells you what the objection might be.

However, I think you will find there is more power in it when you don't <u>let</u> the company verbalize that particular objection. Overcome it before they ever say it! What you are trying to do is to "trade seats" with the client's hiring official. Watch....

I go in and use the same, "How did it go?" question, but at the <u>same</u> time give the hiring official the feedback that my candidate gave me. Then I make a ***recommendation*** on whether or not to hire. I have now put the client in my position. They have to listen to my feedback and my recommendation. Then they have to quickly react to that, and either try to follow or change my recommendation.

By doing so, we call for an immediate response that not only gives them proper direction, but greatly reduces procrastination.

It is a very powerful way of quickly "switching seats", and putting the other person in a position of having to respond.

A Positive Example

Suppose we called the candidate, and the information that we got was that they liked the interview. One of the things I like to get from my candidates is whether or not they liked the hiring official. It is important to them that candidates admire them or perhaps see them as a mentor. Try to get that personal touch from the candidate about how they felt about the official. Remember we are also trying to get any areas that were perceived as good or bad by the client during the interview.

Let's say that this particular candidate was interviewing on a project manager's job in which it was important to revamp the unit there. Upon successful completion, he would be promoted. The candidate feedback to us was very positive about the overall feeling from the interview. He gave us a value statement in that he said he could go ahead and have no problem in revamping the unit, so the company would not have to buy a new one. But there was a concern, because the hiring official never seemed to find the right area of his background to question. The Key to the Hire was in revamp project, not in operations.

Despite this, the hiring official centered the discussion in the operational area. The candidate was concerned that he did not get across to the hiring official the depth of revamping experience that he had. He felt good about this situation. If offered a position, he did not see anything that would stand in the way of accepting a fair offer.

The Client Call in our Example

Based on the above information, let me give you an idea on how to approach the company hiring official on the follow-up call.

"Hello, Bill. This is Larry Nobles with The Reality Group. I wanted to follow-up on the information that I received from John Jones after debriefing him after the interview earlier today. I have to say it is probably it is one of the most positive feedbacks that I have received. You obviously did a good job in welcoming him and being enthusiastic in the interview, because he really does have a high interest level in the position right now. As a matter fact, he said you and he really hit it off. Apparently, you have the same philosophy on project management. He did not see any obstacles or any real differences of opinions.

Now he did say that he was uncomfortable with how he had explained his revamp experience, and that the two of you kept talking about operation. Well, we know that he is excellent in operations, but we also know that your current unit will need a revamp before we really get into that area. I guess he really never got to tell you about the last three revamps that he had done. He had done two in his previous job, and one in the company before that. Both of these revamps were highly successful, and they did the turnaround and got it operating in great shape. He has the skill to be able to do the revamp with his hands tied behind his back! His references are exceptional. He said that he could successfully take that project off your hands and in the first ninety days should have it finished and running. So in the long run, you can save about 18 to 20 million with the revamp.

He has a great attitude! I asked him if there was anything he saw that could keep him from accepting a fair offer, and he said no. I guess I have to say with his great communication skills, project management background and revamp experience, that could be worth up to 20 million easily. With all of that value, my recommendation is unless you have some other thoughts, to proceed to the second interview or offer. What are your thoughts?"

It is important to point out that while this is the way the call will go, there will be pauses, back-and-forth exchanges, variation of pace, etc. here. Just running all this together sounds as though we're overtalking. That is not the case, but if we really printed up honest dialogue (note: this means a two-way conversation), this book would be three times as long.

That's why most serious complex script as in Direct Recruiting or more sophisticated rebuttals to objections or closes are best presented in video format (or perhaps audio), and I've made reference to the best ones in this book.

REVERSING CHAIRS

Now what you have done is reverse chairs with that presentation. You have put the hiring official in a position of reacting to the recommendation, rather than putting yourself in a position of <u>reacting</u> to the official's off-the-cuff opinion. This is an excellent concept that will absolutely change the way many in our business go about following up on an interview. Should we be doing this? Yes! This is what consultants do.

Consultants, no matter what field they are in, are hired to evaluate and make recommendations. You are bringing a candidate to a company, and your job is to help the company hire the best individual possible. Part of your job is to evaluate that candidate on value, abilities, and attitude. Once you have evaluated that after the interview, then you can call the company representative and make a ***recommendation***. That is consulting. That is what is expected of you to do in every area. And when you do your job right in this regard, it will also be far more profitable for you.

Negative Example

Now what do we do if the feedback was not good? Well, we are paid to evaluate and make recommendations, and that is what we still have to do.

Let us say in this same scenario this candidate had the same positives as before. But when he got to the end and I said, "Is there anything that would keep you from accepting a fair offer?", we got thrown a problem. He said, "You bet. I would not go to that company if they were the last one on earth." I would ask, "Why not?" He replied, "Because my interaction with the construction manager there who would be on a peer level with me and co-operate with me, was oil-and-water. We absolutely did not click and we could not communicate. I don't think he was really impressed with me. As long as that man is construction manager, I would not consider the job under any circumstances." Wow! What a terrible feedback from the candidate.

One of the things that we should not do when we get that kind of feedback is to go back to the company and make ourselves look good by saying, "I am taking this person out of contention. He is not good for your position and is not well-accomplished." We make ourself look great by yanking a candidate of ours that was under consideration. But it is not a service to either candidate or client.

Remember your job is to evaluate and make a recommendation. In this instance, when you make the negative recommendation, just say, "These are the positives and here are the negatives." Then I would let the hiring official make the decision.

Don't make the decision for the hiring official. Don't dismiss the candidate just because they gave you some negative feedback. Go to the company, cover the positives, evaluate the negative, and make a recommendation as to what could be done to resolve it. Indicate that you are not proceeding forward unless it could be resolved. If you handle it that way, you will find some good things happening.

The Client Call on the Negative

Let me give you a different presentation based on that negative feedback. "Hello, Bill. This is Larry Nobles with The Reality Group. I wanted to give you the information that I received from John's feedback on the interview that you had with him earlier in the day. He said that you two hit it off fabulously. You not only communicated well, but he said he would rather work for you than anyone he had worked for in the past.

The only thing that concerned him was that he did not seem to give you enough information. Somehow he failed in explaining his revamp experience. He is good at operation and knows it quite well, but he said your specific problem right now is getting the old unit revamped so you can use it without purchasing a new one. John was concerned that he did not get across that he had already revamped three before. He wanted to tell you that he can take that off your hands in the first ninety days on board. You won't have to spend up to 20 million to get a new unit. So he does appears to have all the engineering experience and project management.

It all seemed to go well, and then he dropped the bomb on me! When I asked him about an offer, he said he would not join the company as things are now. Now Bill, I don't know what to tell you, except I tried to find out what was wrong. Frankly, he expressed that he had a conflict with the construction manager. They are not compatable at all. Nothing he said was right or well-received. So he has no interest in joining the company.

Bill, I thought we had here the best engineer that could make you the money you needed, revamp the unit, and wanted to work there. Then this came up. My evaluation is that the situation is not workable. We cannot proceed to an offer or second interview unless you can think how to overcome this construction manager problem. If you can think of a solution there, then we can move forward. What are your thoughts?"

Again, we are not over-talking, though it appears so based on the limitations of a written format.

What have I done? I have gone back over the situation and made my recommendation. I have also said it was dead unless he could think of how to overcome the problem. Now I am going to hear what the client has to say.

Guess what? This did happen to me, and that is how I handled it. What happened? In this particular engineering scenario, the hiring authority said, "This is the candidate that I want. I know that he could do the job. Yes, we did hit it right off and I want him to work for us. You tell him that if he would consider an offer from us, then I will take care of the construction manager."

I said, "Well, what does that mean exactly? Does that mean you will overload him and make him do more work?" "Larry", he replied. "This construction manager has run off the last two project managers, and now he is keeping me from hiring a third one. Tell him if he will take the offer, I will either fire or transfer that construction manager. I will then let him hire his own construction manager for the term of that project and after that is over, we will release the construction manager. Then we can go about hiring a new one."

We put the placement together. Later the candidate hired a new construction manager through me. That would not have happened if I just yanked the candidate. Instead, I told them honestly upfront what the problem was, and that we could not proceed unless they had a solution. Just evaluate, and make your recommendation.

THE "YES" RESPONSE

Once we make our recommendations, a couple of things are going to happen. They are either going to say "yes", "no", or "maybe". If they say, "yes, I agree with you", then you need to ask about the projected offer level. Or set up a second interview, depending on the situation. Here we'll assume an offer is our next step.

What does the company think they could offer up to? The reason that you do this is not to pin them down or force them to make a hasty decision. What you are trying to do is to help hire the person if they are ready to hire him. "Tell me what you are thinking of" is the correct phraseology. Then you can go back to the candidate and see what <u>they</u> are thinking, and determine if we have a compatible decision here.

We don't want to make an offer that is not what the candidate is looking for. If we do, one of two things could happen. He could turn it down, and we would have to go to someone else. Alternatively, we are going to have to come back with a higher offer. We don't want to do that. We want to make our best offer upfront so he can accept or reject.

Tell the client to say what he is <u>thinking</u> of. Then go over with the candidate, and see what he is thinking as well. Based on that information, sit down (over the phone) with the client and come up with an offer. See next chapter for specifics.

THE "MAYBE" RESPONSE

Sometimes we have clients that give us a "maybe". "Well, I think the person looks pretty good, but I am unsure. I don't know exactly where I would go with this person."

I call these "maybe" answers. They don't want to turn the candidate off, but they don't want to turn them on either.

If you allow this to sit, it will turn into a "no". Candidates who are not hired fast probably will not improve with age. The longer we let this situation sit, the greater the chance the hiring official will say no. Follow the technique we have just discussed, and make a recommendation after your feedback.

Will that sell someone a candidate that they dislike? Absolutely not. If they dislike the candidate, they are not going to hire them.

If they really like the candidate, however, the presentation that we discussed above is going to encourage the good feelings they already have about the candidate. If it is a "maybe", that presentation moves the fence riders to the positive side of the fence. It gives them a reason to say, "Oh, I did not know that. I think I will go ahead with this individual."

Resolving Doubt

Your fence riders are who you are trying to affect, because the "yes" and "no" are already effective. When you have a "maybe", you have a fence rider. You have someone that cannot make a decision; in most cases a "maybe" is a "no". What you want to do is take the hiring official back through the key areas of the position, and find out where there may be doubt. Wherever there is doubt, you need to get further information.

For instance, suppose they have a doubt that the candidate has enough experience in a narrow portion of your field, but an important one for this position. OK, if they have a doubt about that, it may be a good reason to think "maybe".

Go and check out what the company needs, and ***bring it back to the candidate.*** How much experience is the client looking for in that area? Find out before you go to the candidate what the client will say "yes" to. Then go see if you can come up with that much experience from the candidate.

Here is the thought process you must understand: when you ask a person to say "yes" after you get a "no" without giving them further information, then all you are saying is "You're stupid. You made the wrong decision." To change a person's mind in sales, you must give them further information, or re-direct their thoughts (off-setting the objection or rebuttals, as examples). By doing so, you improve your chances of their saying, "Oh, yeah. Based on that new information or thoughts, yes, I would go forward with an offer."

Go back through the keys areas of the position and the specific things we are looking for. Find out where the company's representative may have doubt on this individual. Them go check out the information on that doubt, and bring it back to the hiring official and get a definite positive or negative.

It is all right if you come back and get a definite "we will pass". Do you know why? Because when you have a "maybe", then you have a "no" anyway! All you are doing is finalizing it, and you can quit carrying that thing around like luggage while the hiring official decides not to hire. I would rather get it over with now than to get it over two weeks from now. I have other and better things to do with my time. So do you.

Seeing Other Candidates

If the hiring official says he wants to put the person "on hold" so that he can see others, then again you have a doubt situation. Ask, "What is it that you are trying to find in these other candidates that you may doubt about my candidate?" In other words, "if this candidate is perfect, then why are you interviewing others? If you are not proceeding immediately with him, you must have doubts. What are they? Let me go and check it out."

I have had clients say, "Well, I don't know. The candidate was right on and the best that I have seen. I promised to interview a few other people, and I want to get them out of the way." What is it that the other candidates are going to have to measure up to that would cause him to risk losing my candidate to someone else? If he is going to be two weeks in the process of interviewing two other candidates, then he is giving every other company two weeks to hire the individual they want to hire. Point this out! Ask him if that is the way to go about hiring top talent. Sometimes you can get them to cancel the other two interviews, because the person you had is the right one.

Motivate him to make a contingency offer to the person that says, "I want to hire you. Here is the possible offer that I am thinking about if these other two interviews don't go well."

If you get that done, then you have a leg up because the other two have to significantly beat your candidate out before he will reassign the contingent offer. Make an offer contingent upon seeing two other people. It is more a "statement of intent" to the candidate, and obligates the client in no way legally. But he will probably stand by that intent.

THE "NO" RESPONSE

Now if he says "no", don't panic. You can sometimes turn around a no.

However, I want to warn you about the all-or-nothing approach to the word no. Too many times with consultants, I have seen them buckle under when the client says no and not challenge it at all. Wrong. Or the hard-nosed sales type that challenges <u>every</u> "no". Every time the company says no, they have to go through an argument and sales pitch from that consultant. Also wrong.

The top consultants that have a lot of clients know when to "challenge the no", and when not to. If you realize that "no" is valid and the person simply does not have those areas that they need to have, then admit it. Find the client someone else.

But suppose the client is making a decision that you think may not be in his best interest. As an example, he may say, "Well, this candidate was not confident enough," and you have no indication that the candidate was unconfident in his past endeavors. You can challenge that and say, "Bill, I understand your feelings. But I don't believe that is accurate. That probably showed up in the interview, but certainly did not in the marketplace or his past job positions. Let me go and check his references. If I find out that he is not confident and has reduced professional results in the past because of it, then I will accept that and we will go on to someone else. However, if I find out that he is confident in his job, then we have just assumed something in an interview that may not have been true in the workplace.

If I find that out, then I will call you back with that information. We will set up a second interview for you to talk to this person, and find out whether or not the confidence is a real problem.

That is, in general, how to answer any of the "yes", "maybe", or "no" answers after the company follow-up call.

I'd like to refer you to a source that will cover the entire subject of overcoming invalid objections of all types in far more depth. Steve Finkel's background consists of the best classical corporate sales training obtained from three Fortune 500 companies, followed by 25 years on a desk in our industry.

His 8-module, 4-hour video training series, *"Book More Business"*, is the ultimate work on overcoming objections and closing for our industry. I recommend it for more experienced or more sales-oriented people at every speaking program that I do.

Let us talk about some ways we can get the right offer and close those sales.

NEGOTIATING THE OFFER

21

*T*o most sales-oriented people, this is the exciting part. We all love doing battle in the middle of all these different minds. Frequently, you don't get what you deserve in business; you get what you <u>negotiate</u>. When we are in the midst of talking about offers, salaries, trying to put that deal together and actually closing the situation, many of us are in our element. Even if it is not your element, it is where the money is. Those are the areas that are really the bottom line. A great job here will make us money right now!

We have made a presentation and set an interview. You have scripted and controlled that interview. The candidate came out of there and called you as instructed. You followed up with him properly, called the company and gave them the debriefing information. You made a recommendation that they move forward to an offer. The company said, "Yes, I agree. This man is the type that we want to hire and we are planning on going forward with an offer."

Here is where there is a <u>critical</u> <u>difference</u> between the top producers and the average producers. Average producers drop the ball. They do not follow-up to <u>help</u> the company hire the individual.

Our Real Value

Understand where your value lies to your client. Why does your client pay you money? Since we generally work on a contingency basis, the client pays us money when the search is completed. But we are called recruiters, right? We are paid to recruit. Well, yes, we are. But that is only part of our job. Your value also frequently comes at the <u>end</u> of the interview process, not at the beginning of the search.

Look at it this way. If you were given an assignment and presented fifty candidates, all of which were interviewed, none of whom were hired, then do you have any value? No. Everybody's time, including yours, has been wasted. We must understand that our value is in helping clients <u>hire</u> top talent. Your objective must be to put the best person in that position.

How does your client make money based on the fees that they pay you? They make money when they hire someone from you whose talents are so good that they make or save the corporation a good amount of money. But what if you do not control the process and allow the candidate to turn down the offer, or you don't give the advice necessary to your client company? Then you are hurting them. You are not doing your job. You must operate the recruiting scenario so that when your company client makes an offer, that offer will be accepted. That is where significant value lies, at the end, as well as the beginning. It is absolutely critical to maximize your recruiting skills. If not, you'll be at the mercy of those people who hustle the same questionable people on the internet which your clients can find on their own. But it also takes a talented and knowledgeable recruiter to negotiate the offer, and get that highly-qualified candidate to the point that the correct offer is made and accepted.

Have you have taken the time to explain to your hiring official that this is your job? In many instances, companies that decide to go forward with offers just go forward with whatever offer they want and whenever they want. And they blow it. They lose the best candidate. They have never been told that the value of a good recruiter's job is also at the end.

A Learning Experience

I had a client once say to me who had hired three or four top level people from me, "Larry, I love working with you. But do you know where you really have value to me?" I said (creatively), "No. Where?" He said, "You don't just find me these people. I get lots of resumes from recruiters; you give me the information necessary that allows me to <u>hire</u> them. I am so tired of losing good people. You even tell me if we have a problem with the spouse finding a job in the new location, or if they have a problem with hospitals because they have a child they have to take care of. Those things are important in the hiring process. That is your value; you <u>help</u> me to hire!"

I learned something from that client. You should too. From that point forward, I educated every hiring official that much of my <u>real</u> job was at the end. Once I make it a value to the hiring official, they allow me to recommend and control the offer stage. They will put off an offer a day or so, if I recommend it. They will add a thousand or sometimes much more to the offer, if I recommend it. Why? Because they know that helps them to obtain the candidate that they want!

Persuading the Client

The way to sell this to a client is to remember if you want something done for you, make it a <u>value</u> to the person. All you have to ask your hiring official is, "Have you ever lost a top candidate because they did not accept your offer?" Of course, they are going to say yes. When they do, you say, "I don't want that to happen to you. My job is to give and provide to you the information necessary to hire the top people, so that you don't have to start all over again or hire secondary talent."

What we are going to do is to make sure the offer is right and get that all together <u>before</u> they make the offer. I have had them hold off on an offer on a Friday to give me the weekend to work with the family, so the candidate is not under the pressure of an offer over that weekend. The client waited until I could get back to them. The candidate and his spouse were prepared for that offer. When it was made, it was done at the right time!

SEARCH CONSULTANT AS AGENT!

Should you be involved at this stage? Is this a good thought process? Why can't you just let the company go hire the person? Why can't you just let them talk to the candidate about the money they want, and put things together themselves?

Let us look at some parallels.

How about real estate sales? Have you ever bought or sold a home? Suppose a real estate agent finds a buyer and they go into a home, and the buyer says, "You know, I think I would like to make an offer on that home." Does the real estate agent take those two in and say, "Mr. & Mrs. Jones, this is Mr. & Mrs. Smith. They would like to buy your home. Why don't you four here sit down here, and call me at the office when you arrive at a price?" Does that ever happen? No. Why not? Because they would be killing each other by the time they got finished with the price on the house.

So what does the real estate agent do? She stands between the buyer and the seller and says to the buyer, "How much <u>will</u> you offer?" And then, to the seller, "How much will <u>you</u> take?" They do that between the two of them until the price is right. And when the price is right, then they close the deal.

This is the same thought process that we should have as recruiters. That is, we stand half-way between the candidate and the company, and we say to the candidate, how much will you take? Then we say to the company, how much will you offer? And we stand there and keep them at arms length until the price is right, and then when that is right, we get them together and close the deal.

There are parallels in all sales; our job is one of high emotionalism at the end. If you allow the wrong offer to be made at the wrong time, then you are injuring your client's chances of hiring top talent. That top talent is either going to some another firm, or they are going to totally turn down the situation. The sale will fall apart ... to everyone's detriment!

Back and Forth

How do we go about getting the offer correct? First of all, when we find out that the company is thinking of making an offer, we should have a clear indication of a rough amount from them. We may not have an actual figure, but at least an understanding of about where the offer will come in. You should have that knowledge before you go to the candidate.

Then, however, we need to go to the candidate and let him know that the company is thinking of getting serious about putting the deal together. Start asking him about what level is acceptable in money terms. When you ask this, you must understand that the candidate is going to tell you what he wants, and it may not be necessarily what he will accept. But it will definitely be sent up the flag pole to see if you will salute to it. The idea here is the first thing that comes out of the candidate's mouth is on the high end of what they are willing to do, and you need to find a way to get to the low end. Your intent is not to get him to accept a low offer; it is to know what he will accept.

It is not going to be good if your candidate says he wants fifty-thousand and your hiring official says they are going to offer forty-eight thousand, and your candidate was ready to accept that! If you kept beating the official for fifty, they may make no offer at all! It is extremely important that you know exactly where the candidate stands, or you cannot represent him as his agent to the client company.

"BOTTOM-LINE YES-NO POINT"

At this point, you must find out <u>two</u> figures. Explain to the candidate that you need to know not just what it is they would like to have; you also need to know that "bottom-line yes-no point". What is a "bottom-line yes-no point"? It is the point at which they will say, "Yes, but anything below that is a no."

How to Get There

The way I present it to these people is "Look, my job is to help you obtain this position if that is the one that you want. You have already indicated it <u>is</u> the one that you want. You have said to me in the past that there was nothing that could stand in the way of a fair offer. Obviously, I want you to get a fair offer. In fact, I want you to think about this; I have your best interests at heart. The more you make, the more I make. My income is based on your salary. So believe me, I am going to get you the best offer I can possibly get you. But my company is going to ask me about my recommendation. If you say to me fifty thousand, then they may come back saying 'No, we cannot do that; let us hire someone else.' The offer may have been fine at forty-eight thousand, but I have damaged your career because of inaccurate information from you. So let us do this; let us sit down and say what figure do you want from this deal? What figure are you willing to accept, but below that, then it is a no?"

So the candidate says, "Well, I do want fifty thousand. That is what I really want and anything below that will not be very acceptable. But put it that way, if the company can't do that, then my bottom line is umm…forty-eight thousand."

So now you have asked the candidate and obtained an understanding that if the offer comes at forty-eight or above, he will accept. But if it comes at forty-seven, then do they want you to tell the client to go to another candidate? Now, is that accurate? Many times a person will say, "Well, no. Now wait a minute. Forty-seven is not that big of a deal over forty-eight. Hmmm…"

I say, "If the company says we are thinking of offering forty-seven, how do you think that will fly? If I know that your bottom-line is forty-eight, then I am going to say that it won't fly. They either have to come up with another thousand or hire someone else. The company may decide to hire someone else, and you jeopardize your chance of getting an opportunity if I don't have accurate negotiating amunition. Again, I will get you all I can because of the financial picture of the entire deal. But I don't want to lose it for you because you have not seriously communicated to me the correct bottom-line." And then find out what that is.

Put the Deal Together

Once you find out that we have an offer of fifty thousand and a bottom line of forty-seven, and the company says they are coming in at forty-eight five, you now have a good deal that is makeable. You know the candidate's head is working correctly. You just spoke to him about forty-seven, did you not? And what did the offer come in at? Forty-eight, five. He also appreciates that you did not beat him around the head and shoulders to find out his bottom-line number, and then go and run and tell the company about that. That is not your job!

Your job is not to get the company to pay more, or the candidate to accept less. Your job is to put the deal together so it works. Only then do the parties involved receive value from your services.

Don't "Go to the Chapel"

Don't let the offer be made until you know what those numbers are, or it is going to be trouble for you. The deal will close if you do! It will not close if you have the wrong number, and don't know it.

I have seen consultants walking the halls and wringing their hands, and I say, "What is going on with you?" And they say, "Oh, I have got an offer going out today." And I say, "Oh, really. How much?" " I don't know, but they said it was going to be a good one." "Well, what is the candidate going to say?" "Well, I don't know, but I think that he will be impressed."

That is what I call the going-to-the-chapel, lighting-three-candles method of placement-making. You don't have a clue as to what is going on, and you are letting a buyer and a seller get together without knowing what their attitudes are about the situation.

If you do know and the offer will work, get it done in 24 hours. The quicker you move when the money is right, the greater the chance the company has that the candidate will say "yes".

IF THE OFFER DOES NOT WORK

If the numbers are wrong, you have to do some work on either moving the candidate down or the company up. Ask the client for more time before extending an offer. A day or two to give you a chance to do some work should be time enough.

Now who do you sell? Do you sell the company up, or do you sell the candidate down? *I would sell the one that is being most unreasonable,* because I have more ammunition.

Is the company asking the candidate to make a lateral move that is on the low scale of the market? Do you know that the salary range the company has would allow them to offer more? Sell the company up! They are the ones being unreasonable. The candidate is not asking for anything unreasonable, but just a decent increase over what he is earning. He deserves it. He should get a raise to make a move, because the client is on the lower level of the market.

But is the candidate asking the company to bleed and give him more money when he is already well-paid, yet is asking for a 20% increase over that? Then he is being unreasonable. It is easier to talk the candidate down than to talk the company up. And it is more than fair.

Reduction to the Ridiculous

Utilize the "reduction to the ridiculous" technique if you are talking money, either to the client or the company. Don't talk about a thousand dollars a year; they don't get paid that way anyway. They probably get paid weekly or bi-weekly. How much is a thousand dollars a year? That is about twenty bucks a week.

Say to a candidate, "You mean you are going to let this get by you for twenty dollars a week?" That sounds a lot better than talking to them about $1000 a year.

You can do the same thing with a client company, "My goodness. We are talking 26 cents an hour difference in what you are willing to pay, and what the candidate will accept. You could get that much out of the soda machine, if you would just rob it!"

Multiply the amount in dispute appropriately, of course. An extra $3000 is $60 a week (or 75 cents an hour), but *after taxes (or tax deductions), it is*

half of that!   Point that out!   For minimal money, the most unreasonable party of the two can have what they want — the right candidate or the right career.

There are all kinds of ways to address the dollars that you are talking about to make it seem a lot more acceptable, and to achieve the more unreasonable party's goals. Put the deal together!

Sharp-angle Method

If the candidate wants more money, then make sure that you use the "sharp-angle close" when they ask you about it. Some candidate may say, "Well, it sounds real good, but I need another thousand dollars." Sometimes that is a smoke screen; you go and push for another thousand and the client goes to the Vice President and gets approved and comes back, and the candidate <u>still</u> turns it down. You do not want that professional egg on your face.

When the candidate says, "I want more money", get them to commit. Say to them, "Do you understand the seriousness of what you are asking? Do you understand that I too have to put my professional reputation on the line with my client to get you that money. That my client has to put his neck in the noose with the VP to get you more money? Before we jump through those hoops, do I have your assurance that if I get you that money, that you will accept on the spot?"

If they say yes, then see if you can get them the money.

The Real Objection

If they say "no", then the money was a smoke screen; now you can smoke out the <u>real</u> objection and close the deal. Many times that claim of not enough money has nothing to do with the situation. They don't want to talk to you about the real problem, because they are afraid you will solve it, and then they will definitely have to accept. That would require them to move, and encounter fear and uncertainty. The reduction to the ridiculous and the "sharp angle methods" will help when you are talking about money with candidates.

There are also qualifying questions that you can use if the candidate is asking for too much, to determine the real problem. Frequently, it is simply Fear of Change, but you must find out and have him admit to the problem.

To do that, go back to the Reason For Leaving, and requalify the candidate as to the value in this company. "We did not talk about money at all when we first talked about your reason for leaving. So why does the decision hinge on that now? Don't you still want (the Reason For Leaving)? Does this opportunity have (the Reason For Leaving)?"

Foundational Question

Or go right to the Foundational Question. Say, "Forget money! Do you want the career that the situation offers you, regardless of money?" That gets the money out of the way if it is a smoke screen. If they say, "Yes, I want this career opportunity", then say, "Well, why are you pricing yourself out of it?" Or if they say, "No, I don't want this career", then ask why not?

Assure yourself that there is not another problem. You can always ask them if they are pricing themselves high as an easy way to get out of the situation.

In any instance, what you are trying to do is to find out if the problem with the offer is the real problem or only a smoke screen. If you handle the money that way, you will have a much better handle on putting a deal together that the company can offer and the candidate can accept.

Is this serious closing? No. Rather, it is helping the candidate and client to obtain what they both want, and smoothing the path to an agreeable starting relationship. By doing so properly, you greatly increase chances of an acceptance, and assist all parties involved in achieving a happy and mutually beneficial future.

CLOSING

22

*W*hy Close?

Some in our business feel that candidates can make decisions entirely on their own. Sometimes that's true. But not often. And if you take the chance that they can, it will cost you business, and it will cost many candidates a superior career path. In point of fact, we have a moral obligation to assist them. Why? Because the reality is that these people need all the help they can get about making a business/career decision.

That is a true statement. Most of the people who do not maximize their careers sow the seeds of life-long under-achievement by staying put in a bad situation. In my many years of recruiting, I have only had one person who was sorry that he made a move, and that was for a reason that neither of us could see in the upfront scenario. But a lot of people get cold feet, become nervous, do not move, and pay a big price for their indecision.

Why is closing necessary? Poor closers say that if you put the deal together right, then there is no close necessary. In some instances, that is true. There are placements where the deal is so good that everyone is happy and unhesitant. At the end, you say, "Gosh, wasn't that easy?" But those are few and far between.

Emotion Rules

Most people, deny it as they will, are emotional animals. And yet we have many major decisions to make that should be based on logic. Sometimes we lose sight of how difficult it is for people who are trying to make those decisions. Frequently a career determination is made not because it is the right decision, but because the pressure is so great that the easiest thing to do is nothing. If you don't lend some objectivity, "fear of change" will take over.

The top five stress factors that have been rated in a person's life are death of a spouse, death of a family member, divorce, job change and relocation. And the first two are not optional. When logic and emotion have a tie, emotion always wins. Your job is to focus the candidate on logic. But don't feel like you can just sit back there and logically tell these people how great this company and job is, and they will just fall all over themselves to go to work. You must learn to close.

They Will Thank You

You may be a little reluctant about closing. If so, I want to say this to you; it is an absolute necessity for you to be able to help some people change jobs, improve their careers, and improve their lives. And after you do so, they will be grateful to you! I have received notes and phone calls from some of the people that I have had to close the hardest, saying "Thank you." Once they have made the change and are reaping the rewards, fear does not seem to have much meaning. But boy, during those times we really had difficulty! In fact, there were times in many placements that I wanted to give up. But we stayed at it and hammered it out. They overcame their fear, moved forward in life and were much happier as a result.

Your job is not only to help companies find people. It is also to help those people find their way through tough and important decisions about their family, location, kids in school, hobbies, bonus and vesting periods, all sorts of problems.

But how do you close? What do you say when someone says, "I am not sure" or "I am not going to." I would suggest first of all that you find several good sales books on closing. Steve Finkel's book *"Breakthrough!"* has an entire chapter of book reviews on this subject. I've mentioned some authors in this book. Study, underline, and implement. Why read these books? Because many of the general closes that are used in any sales situation are effective in our business. There are also very effective sales techniques and closes that are specific to our industry in audio or video cassette programs which I've recommended already for you.

I am not referring here to softball "relationship selling" touchy-feely foolishness. That's designed for people who want to pretend they are doing their jobs. They are not, and their production will reflect it. What you need are closing skills!

Paul Micali, who has been mentioned earlier, was the founder of the world-wide franchised sales training organization, Lacy Sales Institute. In his outstanding book *"The Lacy Techniques of Salesmanship"*, Paul Micali addresses this topic. "It is great to be everyone's friend", he writes. "But to bring home the bacon on a regular basis demands that you know how to close. It demands that you have the willingness and determination to study and learn, and the courage to implement. If there was ever a secret for success, this is it." Words to remember....

Handling Objections

Let's say this about objections in our business that will help you work with them. There are two ways of handling an objection. You can either overcome the objection, or you can solve it. If it is the real objection, overcoming it works. But solving it is also effective.

Let's say a candidate says, "I want another thousand dollars to be able to accept the job. They have offered me forty-nine, but I want fifty." If you get him to accept forty-nine, then you have overcome the objection. If you go to the company and get him fifty, then you have solved the objection. There are always two ways of handling any of them. Remember both when you are trying to do so. Don't get too "structured" in your responses to difficulties.

"Objection Tennis"

There are also closes that aren't really closes, but rather identify real objections. "Objection finders" are required in our business, because many times we are being screened from the real objection. Why is this? The person is afraid to voice it. If they voice an objection and we overcome it, then where do they go from there? So they are not going to tell us. We need something that smokes them out.

There are two "objection finders" that are really not closes, but they are in the closing area of getting answers. One of them is the "is it close" and the other is what I call the "objection tennis close".

Objection tennis comes when someone is playing the game of "can I bring up more objections than you can overcome?"

My people get two objections that I will overcome or solve. On the third one, I realize that I have a different problem. At this point, I see the term "objection tennis" going off in my mind and realize I must put an end to this.

My statement is, "Is this the only thing that we have to resolve that stands between you and the acceptance of the job, or is there something else? Is this it? If not, lay your cards on the table, and let us talk about what is real." If they say, "Yes, it is the only thing" and then I resolve that question, then they accept. If they say, "No, it is not the only thing", then the real objection is probably about to come out.

Then I can handle it by either of the two previously-mentioned methods.

NON-TALKERS

The "is it" close is another objection finder. It is meant specifically for those people who have a hard time expressing themselves.

Suppose you work in Engineering or Information Technology, where many are non-talkers. Many of your hiring officials are going to say, "Well, I don't know. There is something about the person. They look good and yeah, they are probably qualified, but I just don't know." The easiest way to keeping you from selling them is to say, "I don't know." There is nothing that you can grab on there. There is no objection to address here.

Your candidates also will be equally reluctant is to express themselves. It isn't you and it isn't the opportunity; they are just non-talkers. There are solutions to this.

What you want to say is, "I understand your decision in not being able to put your finger on something. You know something? Most of my clients who have that problem were able to determine that it is only momentary indecision, and there is nothing wrong. Or perhaps there is something wrong, and we need to find out what it is. Let me ask you some questions, and we will see if we can find out what the problem is."

"Is it this person's education?" "No, their education is fine." "Is it the amount of experience that they have? They do have five years." "No, I was really looking at two to three years, so five is really good for me."

Obviously if you are closing the candidate rather that the client, you would follow the same principle.

What you do in the "is it" close is that you ask all the "is it's" upfront that you know are positives. You get them in the habit of saying, "Yes, it is OK." One of my favorite classical sales books is Charles B. Roth's "Professional

Salesmanship", which you should read. As he says, "One thing all salesmen strive for during all stages of the sale is what they call 'the yes response'." We see it here. In the end result, they can not find anything, and they say, "Aah, yes. I guess there was no problem." Then you close them because there is, in fact, nothing wrong. It is only a fit of indecision that is causing their lack of moving forward.

But what if they say, "Yes, that is it! They are weak in this area." Good! Now you have an objection that if you can resolve, will get the hire done.

Again, you should do the same thing with non-talking candidates. Segment the possibilities, and walk them through one by one.

The "is it" and the "objection tennis" are objection finders.

THIRD-PARTY CLOSE

The third party close is frequently effective, especially for younger candidates or for those who have not made many previous career changes. Many times you will find that people who are indecisive want to talk it over with others and get reassurances that they are doing the right thing. I have had third parties come in and help me close my deals. Look for candidates who have had similar concerns in the past, and accepted the opportunity. It will really smooth out a difficult close when you put them together.

As an example, I have had candidates who were very reluctant to go through the trauma of relocating, but after doing so were quite happy with their new jobs. They call and thank me. You will have this happen too; keep a list of these people.

Then what? Put them on the phone with a candidate who is going through the same thing! Now this person has no real interest in making the sale. He is simply there to say, "I know what you are feeling and have been through it before. Let me tell you what happened to my wife and I, the fears we had, and how it all worked out. Let me also say how glad that we did it."

Having someone who seems to have no monetary interest in the situation giving positive and supportive advice is a very powerful third-party close that will be very useful with many candidates.

"COST OF LIVING" CLOSE

If you are involved in an offer involving relocation, this is mandatory.

You can get the cost of living index from the American Chamber of Commerce Research Association (ACCRA); they put out a cost of living on every city in the US that responds to their poll. They also put out special reports such as cost of housing, food, utilities, transportation etc. When you are moving somebody from one cost of living to another, you must focus on comparing their standards of living, rather than the offer.

For housing costs only, try www.coldwellbankers.com. This information is readily available and will gain you quite a few fees, if utilized properly.

The "Cost of Living" Close in Action

Let me give you an example.

We had a candidate in a Northeast city with a Cost of Living that was a hundred and twelve. The hundred and twelve figure is represented by the average city being one hundred; you can think of it in percentages if you would like. This city was therefore twelve percent higher than the average city in the US. Now we had an offer in a smaller metro area in the South, whose Cost of Living was ninety-three.

The candidate was making forty-eight thousand. We got what we considered to be a reasonable offer under the specific circumstances of fifty-two thousand. The candidate, however was of a different opinion. He was not going to accept the job, because it was not enough money.

The first step is set up this close right, and focus attention on what's important. You do this by asking the following questions. "Why is that you want the money? So you can tell your friends how much you are making? Or is the money important to educate your children, to have a finer home, to feed and clothe them?" He replied, "Obviously, it is the second. I am not trying to put on a show here. I need the money for those things."

Most closes are multi-step. It is rare that one phrase will achieve your goals. Only amateurs think that is the case. Having laid the foundation, we now progress on to the next step.

"If that is your value, then let me ask this. If you were shown that you could earn more money to do those things, would you accept the offer?" He replied, "Absolutely. I want the job, but that is not enough money." Note that we have now obtained commitment.

We said, "OK. You must understand that you are moving from an area of a hundred-and-twelve Cost of Living to an area that is ninety-three in Cost of Living, according to the American Chamber of Commerce Research Association. When you subtract ninety-three from a hundred-and-twelve, you have a nineteen percent cost of living differential in these two cities. What that means is when you can buy a larger house for less money. Everything costs you less money. You can provide your family with a higher standard of living than you currently enjoy, and save money for their education at the same time." "Hmm," he said. "I see your point. What would the offer be worth in that town?"

"Let me tell you exactly what it would be worth. If we have a nineteen per-cent cost-of-living differential, we take fifty-two thousand which is the offer in the south, and we multiply times 1.19. In other words, we increase it nine-teen percent, which is the cost-of-living differential. That comes out to sixty-one thousand eight hundred and eighty dollars worth of buying power that you would have to earn in your current position to have the same standard of living. Do you think there is any company around your current home that would offer you sixty-one, eight?" And of course the answer was, "absolute-ly not."

Did the candidate have a fifty-two thousand dollar offer? He did have that in actual monetary compensation that would pass from the company's end to the candidate. But he had a sixty-one, eight thousand dollar standard of living!

We got an acceptance. You will, too.

Using that cost-of-living differential can help your candidates to see the dif-ferences in the standard of living that they are actually looking at.

LIFE DECISION CLOSE

Another close you will find quite useful is what I call the "Life Decision Close". A lot of people seem to be myopic, and believe they are only mak-ing a decision about a job. As the pressure is on them to not relocate, not take the kids out of school, not take the wife out of the Bridge Club or deal with finding a new position for her, they tend to think "it is just a job and I will get another one in the future." This is especially true if this is the first job change or if it requires a relocation. Start talking to them about their entire life, not just this job! That is why we call it the "Life Decision Close".

When they are thinking of turning it down, re-focus their thoughts by saying, "You know what really bothers me about your decision? That you are not just deciding about a job. You are sitting here saying to me, 'I am career-conscious and want a better position that will lead to a better life for my family and better education for my kids. When I move up the corporate ladder, I improve my lot in life, my stability in employment, and my earnings power over the length of my life.' Yet here we are at your first job change, and you have been exactly where you are for the last five years. You are dead-ended, not going anywhere, and have been unhappy for two years. You have not had a salary increase for two years, yet now you have a great opportunity to move up. But because it is in another city, you have decided to say no."

Pause, and wait for a response. Again, multi-step closing will be needed, and you should plan for this. Almost regardless of the response, continue as follows.

"You are not making a decision about a job! You are making a decision about how you are going to spend the rest of your life. (Name), once you decide to stay put and not accept a move up, it will be much easier to make that decision again. I have seen this before. When you make that decision a second and third time, soon you will quit even looking. You will be one of those poor people that you probably see in your plant right now who hates their job and boss, but won't do a darn thing to change it. If you want to be one of those people, then be hesitant and stay put. But if you want to be one of those who move up the corporate ladder and do something, then you need to change. Let me ask you, how do you plan on spending the rest of your life?"

That is the Life Decision Close, and it will gain a lot of ground with most candidates, and close the deal with some.

EXISTING CLIENTS PAY FOR RESULTS

I have mentioned that a major portion of your worth is delivering talent, not in screening and referring resumes. It is clear that good selling and solid trained closing skills will directly increase production for a minimal investment of time once those skills are acquired. But what does this mean?

An Example

I once made a call to a client of mine who was Vice President of a major consulting engineering company, and presented a candidate to him. He said, "Oh, that is ____ (and named the candidate), is it not?" I said, "Yes, Ralph. It is. How did you know? From my little short presentation, you could not tell who it was." He said, "I know that background very well. I have interviewed that young man twice, made him two offers, and have been turned down both times."

Now in the old days of not knowing where my worth was, I would have hung my head and thought to myself, "A day late and a dollar behind", and would have given up. I would have said, "Well, let me see if I can find you somebody else."

But realize that our job is not only to find the right candidate. Rather, it is to get the top person to go to work for my client. So I said, "Ralph, it sounds to me as though you are quite interested, or you would not have made him the offers." He said, "Well, yes. He is one of the best in town, and he would be worth a lot of money to my company."

I said, "If I can get him to go to work for you, will you pay me my fee?" He said, "How much is your fee?" I said, "At this level it is about $21,000." The client replied, "Yes. I will pay you your fee. He is worth a hundred times to me."

Aha! He was my candidate. You have already read how to gain to complete understanding of a candidate's motivation in previous chapters. Here is what it will get you.

"Ralph, if you do what I suggest, say what I tell you to say, and work with me on the offer stage, we will have the greatest odds that this man will say yes. I can not guarantee it. Let us give it a shot." He said, "Well, alright." We put our heads together and I sent Bill in there. I knew what he wanted. All I had to do is transfer that information to my hiring official. Then I had to have him relay these qualities which the client did possess to Bill in the interview to get him enthusiastic.

At the end of the interview, I followed up with the candidate. I contacted the client and said, "Call him now at home, and make him this offer." One hour after the interview, Ralph made him the offer. I closed Bill the next morning. Within a forty-eight hour period, I had earned a $21,000 fee from a client that had already interviewed this candidate twice, and made him two offers. Why?

Because a great deal of your worth is at the end of the placement, in your sales skills, and in your total understanding of the entire situation! Should I have given up and cried big tears because the candidate had already been there before me? If I had the idea that I had find someone else, I could have done so. But I would have injured my client if I had found him a second-choice engineer just because he had never heard of him. It makes no sense. And I believe in my skills. When you work, study, and practice to achieve good selling and closing skills, you will too! And your production will soar.

Placements Are Made By Skill

A repeat client of mine once needed a plant manager for a small drum manu-facturing plant. When I searched and took the order I asked him, "Is there any-one that you would like to see in this position?" He said, "Yes, there is a man here in town. I have already approached him and he ran like a scared rabbit. So there is no way that we can attract him." I said, "Is that the man you want?" "Well, yes, Larry. He is the best there is, but we can not get him." I said, "Look, it is better for me to get you the best talent, because that makes you the most money. If you say this person happens to be the best candidate, then I will go and get him. Why should I not go after this person, rather then go off and find a candidate from across the nation? If I were to do that, you would have to relo-cate and worry about they are not going to like it and leave, when you know that this one candidate is your best person."

He said, "Larry, I don't mind if you do that. We can not just get through to the person. I have tried it." I said, "Tad, you know as much about recruiting as I know about running your can factory." We had the kind of relationship where I could talk to him like that. Well, he laughed and told me the name of the man he wanted. With my knowledge, skills and ability, I recruited the young plant manager. He went to work out there and he had a great career with the company.

And Tad the client called me up after and said, "Larry, after I gave you the candidate, can we reduce this fee?" I said, "No. You have to pay the invoice. The fee has nothing to do with that and besides, you did not give me the can-didate; you gave me a name. I gave you a candidate, because you utilized my recruiting skills to make a person a candidate when you could not." We talked about it awhile, but he ended up sending me a check. And he had a smile on his face when he did. He had the right candidate running the plant for whom he had a desperate need. That candidate could get in there and make them some money.

How did it happen? You have got to have candidate qualifying and excellent closing skills, so you can do the job for your client. What you are supposed to do is deliver top talent to their door. Only then do you have the worth to the client that gives them a great return on their investment.

Other Closes

The difficulty with explaining closes is that intonation, pace, emphasis is so significant that a written format has great limitations. To a somewhat lesser degree, this is true of rebuttals as well. The words can be the same, but effectiveness is significantly impacted by your manner of presentation. No, it is not "personality" or "relationships". It is hard specific skills. But a precise manner of presentation is a skill that must be demonstrated. The more sophisticated the rebuttal or close, the more this is true. Yet without rebuttals or closes, you'll have to rely on quantity — making more calls, working on more deals. To improve results after you have a solid foundation, those areas are critical.

That's why once the foundation is down, you'll benefit enormously from other products I've recommended in video format and, if you commute, perhaps my own audios. This business is remarkably complex. An ongoing learning program is mandatory to your success. This means not here-today, gone-tomorrow public speaking programs, but repeatable reviewable products such as books, audios, classically sales-based videos, or in-house training.

Closing and overcoming objections are not the basis of this business. But once you have a strong foundation down, that is your next step.

DEVELOPING CLIENTS

23

*C*ongratulations! You've put together your first placement! Or maybe your tenth, or twentieth. Or perhaps you are about to start in our terrific business soon.

Regardless of where you are, I have news for you from one who has long ago passed into triple digits in terms of deals. The thrill never fades! It is <u>always</u> an adrenalin "rush". It is called Big-Ticket Selling. And the charge of victory and success will be there for you over and over again.

So why doesn't everyone stay in our business forever and ever, enjoying the vast rewards, becoming addicted to the thrill? Well, many do. And they are very happy and very prosperous people. If you are lucky, it will happen to you! But others don't. There is no denying that our field, like any sales endeavor, has a "turnover rate". When you re-read this book, pay attention to the introduction to see what qualities are required. Not everyone is right for our business. People are different.

But what about those who <u>might</u> be right for our business, who <u>do</u> get the charge of victory, who deeply enjoy the mental and psychological rewards as well as the monetary? Are <u>they</u> always successful? Sadly, no. Many could have a wonderful long-term career in our industry…yet after a year or two, they drift away. Why is that? And how can you stop it?

Initial Success

The first answer is one we've alluded to throughout this book, and it is that of on-going learning, training, and self-improvement. I can't count the number of young "hotshots" I've seen who do well early, and ultimately fail. Sometimes their early success is due to raw talent. Perhaps a background in a different type of selling yields quick success in our industry. Sometimes it is luck, though you sure can't convince them of it. It is also possible that the managers gives <u>too</u> much help in terms of clients or candidates early, and success cannot be sustained when that help is switched to other newer people.

Such people have a problem. However, even if you don't meet with early success, the same problem can happen to you. That is, they quit learning! They think they "know it all". This business is not easy to master. It requires extensive in-depth serious <u>study</u>. That does <u>not</u> mean going to a conference, hearing a speaker, and <u>pretending</u> you are learning! It means honest reading, re-reading, watching videos, listening to audios, <u>working</u> at it.

Long-term results require a long-term investment in education, and it is best done at home after hours.

Long-term Thinking

But there is another reason why even talented and hard-working people sometimes fade after a few years in our business. They tend to think short-term. Put a deal together. Get a search. Find a candidate. Collect a fee. Do it again. You can make money that way. But can you develop a career?

The ability to identify, acquire, develop and retain a good repeat client base is the <u>key</u> to our long-term success! It will not only yield major income, but an income with great <u>stability</u>. But do you have a well-thought-out <u>program</u> that you work at on an annual, monthly, weekly, and even a <u>daily</u> basis to achieve these goals? Most in our industry do not. Lack of such a long-term conscious program leads eventually to long-term problems. But it doesn't have to be that way.

Making Clients

The ability to have clients utilize your services multiple times during the year and to use you exclusively really adds money to your bottom line. Most of us focus on trying to make <u>placements</u>, but we spend little time making <u>clients</u>. If you spend your time making clients, then the placements will almost make themselves. Sometimes it is so easy when you have an exclusive client, it really seems ridiculous. Wouldn't you rather work for a client that returns your phone calls, agrees with you, co-operates with you, and gives you information? Isn't that better than the customer that gives you an order on which you work and send in resumes, and you can't even get a return phone call? Most of our good, quick, easy placements come from the type of people that we should develop as a <u>client</u>, rather than a <u>customer</u>.

What are clients worth to us? Clients are worth <u>stability</u> and <u>survival</u> in the down times. We are a service business. We sell a service; we don't sell people. And any service industry is not going to survive very long if they don't have an adequate, widespread and solid client base. Many of us do not. We come into the office every day, get on the telephone and try to burn it up, trying to find our next search or placement.

Who Do You Call?

I remember when I started having this thought process about clients. I was placing accountants and administrative-type people at the time. My boss came to me and said, "Why aren't you making any placements with banks? I said, "Well, I am calling them but no one is responding." He asked, "Who are you calling?" I replied, "I am calling Human Resources. He said, "Don't call Human Resources; call the President of the bank." I about died! I was young in the business, and I was going to call Presidents of the banks? I had some problems over the idea, but the next day I grabbed the telephone and called those bank Presidents. What a difference in the response! After not doing any business with banks in the past, by the end of the day I had two search assignments and four invitations to their offices to meet with them. One even said, "My goodness, Larry! Why did you not tell me that you were in town? I have been using a search firm out of Kansas City and one out of New York." I realized that clients used recruiters, and smart clients realize they <u>need</u> recruiters. But here I was beating a telephone to death trying to find job orders from lower-level people who had never heard of me or my firm, and didn't much care.

I was looking for fees. But I should have been looking for clients.

HOW MANY CLIENTS?

How many do we really need to make a good living? I chaired a group of $300,000+ producers panel at a major industry annual meeting a few years ago. The question from the floor to these $300,000+ producers was, how many serious clients do you need to produce $300,000+? The top answer was eight and the lowest was four! Most of these big hitters don't have thirty or fifty exclusive clients that used them all the time. It does not take many clients to produce a lot of income for you if you are being used all the time, exclusively, or with retainer business. A proper on-going Client Development Program puts some serious money in your pocket, and does that year-in and year-out.

Performance-Based Client Development

Most people in our business limit their efforts to what I call Performance-Based Client Development. They are not out there trying to develop a client. They focus on making placements. All of a sudden, with one company they might make three or four placements. That company gets to know and respect them. Over a period of time with good performance, they continue to use that search consultant. That is what I mean by performance-based; we only <u>perform</u> rather than <u>develop</u>, and a client eventually comes out of it.

Over time, everybody gets a couple of those kind of clients. The problem is we never have more than a couple. It takes so long to develop one that by the time we develop another, one of the others may have dropped off. We continue to mill around in that lower area of client development.

Client or Customer?

It is common in our business to do a good job with a specific company, and receive a nice fee. Then we happen to call some months later, perhaps as a result of seeing an ad or information from a candidate. What do we find? The search is almost completed through another firm. Or perhaps a generic semi-qualified candidate has been dredged up by their Human Resource department after "training" by some internet consultant or by some "trainer" in <u>our</u> industry who claims to teach HR how to "recruit". Then we complain that the "client" was disloyal! What that search consultant who made the placement failed to understand was the difference between a <u>client</u> and a <u>customer</u>.

For instance, suppose you were to buy a copy machine from a good sales person who treated you professionally. Then you wanted to buy a new computer a few months later. I guarantee that you can not remember the name of that individual, even though they did a great job and sold you a good machine professionally. You may not even remember what company they were from without serious digging. Many in our business are the same way.

Without a specific <u>plan</u> to develop them, clients will see us as a one-hit basis. They will see us as salespeople who have sold them one good service. A few months later when they have another need, they may not even <u>remember</u> us. You must take it upon yourself to consistently call those clients until they get to know you, call you, and talk to you on a regular basis.

I've mentioned the sales author Les Dane earlier. His books end with a list of thirty one-line reminders gleaned from previous chapters of his books. He suggests that each be copied on a 3" x 5" card and looked at frequently, one per day.

One of his Master List of one-line reminders in his book *"Les Dane's Master Sale Guide"* is "A one-shot rifle is fine, but a repeater is finer; follow up on the sale!" The wonderful sales author Charles B. Roth in his outstanding book *"Professional Salesmanship"* makes reference to the fact that ***"the best salesmen I have known have been men to whom their existing customers were the most important factors in the world....and who had a specific plan to develop them!"***

WHAT IS A CLIENT?

When we are talking about the difference between Clients and Customers, we need to define a Client. What is a Client? It is very simple. A Client is a hiring authority who pays us <u>multiple</u> fees. He <u>calls</u> us when he has openings. He is <u>co-operative</u>, and <u>listens</u> to our advice.

True Client

Now a step up from that client is what I'd like to call a True Client. In addition to those three, a True Client will also give us <u>exclusives</u> and/or retainers. He is willing to be used as a <u>reference</u> and is willing to talk to other corporate companies about how good we are. Lastly, he <u>refers</u> <u>business</u> <u>to</u> <u>us</u>. People will call and say, "I was talking to Mr. Jones at ABC company, and he said to call you because you could help me with a difficult opening I have."

A Customer sees you as a salesman. A Client sees you as a consultant. There is a serious difference between the two in terms of co-operation, how many times a year that they use you, and whether they can remember and rely on you. You <u>develop</u> Clients from your customer base.

WHAT DO CLIENTS EXPECT?

How do we develop Clients? For us to become client-oriented and to supply them with the service they are looking for, we need to know what Clients expect. Until we can determine their expectations, we cannot fulfill them. Clients only want one thing from you. Trust-Based Performance. Only this type of performance will draw people to you and your firm to use you time and again. If you perform but they can not trust you, they are not going to use you very often. If they trust and love you and have a great rapport with you, but you do not perform consistently, they are likewise not going to use you very often.

Rapport Follows Performance

Rapport follows performance. Too many in our industry think that client development is going out, talking and entertaining. That's all right for an introduction. But until you get in there and perform, you are not going to have the respect or the business from that client.

I remember early in my own career when I first learned this. My boss and I had two major clients out on the golf course. He was off to one side looking for a ball, and I was walking down the other way. Now this was a client with whom we were making one or two engineering placements a month. I asked him how he liked working with my boss. "I don't like working with him." I said, "Wait, I am sorry. I don't understand. You don't like working with him, yet you hire from us multiple people monthly and yearly? Why is that?" He said, "Because that man can find me any engineer I want, any time I want. That is why. He is a performer!"

I understood two things. He trusted my boss' work, and he could perform. The fact that he did not like working with him was because my boss tried to push and move the timing up, and frequently was successful. They were a huge bureaucratic corporation and had difficulty moving forward, getting things done. He changed their hiring habits for his candidates, forcing them to move more rapidly. And they used him multiple times every month.

Performance does not follow rapport; the rapport follows the performer!

An Example of Developing Trust

Use your rapport to only open doors, and get to know people. Then you must perform to get that client to use you multiple times.

I remember I was quite young in this business and was about to make my second placement ever. I talked to my candidate who had an offer and asked if he was going to accept the offer? And he said, "Yes. Of course." I responded, "That is great! Do you really like that company then?" He shocked me when he said, "No. I don't like the company at all. The only reason I am accepting the offer is there is another company in that town who wants me. But their opening is not available for six months and they don't pay relocation."

I had a decision to make. It was my only second placement in the business, but I understood that I had a choice. My only thought was to pick up the phone and call my client and tell them to pull the offer from this guy before he accepted and then resigned, so they had a contract. He asked, "Why?" I said, "I will tell you later. Call up and make a excuse. Tell him that corporate pulled the position, and it is on hold. Tell him anything, but take the offer back." So he did and he called me back. I told him what the candidate was going to do, move up there, jump ship and leave them in six months before they even had the project started.

He said, "Larry, I have been hiring from people like you for fifteen years, but I have never had a consultant pull a candidate that had an offer." I hung up the phone a little depressed. I watched the packet of money just fly away. My fat commission was gone! I tell you, I was a sad puppy. The moral of the story? I made eleven placements with that company over the next year and two months. What happened? Trust-Based Performance!

TRUST-BASED PERFORMANCE

I have had clients — True Clients, not customers — fly candidates in to interview just on my say-so, without ever presenting their credentials. The clients were rushed or on the road, and just asked me to line up three candidates to interview. They gave me the name of an HR clerk who mailed out the airline tickets and sent paperwork, and I just set up the interviews. That is trust, based on my performance, my ability, and my judgement. If you follow the program we are going to lay out, it will happen to you too. Don't ever trade your integrity for one placement. It will always come back to you ten-fold if you do your job professionally and do right by your client. Repeat business many times depends on how much the client thinks that you have their best interests at heart.

A client who has an opening has a problem. There is something that they want resolved within their company. When you are a consultant trying to discover what that problem is, when you try to refer the right person to the right company and when you have the genuine <u>real</u> Recruiting expertise to find that talent, that will solve their problem. Then you are going to find that you make a lot of clients. Your client will feel you are trying to find the candidate to solve the problem, rather than just any candidate they will hire to earn yourself a fee. I call it being an industrial problem solver.

That's what they pay you for — and combined with the Client Development program you'll see here, they will pay you a lot!

CLIENT DEVELOPMENT: ISSUES AND EDUCATION

24

Client Education

*C*lient Development equals for the most part Client Education. You have to understand that these people don't know how, why or when you do your job. And sometimes they don't know what they should be paying for it.

Retainer through Education

I once had a hiring official who hired from us for several years, and used us multiple times per year.

After a few years of a client relationship with this gentleman, I was doing well. But I started pushing him for not just middle management positions, but top positions. When I did so, he turned to me and said, "Larry, let me ask you a question. Why don't you give me a dossier like Heidrick and Struggles? I use them for all my director positions and use you for all of my lower positions. All you guys do is call me up with candidates. Why can't you take these people out to dinner like these guys do? All I get from you is discussion of their backgrounds."

I said, "Hugh, I will be straightforward. I can take these people out to dinner in Houston. But I want you to understand one thing; <u>you</u> are taking these people to dinner. The agency is just eating the roast duck and drinking the wine. I can do that if you want to pay me to do so. But Hugh, you pay me on a contingency basis. I don't get the up-front capital to be able to provide you with that kind of a service. It is business suicide for me when you are paying me nothing to go and travel and meet people all on my money. The odds are great that I may not make the placement and that is just too much overhead. I can personally interview out-of town at expensive restaurants any time that you want. All you have to do is pay me up-front plus all expenses, the way you do Heidrick & Struggles."

He had never thought about it in that sense. But from that point on, I got all his business. When you develop mid-level business, don't be happy with what you have. <u>Develop</u> the account.

Multiple Sources? Educate!

Does a client or potential client want to use four or five search firms at a time because they believe that creates competition and better service? It does <u>not</u>! *Tell them so.*

Say, "It does not create competition and better service. It creates <u>no</u> service."

"Well, what do you mean?", they will respond. "If you have four or five recruiters on it, then you have got to hustle if you are going to make that sale."

"Well, first of all, we don't see it as a sale. We see it as a service. Let's say that you give this to me as an exclusive, Bob. I have a 90% chance of making a profit. If you put 5 recruiters on it, then I have 20% chance of making a profit. Now you want service. Let me ask you if one of your people came to you and said, 'I have two business deals for you. With one of our prospects, we have a 90% chance of making a profit. This other one over here has a 20% chance. Which one do you want me to work on?' What would you tell him? Certainly you would tell him to put effort in the 90%. That is what recruiters do."

"Bob, if you have 5 recruiters on that search, and I have a 20% chance, then you are on the bottom of the stack! You get no priority, little attention and no commitment."

We as recruiters do not tell our clients enough of those things so that they are informed enough to know how to set up the search. You must help them understand that how they set up the search will determine the service that they get. You must always sell service, and teach your clients what they must do to maximize that service. Straightforwardly informing prospects of flaws in their thinking sometimes leads to expanded business as well.

The Client's Choice

I had one uninformed individual who wanted me to thoroughly qualify candidates before I sent them to him and pay a discounted fee to boot! I said, "Wait a minute. You have a first-resume-in wins rule." He said, "Well, yes." I said, "Twice last month while I was qualifying a candidate, some other recruiter shipped the resume in to you, and you rubber stamped with a date. Now they get the fee based on my hard work. I spent three days chasing this guy and qualifying him. How can I qualify candidates when the rules of your company causes me to lose when I do that?"

Did he change his rules for me? In that instance, no. I shipped him my junk that I couldn't place anywhere else, and sometimes I got lucky. But after a while, he was replaced. I set up a meeting with his replacement, and presented the problem to him. We proceeded on an exclusive arrangement for a 90-day test. I broke my neck in trying to get him top people, and turned the account into a permanent exclusive multiple-hire account….at full fee.

Did I find better candidates faster for the second method of hiring the first? I sure did. And the client knew it.

Let the company contact determine the level of service that he is going to purchase. But tell him what he'll be getting and why.

Experienced Recruiters Only

As you develop more true clients, don't be afraid to go outside your area of specialization if you believe you can do an effective job and solve a problem. This is not recommended for newer people. That's a good reason you must own this book, and re-read it even after you get successful. Experienced people and solid recruiters should consider this on rare occasions, though, for True Clients.

I have recruited warehouse managers for True Clients! Why? Because the client had a warehouse manager with a history of missing shipment deadlines, customer complaints, breakage and spillage. He had a major problem. I found him three, he hired one. Did I ever place another warehouse manager, or even try to? No. Did I get on-going repeat business with that client by solving his problem? You bet I did!

Fees

A client relationship is a two-way street. What do I mean? A two-way street means when you give something, you get something.

I always tell my clients when you pay full fee, you get full service. When you pay a cut-rate fee, you get a cut-rate service. No matter what any recruiters have told or sold you, you get what you pay for. I make a certain profit at a full fee which keeps my firm alive. If a client says to me, "I will pay you two-thirds of that", the only way that I can make the profit is to cut my services by a third. I cannot give the same amount of time, effort, hours and service on a cut-rate fee that I give to full fee. It is impossible. If you try to do so without getting something back, it will cost you and your firm money. It goes against every basic business law and teaching. Your good clients will understand that if you will tell them so!

One of the great thought processes was developed by Jack Maxwell, the gentleman with whom I used to work. He had a little form that had thirty things on it that he did to earn his fee. When a client said to him, "We are going to pay you 20% instead of 30%", he pulled a form out and said, "Let me tell you the thirty things that I do to earn my fee. But since you are only paying me two-thirds of the going rate, I would like to fax you this list of thirty. If you would please review and mark off ten of them that I am not required to do, I would be happy to work with you at 20%."

It was a graphic way of showing the client that whatever they pay for, they get, regardless of what any recruiter is telling them. The law of business is that you can not put the same amount of service and effort into a lower-paying service, because you can not make a profit in doing so.

Exclusives

I had a client one time who was angry with me because I had sent some of the candidates he was interviewing to another company.

He said, "Larry, do you mean to tell me that you are working with me, yet you are not giving me exclusive looks at your candidates? You are shopping them to other clients and giving me competition?" I said, "Well, yes sir. I am." He asked, "Well, why would you do that?" I smiled happily, and replied, "Because you are not giving me an exclusive. I have other recruiters that are competing with me. Since my odds are low that I am going to make any money here, I have to protect myself in business. I will make a deal with you. Since I believe that a client-consultant relationship is a two-way street, when you give me an exclusive and use no other recruiters, then I will give you an exclusive interview with my candidates before I send them somewhere else."

Did I get exclusives from him? Yes. In fact, I had "set him up" by mentioning that my candidates were going to other firms. I made a few placements first, so he valued my services. Then I sprung the trap! Try it!

Guarantee

Don't let clients take advantage of you in your business. Do they want an extended cash refund policy? No chance! Don't start agreeing; start negotiating. Many in our business are shy about fees and sell the guarantee. Understand your worth to the client. Be proud of the fees you charge because you earn them.

I personally give no refund guarantee, but I will give a replacement guarantee for sixty days to replace the candidate if they lose them. But I am not going to refund their money.

You must finally understand your worth before you can go out and sell fees.

OUR VALUE

Our value to clients is in the economic investment they make, and the return that they make on that investment. We are not an expense to industry. We are an investment! They get a return on an investment in two ways by paying you your fees. You save your client's time. You bring talent to their organization that makes them money.

Moreover, you bring them top talent, not just what is available on the street or the public square of the internet. Through the talents of that candidate, they earn more money and the manager's career is greatly enhanced by a more productive staff. Your job is to recruit talent, not just to refer resumes.

You are a talent broker. You are the ***most important vendor that calls on any company***, because you as a talent broker directly generate a great return on investment. A top engineer can make a company millions of dollars; an average engineer can make them much less than that, and a poor engineer can cost them millions of dollars. You have to understand where your value lies. Explain to the client why they should invest in your services.

Clients frequently don't understand the monetary reasons behind the fees. You need to get out there (on the phone), look them right in the eye and explain the difference. When they use you, they get a great return on that investment.

How Do Clients Lose Money?

A client begins to lose money when they don't have that position filled. They runs ads, they look through all those resumes, they interview people that do not fit. They may go through word of mouth; they may slug through the unemployed, unhappy and unqualified internet referrals. The longer they wait, the more money they lose. The client goes for two or three months without the position filled, and loses tens of thousands of dollars. They end up using a recruiter, and still paying a fee.

Sometimes they don't use a recruiter. The result? They can end up losing hundreds of thousands of dollars! Ask any department manager or human resource representative what a bad hire costs the company. It will be ten to one hundred times your fee!

They need to use you from day one! Not three months later, when they have failed in all of their efforts. Tell them why! Timing is important; they need that chair filled now to start earning or saving money, depending upon what the job is meant to do. This is especially true when the position greatly impacts the bottom-line.

A very high-impact bottom-line job, sales manager, marketing manager, engineering manager truly has a dramatic affect on their firm. They can not afford to go any period of time without that person, and can't afford to hire second-rate talent. They need to hire a skilled well-trained recruiter who is willing to make the phone calls and go out there to find the best possible person, not just submit any resume that happens to be laying in their file or dredged up off the internet.

Sell your fees based on economics, and leave the fluff at home!

Fee Cutting or Fee Negotiating?

Is there a difference in fee cutting and fee negotiation? Yes.

Fee cutting is when you call a company and present a 30% fee and they tell you that they have another recruiter on it at 25% fee. You say all right, to get rid of the other recruiter and get the deal, I will go 20%. That is fee cutting, undercutting someone else's price to try and get the deal. That is not fee negotiating. Yes, sometimes we work a little below our full fee. But not much if you are smart.

Sometimes, however, the thought process is valid as long as you are <u>negotiating</u> your fee, not cutting it. Negotiating a fee means when you are giving something, you are getting something in return. You might get an exclusive. You might get client visits at <u>all</u> the locations to develop a relationship or multiple placements. Perhaps the President or top manager will send a letter to all of the firm's managers urging them to use you, and speaking well of your skill, professionalism, and track record with their firm. If you agree to reduce your income, then you should get something back. Quit agreeing and start negotiating.

When you negotiate fees and guarantees, if you have to give something, then get something back. Get exclusives, retainers, partial retainers, client meetings or written recommendations from top management to all managers out of it. But get <u>something</u> from it. Don't let yourself be taken advantage of by industry.

Retainer

The retainer may take more time, or the partial retainer. By this is meant, you charge one-third down and two-thirds contingency, plus expenses. What it does is fund you one-third of the fee, regardless of what happens. The client does not have the entire risk of the entire fee, but they do that commitment.

A full retainer is a bit different. Unlike contingency where you simply refer resumes or call up and present resumes, the client expects you to document strongly what you are doing for that retainer. They are not going to pay a retainer to someone who asks them how they would like the business done. They expect you to know the recruiting process and help them through it, so that they can hire the best person available. They will expect references to come with the resumes on the candidates that you refer. They may even expect you to travel to interview these individuals (at their expense). Sometimes when you get the partial retainer to fund the expenses upfront, you do not have to travel all over to see these people.

Why should a client do a retainer with you? How do you sell a retainer? The reason is the client has got to be one of those people who are tired of the contingency rat race, resumes, resumes, coming from every direction, conflicts, lots of phone calls etc. They want 100% attention by one firm and a focused effort on their search, so that they get top level service. They want top talent, not what is just available, and <u>no</u> problems.

It is very difficult to sell a retainer upfront when a company does not know you, or have any idea about you. You will have to use references to get that sold. Through your reputation or references, you build a relationship with a client that is willing to pay you that retainer. Frequently, you start with contingency, prove yourself, and work a client into retainer business.

Sometimes the only way to get the retainer business is to state that you <u>are</u> a retainer company, stand on it firmly and not do contingency with them. A partial retainer as stated above is to reluctant clients a lot easier than the full retainer.

It is worth remembering that, with very <u>few</u> exceptions, the top producers in our business are not retainer but contingency people. Don't let your ego interfere with your income! The ability to walk away from a troublesome client or assignment is, on average, worth <u>much</u> more that a one-third deposit which forces you to do far more than the assignment is worth. For most people, retainer is not the way to go, in my opinion. It may <u>sound</u> impressive, but is usually less financially productive despite the neat sound of it.

If you have a reluctant client, guarantee that if in thirty days that client is unhappy with your service or results, you will refund the one-third retainer that they paid you. People who use this technique almost never have to refund. Sell for the exclusive and the retainer if you wish, because they can not assure themselves top service or commitment <u>without</u> a retainer or exclusive. Explain that to them, and you will have more retainer and exclusive business.

Switching to Long-Term

The issues addressed in this chapter and the one before it need to be considered, contemplated, and truly understood before you launch your long-term Client Development campaign.

In the early stages of your career, there is much to learn. It is certainly true that your first step must be a solid foundation of understanding the mechanics of this business. Continued improvement of your industry-specific selling skills is a major foundational key to success, and will allow you to produce more and more revenue without additional time in the office.

Once some adequacy of technique is achieved, however, and the fees start coming in, you must add a long-term component to your thinking and methodology. This requires a true understanding of the philosophy of our business, pricing levels, what we have to offer, and how to sell it to serious clients to the benefit of all concerned.

Don't just "put deals together". That is obviously your first step, and you must continually improve in doing so. At some point, however, switch your thinking. Put a brilliant career together!

THE CLIENT DEVELOPMENT PROGRAM

25

*I*t would not be too far off the mark to think of Client Development as a baseball "farm team system". Your intent is to end up with a select group of absolute top-notch Major League Clients. However, you would not accord a young prospect the same attention as you would an All-Star. Neither would you treat a prospective client as you would a True Client.

Rather, you would put that young prospect in "Class D" league, also known as Rookie League. Then, depending on how he performed, you'd move him along to Class A, AA, or AAA. He ultimately might stall at a particular level and remain there. Or he might make the Majors.

Developing a prospect to the point of being a True Client is the same thought process.

The program you should develop has four different levels of clients. You are going to start them at one level and move them through all four levels until you have them in "the majors", getting their exclusive or multiple business and maybe retainers. Only by doing so can you achieve the group of consistent reliable repeat client you require for long-term success.

How Many Again?

When we discussed about how many do you need, we said between four and eight; that is true if you can get <u>multiple</u> <u>hires</u> from each of those clients. However, you may need <u>more</u> than eight if you work in a very narrow departmental specialty in which even a big company may only have two or three of the people that you would place. If you could work company wide, you may only need four or five clients. If you work departmentally, you may need five or six clients. If you work in a narrow department specialty with limited staff per firm, you may need twelve to fifteen clients to create enough on-going business to supply you with stability and income that you need.

The Four Files

The first step is to prepare four files and label them in four catagories. File one is to be labeled *Client by Identification*. File number two labeled *Client in Transition*. File three, is *Client in Development*. And file four should be labeled as *Clients and True Clients*.

What we are going to do is implement a methodology of identifying, acquiring, developing and retaining a solid client base. This program will put a least a dozen clients in your hip pocket over the next two years and set you up for permanent conspicuous success!

If you are developing clients, you are building a business. If all you are doing is making placements, you are only operating a practice. If you don't have many clients after five years in the business, then you don't have five years in the business; you have one year five times. This business should not be a hundred-yard dash every day... or every year.

You must break that cycle with a well-thought-out logical Client Development Program. Focus on learning how to move them through the different folders/stages until we get them to be a Client or True Client situation.

CLIENT BY IDENTIFICATION

Let us start with folder number one, Client by Identification. You need to go out and discover which clients seem to be worth working with, at least potentially. We do it sometimes the other way; we let the clients select us or give us the business. A logical thought process as to which firms we want to work with is needed.

Let us think about how we acquire clients to begin with. Where does every client come from? What is the very beginning of client relationships? The marketing call. As stated in early chapters there are options for skilled people with sophisticated industry-specific in-house training. I have seen this be very effective. But for most of us, we start with a marketing call. Generally, the way to begin this folder is to go out and market to one industry at a time.

A Client <u>Development</u> Call

Because of the way we are going to approach this, let's start calling these Client Development Calls. Think and focus on long-term client development. Market to one industry at a time. Industry knowledge is paramount when you are trying to deal within that industry. Develop it and dominate it for your own client development, and for income and stability.

Suppose I am going to open up the rubber industry. Is Firestone the top company in rubber? Or is it BF Goodrich? Who else? If I don't know, then I need to go and find out.

In each industry, there is an upper tier of companies, a medium or middle tier, and a lower tier. If you develop the habit of marketing to one industry at a time, you will begin to find out who is who. You can not have everybody in industry as your client; you have nowhere to get people. Determine who is on top and who is on the bottom. Anywhere there is a difficulty in placing people due to their intransigence with you and candidates reluctance to join them, there is an equal and opposite ease of recruiting people from that company. When you are going through your marketing, try to determine at which level this company resides.

Don't Be Fooled

The thing you must understand about your initial pass through those companies is that you could get fooled. Many times much of your immediate or initial searches will come out of the lower tier. They have more openings than anyone else, and need more help. You are getting initial orders from a company, but that does not make them an upper-tier company! You have to be careful.

The way to identify a lower-tier company is that they are fee cutters. They don't want to co-operate, don't want to use you and you are a last resort. They put barricades in your ways. You have to work with HR, send resumes and not call, all those things that make it difficult. Begin to identify those lower-tier companies.

Make the determination of who is going to be your client. Find out who the good companies are, and put them into your <u>development</u> program. The specifics for doing so and other purposes to be achieved will be found earlier in this book.

Total Objectives

Let's briefly review our objectives to the Marketing or Client Development Call. Remember that there are five objectives. When many people market, they only do the first two. The first objective of a marketing call is to get a send-out. The second objective is to get a search.

Add these <u>other</u> three objectives to your marketing call, and they will make your call more effective, build your business better, and support your Client Development Program. After your send-out and search objectives, number three is to gain industry knowledge about that particular industry that you are calling. Four, get client identification information to be able to tell you whether you want to pursue this company and put them on your list. Five is to get advertising for you and for your firm. Most of the advertising that we do is for candidates. We do very little advertising to clients that can give us openings that could earn us fees. This critical "on the phone" advertising is telling them who you are, what your company does, what your firm specializes in, sending them follow-up information letters, etc. This should be an important part of your marketing plan. Don't send "informative" e-mails, either unsolicited or "with permission". Over 50% of all e-mail is identified as "spam", and much of it is business-oriented. Don't think your website will do the job of you on the phone. It won't.

What you want to do is get a feel or flavor of the firm during this call, and impress upon the person your abilities and knowledge. Find this out what the company says about how many hires they make and how many <u>outside</u> hires they make through recruiters. How many people do they have in your specialty area?

If you find that they use recruiters and pay fees, but do not have an exclusive recruiter all the time, then they are a prime candidate for your potential (Client by Identification) list.

Frequently, of course, what you will find out about companies will cause you to never call them again. That's fine. Use a routine of calling that allows you to get all of these questions answered. You are going to present a candidate and find out if they need that person.

If you strive to achieve all five objectives on every marketing call, the amount of business that you generate will be much greater than just attempting one or two objectives. When you finish, don't keep these people on the phone for very long in a straight cold marketing call. The reality is that you might only get in one or two questions about the company or industry. You might get only a few questions about identifying them as a client. You may have to call them three or four times before you get enough information to determine accurately where they belong. Don't worry. Eventually you will.

After you contact and evaluate about fifty companies in one industry, make your decisions as to who are the top companies and who you are going to pursue. Then you can put them on your Potential Client-by-Identification List. These are a set of companies that you are going to do everything in your power to put into your hip pocket, and make them a client rather than a prospect.

Re-Call and Customer Lists

You will also put some on a Re-Call List, meaning you did not learn enough about this company to make your decision. <u>Continue</u> to call them till you do.

You are going to put some on a "Customer List", meaning they are <u>not</u> going to go into your Client Development routine. *Not every company can go in there! It just overloads the system, and causes it all to fail.* Be selective.

What do I mean by "Customer List"? This is a list of companies you can do business with, but it may be only once a year or every two years. You should still work with them, and still call on them. However, they are not going to go into heavy-duty Client Development. Why not? There is not enough business there to justify the time you would have to spend to make that happen. A raw unqualified prospect may be called a customer. Some move forward, some stay there, and some move back to our next list.

Obviously, you will also learn who some of the poorer companies are, as far as their morale, how they work and operate. They don't like using recruiters and you don't want the hassle of trying to completely turn them around. They go on your Source List. You have to know companies that you <u>don't</u> work with, as well as companies that you do work with.

TARGET PROSPECTS PER MONTH

During your marketing, identify minimally twelve great prospects per month to put into your Development Program. These are prospects that you have decided you are going to continue to develop and try to move them through our four folders.

Now we are working on our "Potential Client Identification folder" in identifying the companies we are going to put into the program. Again, don't overload it to the point that it becomes unworkable! Fifty a month is <u>not</u> better than twelve. It is worse.

Continue to put companies in there. It will take anywhere from six months to two years to fully develop the client.

Set up some sort of "tickle file", whether manual or electronic, to re-call the complete Potential Client-by-Identification list on a regular basis. It is imperative that this group of companies that you have identified gets a call from you <u>once</u> or <u>twice</u> <u>a</u> <u>month</u>, depending upon how often you think that you should contact them. Recruiters who work in Office Support will contact their "Potential Client List" more often then technical recruiters that have very few people in their speciality in that company. But don't be a pest! Don't call them too much, or eventually they are going to be tired of hearing from you and you reverse the process.

Information

As soon as you get some rapport with them, ask them for any or all public information that they are willing to send you. Get annual reports, products brochures, their other locations, their affiliates etc., anything that will tell you more about this company. Don't settle for "we have a website". You want more specific information, and just addressing an envelope (or their telling an assistant to do it) to send you material will serve effectively to fix you in their minds.

Make a file on these companies. Your homework is to review these so you can begin to become more familiar and knowledgable about the company and their products. The quicker that you can do that, the faster you can get them to start dealing with you. Your knowledge will be evident when you do talk to them.

If the company is a local one, you may want to consider an introductory visit now to get to know each other. Once you have visited a client, the difference in your phone rapport increases greatly. This meeting on introductions and "who I am" is <u>different</u> from a meeting that we are going to cover in a development phase. This would be just one to introduce our company and get to know them and ask a few questions.

Do not overdo this, and <u>only</u> do so at this stage with local companies. If you can get this meeting, it shortens the number of times that you have to call them to gain all the information that you need to decide whether to put them in the Client by Identification file. It is neither necessary nor wise to travel all over and spend your hard-earned money just doing introductory meetings with people. There are better times to invest time and money, as you will later see in this program.

We want to put these qualified people that we have identified in our "Potential Client by Identification list". They should stay there till you get your first search assignment from them.

CLIENT IN TRANSITION LIST

Once your first Search Assignment comes from that company, then they move <u>from</u> the "Potential Client by Identification List" to the next folder called the "Client In Transition". They have now been upgraded. You should transfer the firm from just one that we have identified into one that we are now going to work with. Since we have our first search, we have broken through to this company, and now have a possible chance to do business. Remember they have been <u>qualified</u>. All searches are <u>not</u> from "Clients In Transition"!

Sometimes the first order you get is not the greatest in the world. If it is the right sort of firm, however, for the good of your Client Development program, put out effort on this order. On your first order from a Client by Identification moved to the Transition List, fill it or perform well. You are going to have to do one of those two to get further chances down the road to progress to multiple hires. Everyone in your firm should do their best to help in transitioning that client into fees and work. You should make it a standard in your firm that everyone tries hard to get the right candidate in front of the company, once they pass from the "Potential Client By Identification" to the "Client In Transition List".

Try for an exclusive. You are probably not going to get it in the beginning, when the company really does not know you. But begin your education process early that the exclusive "use me only" is the best way for companies to get top service. Start that right now!

It may not always be possible. The company may have given this out to two recruiters by the time that you called. Give it a try. If you cannot, then you are going to have to compete and try to fill it.

Clients have certain service expectations and without asking, you don't know what those truly are. Find out.

THREE TYPES OF RECRUITERS

I have found in my teaching around the nation that there are three types of Recruiters in terms of the level of service that they provide.

Level One

First we have the Level One recruiters. This type of person just does "numbers". All they are concerned with is getting as many resumes in front of as many clients as they can. They e-mail to the point of "spam". They don't have time to qualify or take a genuine search assignment. All they are doing is putting resumes in front of people; they believe if they put enough resumes in front of enough hiring officials, something good will happen. Many of them believe computers are the way to success. Very little quality follow-up is done and poor closing skills are the norm. The main focus is just getting a placement started.

Level Two

Level Two recruiters do a little bit more in the search and take more information. They are also a little bit more in tune with the concept of qualifying. They try and send on-target candidates, not just any resumes that may happen to have a few buzz words on it. But they are still as numbers-oriented as can be to the exclusion of genuine in-depth skill, because that is the way that they have been taught. They would rather e-mail a resume than verbally present a candidate, though they won't admit it. They don't feel that they have the time to do a completely a full-blown screening and qualifying service. They rarely do true recruiting, preferring to rely on the internet, though they may claim otherwise. They are weak at following-up after the interview, and trying to get the placement made and then closed. While they are more adept at qualifying and send fewer resumes, they still are not what we would call the "full service" recruiter, by a wide margin.

Level Three

The Level Three recruiter is the one that is full service. They try for exclusives. They take search assignments, sell exclusives and retainers and then qualify. They present candidates. They also probably will only send two or perhaps three candidates per search to a client, and they will work with them to hire one of these. Those candidates are already qualified when they sent them. They have been qualified on the location, job, salary, requirements of the job status. The Level Three recruiter does that with these candidates so the client does not have to do so. They qualify up-front, both client and candidate. They do not simply send the resume, and then wait for the client to call back and say, "I like this individual".

They qualify each candidate <u>before</u> they send the paperwork. They send qualified candidates, not questionable resumes. They work hard to develop strong selling and genuine recruiting – frequently Direct – skills. They or their firms invest in training products, not just speaking programs, and they view or read these products repeatedly to get full benefit.

Expectation Conflicts

Many recruiters have conflicts with clients. Why? Well, perhaps you have clients that expect one level of service, and you are providing a different level.

For instance, have you ever heard of a client complain that all recruiters are nothing but paper-hangers? They say that we sling a bunch of junk against a wall in hope that some of it sticks, and do not do quality work. Why is that? Frequently, when you are talking to a client like that, you are talking to a client that has only been serviced by Level One recruiters. These are paper shufflers that are <u>only</u> numbers-oriented. They only make their money by shooting out as much as they can, and cluttering up the client with e-mail. This leads the potential client to think every recruiter is that way! You have to make them understand that you are not going to give them that kind of service.

Have you ever had a client who once you start giving them advice, draws into a shell, and will not talk to you? You can tell that they believe they are being pushed or sold. They are really not into your advice yet.

That is typical of a client who has been used to Level One service, and you are giving Level Three with appropriate advice on how to find and secure the best talent. They may feel in the end that you are just a pushy salesperson.

Avoiding Conflicts

How do you avoid conflicts? On that first order that is so important, ask what kind of service your client is used to receiving. How do they perceive the service that they want rendered? You can talk to them about the service that you do render, and how it is different. The two of you can compromise in areas, so the two of you are on the same track.

That is one of the most important things you can do to get off on the right foot on your first order. If you will talk to them about service and understand what they want initially, it is much easier for you to deal with and influence them at a later date.

Commit with "Clients In Transition"

Make a commitment to the client on your performance. If they have passed from the "Potential Client By Identification" to the next step, tell them what you are going to do. Say to them, "I am going to put down what I am working on now, and take care of you. I will have a candidate that matches your needs next week. Let me get to work on it, and I will call you back." Remember, these are qualified prospects and are worth the effort. Don't make promises on every search from every firm!

Don't be afraid to make commitments. One of the things that happens is it tells the client that you are serious about performing. It also puts a little monkey on your back, and is the kick we need to get off dead center and find the right candidate for the company.

As mentioned previously in this book, people who commit to an exercise program to the point of betting friends that they will stay with it, tend to do so!

Follow-up

Get back to the Client In Transition within 24 hours with some kind of new information. Many times you get a good potential client that gives out a search, and they don't hear back from the recruiter for three to four weeks. When they finally have a candidate, the recruiter calls. That perhaps good potential client doesn't even know that you are still working on it!

I myself was embarrassed once early in my career. I called a person one time after three weeks when I finally had a candidate, and he had forgotten that he had given me the order. It had been too long since I had called him back. Whose fault? It was mine.

Even if you don't yet have a candidate, get back to them with some kind of information or question. Tell them, "This is what I am finding out in the marketplace" or "I have been asked a few questions that I could not answer, so let me get more information about it." It lets them know that you are still working on it, and you are working hard and diligently. You will find a greater response in getting your phone calls returned or them accepting your phone calls if they know that you are putting in time and effort on the assignment that they gave you.

Make <u>value</u> presentations to these clients when you have candidates. Don't e-mail. Don't just read a resume. Qualify all the candidates before referring the resume. Let them know you have <u>recruited</u> this candidate or utilized your data base of people, and not just pulled someone off the internet.

Placements are made by the skills of the consultant. Period. Some placements might happen without skills, but not many. Developing clients is a <u>major</u> skill. Try to refer <u>the</u> candidate, not just <u>a</u> candidate, and you will find co-operation from your client.

These people <u>are</u> concerned about service and top candidates, even though they may not voice that over the telephone. They are truly tired of reading resumes with bloodshot eyes, and things just don't fit. They can weed through junk resumes by running an ad, or finding the same poor quality on the internet. They don't have to pay us 30% of salary for them. You are going to cause a client relationship to develop when you begin to refer candidates that save your clients time and have value. This makes them want to move forward, and work with you!

Keep Them Informed of Screen-Outs

Call them up and tell about a candidate that you have screened out. Tell them you want to verify that you are doing the correct thing. It is a great technique in letting the hiring official know that you are not just firing resumes at them, but are truly trying to find the right candidate.

Call them up and question them about qualifications. "I have a person here with this kind of experience, but not exactly the right degree. I wanted to ask if they have this experience, would this degree work? Or am I correct in screening them out for you? I really don't want to make a mistake on your behalf." When you have presented the wrong candidate and admitted to it, it raises their trust level.

Make sure your first candidate seriously presented, however, is on target. You will be judged on the first candidate that you send in. Your future opportunities to continue to work with these companies may depend on it.

These companies stay on this Client In Transition List until we close a placement and collect a fee, no matter how many orders that we work. Only when that is completed and the money comes in do they move to the next level in Client Development!

We'll discuss development of that one-time fee into a good solid repeat account in the next chapter. But it all starts right here.

POST-FEE DEVELOPMENT

26

Now that you have put a deal together with the client, you can start to get serious. They are no longer a prospect. They are a genuine client. Many of us speak of prospects with whom we have not done business as "clients". I do it, too. But it is incorrect and may cause us to think that way. *Only when we have collected a fee can they seriously be considered a real client.* We may have taken two or three searches from a prospect before we fill one. But no matter how many searches we take, just remember they are not a client until they pay us money! Only then can they progress to the next stage of Client In Development.

STAGE THREE - "CLIENT IN DEVELOPMENT" FILE

Now, however, we can launch a program to develop the client from one placement into multiple placements, so we can have a stable, efficient, profitable client base. This is an organized tracking effort that we have put together. At this point, it is worth putting in the time, effort, and, yes, money to develop specific companies into multiple-placement clients.

Not Your Only Source

Many placements that we make will not come from this list. Don't see this list as your total business effort. These four folders are your long-term development of clients effort.

You will still be out there marketing to people and making other placements with "customers" that will <u>never</u> be on your client list. That is the way it should be. On-going new client development comes from marketing calls, and there is nothing wrong with a few stray fees. We are, however, carefully taking a <u>selective</u> portion of the customers out there, and working with them until they become "clients". Then they go to the Development Stage, and finally to True Clients. The clients that we have on this list have given us a search and we have filled it. Now we are moving forward into multiple placements. When the search is complete and the fee earned, that is not the end.

Be flexible about your list. As mentioned, you will make many placements with firms which are not clients, but just customers. Reverse that too. Sometimes you will stumble across a potential client that you have never identified, have no background on, and have done no work with. They give you an instant order, and you have a rapport with the hiring official. You make a placement, and you say, "Gee, I would really like to work with this company." Add them right now to the Client In Development List.

In other words, the first time they come on a list is not at the beginning when we identified them, but actually they enter into the <u>third</u> folder, Client In Development. You have discovered them by making your first placement. But you <u>must</u> get a fee before they get in that folder!

Be flexible; use this not too rigidly, but as an organized methodology of identifying and developing these clients. The idea of the development list is getting more and more business from this particular company.

Developing The Client

Spend time in getting to know the company, product, and their business. If you are truly going to develop this company, then get to know them. Don't settle for internet research. Talk to the <u>people</u>. Take notes and add them to the file. The more you know about them, what they do, how they stand in business, the better you can talk shop and understand the actuality of what they are dealing with. Hiring officials not only want someone who is good at recruiting, but also who has real knowledge of what is going on in their company and business.

Be that person.

First Things First

Let us also remember that *your first step — and it is a long step — is to learn the mechanics of this business.* It is pointless to launch into an extended Client Development program if you are not organized, can't recruit well, market, or perform any of the foundational elements of our business with solid skill. Don't think about going out to visit clients until you have reached that level!

Nevertheless, once you have done so and proved it by <u>completing</u> a decent number of searches, the development program outlined here is critical to you for long-term success. Appropriate client visitation can be an important element.

Client Visit?

The best time for a client visit is now, immediately following the first placement. Remember, they don't go on this list until you make a <u>placement</u>. You may not always want to wait to collect a fee. Sometimes that can be thirty to forty days beyond the start date, and that is too late for this visit. Once the deal is put together, you can sit in their office with that feeling of co-operation that you have successfully completed an assignment together. You have their trust, you can talk to them and they will really listen to you. This is a critical developmental moment. Try to use this time. Go see them, and try to develop the client.

Even if you have to travel, an integral part of Client Development is visiting the company. Yes, I know that sometimes it is a long way. Sometimes I will put a trip together to a city and see that one client, and at the same time also see a couple more. The main purpose (and funding) is to solidly develop a client. But you can also touch base with others. You can double up the personal visits and it helps you in your client development, even though you would not travel to visit if a placement had not been made in the same city.

Let us face it. You can afford it now, because the company has just paid you a fee. Allocate a part of each fee from a "Client In Development" firm for the expenses that it takes. If you have a manager <u>and</u> you have completed multiple searches already, offer to split the cost. Don't expect your employer to assume it all. Remember that you will <u>not</u> allocate a part of each fee from every placement made to go visit. All firms are not entitled to Client Development. Each fee is not going to always be from a client, but maybe just from a customer. That's fine...but no client visit for them.

THE CLIENT VISIT

This particular visit has a very specific objective that you are trying to reach. It is not an introductory visit, but a <u>post-placement</u> visit with a client to be developed.

This visit will make a significant difference in how well you bring about the development of this client.

First, the meeting should be thirty minutes <u>maximum</u> in length. A person only works eight hours a day. An hour is one-eighth of their entire day. Extremely business-like corporate people or managers of departments don't have that much time to devote to small talk. Keep it thirty minutes maximum. Tell them when you call and set up the meeting that's how much time that you want. They may tell you that you can have more time, or they may even tell you that they have only fifteen minutes. Find out what it is and keep your meeting to that level. Thirty minutes is an acceptable meeting time. Sometimes it runs over thirty minutes, but only because they have <u>asked</u> you to stay.

If you truly utilize this meeting to begin to get the company person interested in what you can add to <u>their</u> productiveness and how we work together to achieve it, sometimes the meeting will go on. In fact, when it does, it is a clear sign that you have someone who truly wants to improve the quality of candidate and the hiring process, and have a good relationship with you.

Secondly, take a company brochure and a card, and leave it with that hiring official that you are meeting with. Even if you have previously mailed it before, leave something that they will remember this meeting by. Sometimes they don't have that material that you mailed them or it got filed. Don't say "here's our website". Leave something with them, so they will remember this meeting.

Don't do lunch if you can help it. They don't always expect you to spend money on them. A lavish lunch is in the movies. It is not expected, nor does it generally help.

The reason that you should have this meeting at their office is that you see them in their natural habitat. This is a time to observe their office and the company. Notice the kinds of people that are working there and get the atmosphere of the company. Getting the feel for the company that you can't get at the restaurant is absolutely helpful in future dealings.

If you have to do lunch, then don't drink. Period. I don't care if they do, and invite you to. Just politely say no. It is not good for your reputation, or where that conversation may lead after a few stiff drinks. Don't smoke. You never know the attitudes of the person. Don't talk politics, your preferences in team sports, religion or anything controversial that may turn this person off. We really don't know them well enough. You are there to enhance <u>business</u>, not to find a friend! The only good thing about lunch is you generally get an hour or more of their time.

Open with comfortable small talk. Get the hiring official relaxed, but get to business quickly. Remember, you have made a placement already. Do not spend valuable time talking about nonsense.

Improving the Process

Focus on the recruiter and hiring official relationship. However, it will be important to explain how improving that makes the process work better in terms of <u>value</u> to the client.

Talk about the exclusive, and why the client should let you work on some of the openings exclusively. Help him to understand that if three recruiters are on it, his company actually gets <u>reduced</u> service, not triple service! The service is reduced because the recruiters know that they only have one-third chance of making a profit, and two-thirds of losing the thousands of dollars of time, effort, and research invested. So they really put no time into it. They certainly don't recruit on it or spend many hours on it. If they have other exclusive assignments, that is where a recruiter will put his time. Any business person will invest time where there is ninety percent chance of profit, rather than a thirty-three and a third chance of profit.

<u>Explain</u> this to these people; this visit is about education. It is about helping your clients understand how the process works for their benefit.

How We Work

Always educate the client on how we work in terms of value to him or her. Don't just say, "I want you to return my phone calls, it is important. If you're going to work with me, you are going to respect me and return my phone calls." They don't care about you or what you need. They only care about what you need if it has <u>value</u> to them.

Emphasize that the best candidates have a short shelf life. They have other recruiters chasing them and other opportunities out there. You can never control when someone is going to come after this candidate. Tell the client that even though they might be very busy, take the time to return your phone call.

"Give me a quick buzz for a couple of minutes. You may miss the top candidates and let them get taken by someone else, because you did not return my phone call quickly enough, and we could not get something done for a period of days. I won't call you if it is not important. But please be prompt in returning my call if you want to be protected against losing the best candidates."

Stress to them why this is important.

Attracting the Candidate

Talk about how the process will improve as the two of you work together. One of the things we want to do is to teach our hiring officials how to be better at this game of recruiting good candidates. Most of them do not really know how to go about attracting top talent. We are not, of course, going to teach them how to recruit in place of us. Speak of "recruiting" from their standpoint as drawing the best players to their team, the way a football coach might do. Teach them how to work with us so the process becomes smoother and more effective. By doing so, they secure a better candidate for their department and company.

An Example

Here is what you might say to a "Client In Development"

"I want you to help me recruit the best candidate. So I am going to give you more intelligence about the candidate that you are interviewing that you normally get. Rather than just a resume, you are going to get information from me about what the candidates really like. What are they looking for? What are their values? Why are they considering leaving their position? And I am going to ask that you tell them some of the things in that interview that they will <u>want</u> to hear from your company.

What I am trying to do is enlist your help in <u>exciting</u> the candidate about your opportunity. We are going to work on the interview process to make you a better recruiter for your team. The top candidate must walk out highly interested, and go to work for us rather than your competitor. If we don't manage the process correctly and allow them to get away, then we have lost the top candidate and our only options is to hire second-best. That would be a loss to both of us."

Impress upon them that you know what you are doing as a recruiter, you know the hiring process, and will help them to achieve their goals of the most productive addition to their staff. Quit asking clients what <u>they</u> want to do on searches. That is why they hired <u>you</u>. <u>You</u> are the one that says, "This is how we are going to recruit this person, and here is the next step". Then help them manage it. At the end, the best candidate is going to work for them and will say "yes". That is where your worth is; show them your worth, and help them through the placement process.

Teach them that there is nothing more fun or more profitable for a hiring official than learning the important process of bringing the best talent to his team. Soon clients will be saying, "Larry, what about this guy and how do we handle him?" Or, "What do you think we should do next?" This is a person that is in tune with the process, and knows that you know your business. They will use you from then on, when they learn that.

<u>No</u> Searches

DO NOT take a search assignment on this visit. You have just wasted the objective of this visit if you sit there and fill out a form. You have wasted the thirty minutes that you got to develop this person. Even if they offer you an assignment, then say "Great! Let us finish this meeting on our relationship and how we can work better to improve your results. I will give you a call when I get back to the office, and I will take the specifications down then on the search that you want me to handle."

On Time

Don't over stay your welcome, unless invited. You committed to the time allowed that you and the hiring official agreed on. Know what your time is, get all of your things done, get up and say, "I've finished my time, and I promised you thirty minutes." It is a statement of professionalism when you do that. It helps them to understand that you do what you say, and that always helps. They have seen so many recruiters who don't wrap it up right.

Close Them!

Tell them that you <u>want</u> their <u>business</u>. How many times do we tell candidates to ask for the offer at the end of the interview? Then why don't we ask for the business? Don't just be general. Tell them explicitly what you are there for. When you are shaking their hand at the exit, look them right in the eye and use whatever statement feels comfortable. You are there to get to know them. You are there to become the recruiter that they use <u>all</u> <u>the</u> <u>time</u> when they have needs. Tell them that you are a highly knowledgable search consultant who is willing to put forth the effort and time to earn that respect and that business. Then go do so!

Finish it correctly, walk out with a smile, and then send them a "thank you" card for the time. Make sure that that you thank them for the time, and they will frequently thank <u>you</u> for the information! It is a great and powerful meeting when done correctly and will significantly help in moving to the next stage.

FORMING THE CLIENT

There are some critical areas that you should talk to the hiring official about that will help you in placement making. It is better to do this kind of talking to hiring officials <u>before</u> the problem occurs. When you let a problem occur, you try and resolve it. However, if you have not discussed it in advance of the problem, you are forced to get them on the phone, and kind of slap their hands for it.

It is different when you talk about it upfront and try to approach it that way. It is better to form someone's mind than it is to change it. Do this in advance of the happening rather than waiting for it to happen and then going in and trying to correct the problem.

Keys To Improvement

There are five things that your hiring official should do that will help you make and close more placements. Beyond assisting them to obtain better candidates, these keys will dramatically improve your closing ratio. Is your send-out-to-placement ratio eight to one, or six to one? Those are good ratios. There is nothing wrong with that. But a top closing ratio is four or five to one. If it gets too much lower than that overall, it is a sign that you are not expanding your client base continually, or are being too selective. But four or five to one is reasonable.

With True Clients that will use you and listen, work with you and give exclusives, your closing ratios with those firms will go down to as low as two to one. It is an amazing difference in how much money you make per hour of work once you <u>develop</u> a True Client.

Here are five things that will help you with your client. Motivating them to co-operate in these areas will help you in the future to make multiple placements.

One, get them to return calls promptly. When you make phone calls to people and they consistently put you off, never call back, or sometimes get back in a couple of weeks, they always have excuses for priorities or problems. They are telling you that they really don't want to deal with you. <u>Confront</u> them on this, but make it a <u>value</u> to the hiring official to get him to talk to you.

Two, try to get a 24-to-48 hour turn around on resume submittals, if resumes are manadatory. In theory, you should avoid them. In practice with <u>clients</u> (not new firms), they may be necessary. You lose placements when hiring officials allow resumes to lay in their in-basket for weeks without anything ever happening. Talk about that <u>upfront</u>. <u>Explain</u> to them how they are going to lose people if they don't give you a quick turn around. They can not expect to come back to you after weeks and weeks, and have the candidate still be available or even interested.

Thirdly, have them give you feedback on rejected candidates. Don't let them say, "That candidate did not work", and that is all that they will tell you. Find out <u>why</u>. The <u>value</u> to them is it will help you screen future candidates, so that their time is not wasted sending the same incorrect candidate because you did not know why the candidate was incorrect in the first place.

Four, have them commit to quick decisions and actions on interviews and hires. I said <u>actions</u>. Just because they say they will give you a quick decision does not mean they will act on it quickly. If they say, "Yes, I want to interview this candidate, but I can not act on it for three or four weeks," you know that you have serious problems. Same thing with the hire or the offer. It will be of <u>value</u> to them if they do so, in enhanced likelihood of obtaining a top candidate's services.

Finally, have them give you complete information on all aspects of the assignment. Make sure they are co-operative enough that they will talk at length about their problems, where they are headed, and what this person needs to do. Work with complete information.

Can you accomplish these things? Absolutely! That's why you qualify first (Client by Identification). One of the qualifications is whether this hiring authority is serious about bringing the best talent to his team. If he is, he will listen to you explaining how he can better accomplish that goal, and will be happy to improve his own methods to so do. That is what is meant by "forming the client".

Once your client is doing those five things, it will make the placement cycle much easier and you will close more of them, which will make the client happy. Everyone wins!

Expect Drop-Outs

One thing I want to say about clients. It is possible to push too hard on this "top-candidate" thought process, knowing they make the company the most money. It is true that these candidates give the company the highest return on investment for our services. But sometimes you will run up against mediocre companies that want to hire mediocre people; it is very difficult to sell them on this thought process. Sometimes you may have a top candidate turned down, or not even be interviewed by a client.

What you will find at times is that the <u>client</u> does not have the experience or credentials of the person that you are bringing to them. That person may be a threat to them. Many times mediocre companies are looking to hire average people, someone who will be able to punch the time clock and be dependable. The selling of "top candidate" may not always go over well with all companies.

You have to keep in mind that you are working to develop the top tier of high-morale, highly-profitable type companies. That is why we identify them and try to put them in our Client Development program. This process <u>works</u> with that type of high-performance companies that want those kinds of people. However, while you should expect drop-outs from your Client Development program, don't eliminate these firms from occasional calling. Such firms are not your future, but picking up an extra fee here and there also has merit.

Placement Improvement

Placement improvement is defined by where we are in the process . We have made one placement, made a visit to our client, and talked about areas that would work better. Let us say that we have obtained another couple of assignments. Maybe we have filled them or maybe we are working on them. Keep emphasizing the five keys to improvement.

They must view you as the recruiter who can manage the process that allows them to hire the top candidate. What you are going to do now is teach these hiring officials areas of placement improvement. Work on their skills to get the top candidate hired.

Remind them that improvement of the process that you and the hiring official go through will yield a "yes" from the top candidate. If you don't end up with an acceptance from the top candidate, you either have to start the search all over again, with no assurances that you will find anyone better. Or you have to hire second choice. Period.

The constant talk to your hiring official of how critical it is to him or her that you hire the top candidate who will make them the most money and best help their career is the key. You have to instill in them a desire to not hire just anyone walking in off the street.

Key To The Hire

Teach your hiring official that you need to determine a "Key to the Hire". If we are going to decide on a particular candidate, then let us identify that candidate.

Many in our business are troubled by procrastinating hiring officials. They procrastinate out of fear of hiring the wrong person. The reason is they are worried about hiring the wrong person. Frequently, they have not set down the parameters of what the right person would even look like! Help them understand that a "Key to the Hire" is one specific technical aspect. Every job has within it is one technical area that would help the company more than anything else. Help them to think of what is it.

This helps you significantly in completing the search, because it helps you identify and present the right candidate. Many hiring officials don't make decisions because they have three or four really good candidates, and do not know what to do! They can not tell them apart.

Another good way to ask this question, is "How would I recognize the right candidate if I had three that looked just alike? What technical aspect of their background could I go into, so I know that I have the perfect candidate and not just one of the candidates?" Help them get into the habit of identifying the right candidate.

Attracting Candidates

Teach these hiring officials how to attract a candidate. Every candidate in the world has one thought when they go into an interview, and that is "what is in it for me?" Candidates get excited about companies who resolve their current pain or reason for leaving. Find out what it is about this candidate that is causing him or her to consider a move, and transmit that to your hiring official.

Tell the client to take the majority of his time asking questions and interviewing. Clearly, the first step is to ascertain whether this is a good candidate for the position available.

But at the end, I want the client to say, "Let me tell you a few things about our company before you leave." At that point, based on your coaching, the hiring authority should tell the candidate things about the company that relate to the candidate's Reason for Leaving or concerns in his present position. If the candidate never gets the information, then he can never be excited.

I had one old hiring official that I was trying to teach this to who said, "Larry, I don't want to sit there and beg these people to work for me. By gosh, if they want a job, then they can just come in here and go to work for me." I said, "You know, Chuck, you are terrific in your field. I like working for you, and I'm very supportive of your company. But you want to know something? If your local University coach recruited halfbacks the way you recruit people, he would never win a football game. In fact, he probably would not even last as a coach. The word recruiting does not mean hiring, it means recruiting. It means that top talented people have other offers, and for us to compete for their services, we have to do things that cause them to be interested in us rather than some where else. Otherwise, you'll lose that top player to the other team. Is that what you want?"

This sort of explanation works well for hiring officials who do not understand the difference between a looking-for-a-job applicant and a top-quality in-demand candidate.

Consultant As Advisor

Once you get yourself into that advisory role, you have much more effect on the outcome of the placement. When you start having a <u>lot</u> of effect on the outcome of the placement, you will make a lot more.

Tell the hiring official why you must be involved at the hiring stage. Explain to him that you know the candidate and can go to them and check out their thought processes. By working together, you can <u>help</u> the hiring official put together the right offer and secure the right candidate.

Make sure the client will give you co-operation in solving eleventh-hour problems. The client may have to fly the spouse in to see the city before acceptance. There may be problems in finding schools for the children or local connections on hobbies. More information may be required, or additional meetings or phone conversations with others in the firm may be indicated to assuage concerns or answer questions. The client should not force the candidate to give a decision until the true problem-solving is done so they can move forward. Make it clear that you can help as a liason to the candidate. He must know that you are an experienced thinker in solving these problems.

Theodore Levitt, renowned Harvard Business School marketing professor, is the author of the groundbreaking article *"Marketing Myopia"*. It is a foundational study in most business strategy classes in MBA programs. He describes good marketing, like good selling, as "focusing on the needs of the buyer" and emphasizes that "an organization must think of themselves as <u>buying</u> customers by doing the things that will make people <u>want</u> to do business with it". Helping selected clients to achieve their goals is a good example of this.

As you work through these future assignments and the teaching process, you will see a respect for your talents developing between the two of you. A trust relationship will form between you and the hiring official. The two of you will become a team trying to find and acquire the top talent. It will give you a high-performance reputation and, once it is taught, you will make many more placements.

It will also give you much more repeat business. The client loves working with someone who knows the process so well that they can lead him through to a good ending.

This will also lead directly to exclusives. It is the one thing that will cause a client to want to use you and you only. They will not want to fool with the paper shufflers or internet hustlers. They will become tired of the resumes coming in there that are wrong, tired of the recruiters that are not recruiters, tired of paying fees for candidates they could find on their own. Very soon you will begin to get exclusives, because they see you as a major value to them.

CLIENT LIST! THE FOURTH LEVEL

When you have made your <u>third</u> placement with a client, you can now move them off the Client In Development list and put them in the fourth folder or the Client List.

They go on the Client List when they have three things.

We have made multiple placements with them, and think we will continue to do so.

They call us.

They are co-operative and listen to our advice.

True Clients

We also have another group within that fourth folder that I call "True Clients". These are people that we have developed a little further and they are the "All-Stars" in our Major League client team.

They are people that will give us exclusives and retainers.

They will be a reference to other corporate officials who are interested in using us.

They refer business to us.

Once you get those <u>additional</u> three, then you have a True Client.

By following this program continuously, remembering to frequently add new prospects to our beginning level, you will take many from our first "Class D" client farm team up to True Client All-Stars with consistency, confidence, and maximum production results!

Multiple Contacts

Make <u>sure</u> that you get to know more than one person in the company. You really don't have a client as a company if you only know one hiring official. If that one hiring official leaves that company, you will <u>lose</u> that company! The next person that comes in may never use or know you, even if your original contact leaves a file on you. Try to get to your client's boss somehow without injuring the relationship with the primary hiring official. Go as high in the company as you can to get to know people. If that person leaves, you can retain the client's business because you know other people in the company.

Personal Touches

Steve Finkel recommends in his outstanding book *"Breakthrough!"* that you try and get to know birthdays or hobbies, spouses or kids names, and find out from the secretary particular information of this nature. He also suggests you send them a personal birthday card. This is not a corporate card or even anything to do with business, just a nice card so they remember that they are a real person to you.

If they comment that they have returned from a vacation, ask where, why they went there, and what they did. If they have hobbies, then you can send them articles on the subject. If the client has a dog or cat, find out the breed! Send a card occasionally with that breed on the front of the card. Don't over do this! But it is a nice touch and a good idea.

If you can call up someone and say, "Hi Bill. How is John doing in baseball? You said it was his first year? Tell me how it came out?", you tighten the relationship. No one likes to talk about anything more than their children or dogs. The fact that you are interested will give you a step up that really helps to solidify the relationship between you.

Social Activities

Don't just talk business with these people. Find out if they are involved in active social/hobby activities (party, golf course, tennis courts, workout room) or wherever it is that you might meet them. Take them, pay for it, entertain them. Again, we are talking Clients to True Clients <u>only</u>.

However, don't start by talking business. Let them bring it up. They will.

As an example, I am a golfer. So are many of my clients. I take people out to play golf. They can't stand it when we just play, and about the third tee they have to start talking business. I think, "Well, hey, if you brought it up, then it is not a problem!" Socializing appropriately and treating them as a person in the end will help you.

Professional Distance

It is important, however, to keep your professional distance. Socialize yes, but friends and lovers do not make good business associates.

Don't have clients over to your home. Don't have business talks at parties involving a lot of drinking where things can go wrong. You may go to their home, but watch your manners when you do. You may take to them to social places, but don't get involved heavily, either on a friendship or lover basis. If you decide you have to do that, then drop the business aspect and go somewhere else for your business.

Keep your professional distance, or the professional relationship will crumble.

Give Away a Candidate

Occasionally, it is worthwhile to give away a candidate to a client that you would never place and they would not pay for. Let us say they have an opening entry-level position. You don't deal with that, but you have someone in your file. Refer them, set it up, and tell the client that they don't owe you anything. Believe me, they will pay you back ten-fold, especially if you tell them they don't owe anything. Clients are a two-way street. Do them a favor.

Obviously, I am not saying give away placements. But when it monetarily has no value to you, don't be afraid to refer a candidate. Even the offer to do so will help.

Send information to them, articles or anything that can impact their business once you learn what their business is. Anything that can help them, will help you.

Reference Letters

When you reach the point of three placements with a given firm, it is worth-while to request a letter of reference.

To do so earlier serves little purpose, since the reality is that anyone can "luck into" a placement or a good candidate. Such letters will be ignored by prospective clients (and should be) if they reflect a single placement. If you have a website, you may wish to excerpt quotes from single-placement letters (like everyone else) to clutter it up. Don't use quotes from a letter to send to potential clients via e-mail, or you'll get a "spammer" reputation.

Multiple searches completed, however, are a different story. Beyond their obvious real significance to prospective clients, the very fact of <u>writing things out</u> will help to <u>fix</u> your worth and merit in the client's mind! *Morever, if this hiring authority should leave, a letter of reference will allow you to retain the account with the successor.*

If the client asks you to write it out and he or she will sign it, do so! And don't be shy about emphasizing value on a basis of comparison to others.

Send Them Business

Send business their way if you can. If you are dealing with a consulting firm and you know a client that can use them, put them together. Any time you put money in their pocket, I guarantee that they will put money back in your pocket.

I want to repeat that these advanced techniques on development and retention are for <u>after</u> you have developed the business and you are <u>already</u> doing business with them. It is the small add-on touches that will make these people into long-term and good clients for you. It is so much easier to work with a client than it is to work for a customer.

Start Now!

Set a goal today to start this program. Develop twelve clients over the next 24 months. It is a constant process and you must keep this program going, because you will lose some clients along the way. You can't just make three or four clients and quit this program. This program requires <u>constant</u> add-on to your business.

There is nothing other than your skill at this business that will help you to stay highly successful long-term like this four-file program of upward mobility for clients!

Get organized and do this step-by-step. Get your folders in line and build a stable and highly profitable business base for your desk, for your firm and for your lifetime career. This is how you do it.

PERFORMANCE TIME

27

*T*his book would be incomplete if it did not address a critical problem with which many in our industry struggle. While desk organization and sales skills are absolutely paramount, you won't get the most out of them if your effectiveness is reduced by time away from the office, or being in the office, but not on the phone.

Let's take a look at a normal year, and see what happens to many who don't pay attention to the minutes, hours, and, yes, days in which they don't get full results. Note the results of on-going inattention to this critical topic.

How many times have you heard the phrase "time management"? Well, I contend time management is the wrong phrase! Rather than talking about how you "manage" it, I'd rather address how you spend it.

In understanding this concept, let's drop the term "time management" and re-label it "behavior management." Since everyone has the same time available, the critical question is "which behavior do we choose to exhibit during the time available?"

This chapter is entitled "Performance Time" to remind you that only eight of our 24 hours are available for performance. We must work when our paying customers work, which is generally 8:00 A.M. to 5:00 P.M. minus lunch. Yes, we can recruit and re-qualify candidates all evening if we choose, but our paying customers' (clients') time is limited in terms of our ability to reach them. Some in our industry call the East in the morning and West in early evening, and stretch their available time to a 10-hour day. But for these purposes, we'll discuss a normal eight-hour work day.

Let's examine some of our "behavior management" during a regular work week and see what it costs us over a period of a year.

These behaviors we are about to discuss are not "problem behavior" traits, but are the normal ways many of us utilize our time. Observe what happens, however, when we do.

There are approximately 264 working days in a year based on approximately 22 working days in the average month. Two hundred and sixty five days is what you have to accomplish all of your results, and thus achieve your dreams. But how do you utilize them? Let's look at working days <u>lost</u> over a period of a year.

✓ 1.   Two weeks vacation is 10 days lost.
✓ 2.   Average sick days = 6 days a year.
✓ 3.   15-minute break in morning and afternoon is 16.25 days lost.
✓ 4.   One 30-minute errand a week is 3.25 days lost.
✓ 5.   Average 10 minutes before lunch and 10 minutes after lunch (whether you leave the office or not) is 10.83 days lost.
✓ 6.   Family emergencies and special events or holidays we didn't include average 6 days a year.
✓ 7.   15 minutes late to work once a week is 1.62 working days.
✓ 8.   Personal calls, business and general ineffectiveness of 30 minutes a day is 16.25 days gone.
✓ 9.   First 30 minutes of the day in hellos, coffee and office gossip is 16.25 days lost.

If we add up these times, it amounts to 86.45 days lost a year because of these habits. So if we subtract 86 ½ days from 264 we have 177.5 days left. Divide that by 22 days per month, and there are only 8 months that we *even have available* for our work.

Now, if we are less-than-productive during that 8 months (unenthusiastic presentations, no daily plans, not selling hard, calling dial-a-prayer), then we can see that ***many of us are producing our year's volume in less that six months time!***

Some of us do not exhibit all the traits listed. I do not mean to be critical. However, some have even more. The idea is to understand the <u>compounding effect</u> that any sloppy habits have on our yearly performance.

A great sales trainer, Zig Ziglar, once said that top people become that way by not only determining what they will do in a day, but by also determining what they will *not* do! What about you? Will you *not* interview walk-ins if they are not qualified? *Not* come to work late? *Not* take personal calls during prime time? *Not* delay hitting the phones early? *Not* get distracted by office chatter? Each of those decisions have a significant and positive impact on your bottom line.

Ziglar, in his extensive book *"Secrets of Closing the Sale"*, quotes a number of studies indicating that "the second leading cause of failure in the sales profession is improper utilization of time." The average securities broker according to many authorities spends less than two hours a day on the phone, the <u>same</u> amount as mediocre performers in our industry!

"There are two major reasons for this", writes Ziglar. *"First would be a disregard for, or lack of expertise in, the field of time management. Second could be a shortage of energy which causes the salesperson to start the day late, end it early, and go at less than full speed during the day. A focused professional salesman is always a time miser."*

Further reading and concentration on this subject will benefit you enormously. It is absolutely essential to learn the industry-specfic selling skills that will yield you massive success. However, what good is it to be The Best Alive in our industry if you are not maximizing your skills by good work habits?

Paying close attention to performance-based behavior management requires no special training and is available to every consultant tomorrow. As we saw when we reduced a 264-day work year based on poor work habits, *it is possible to increase production by 50% or more just by tightening up and focusing in this area.* Become professional in your work habits. Don't expect $200,000 in production for $100,000 worth of effort!

The combination of this <u>plus</u> continual and effective skill improvement, though, will yield production you may not have even imagined. We have the business in which you can achieve your goals …. and then some!

AFTERWARDS

28

*A*nd so it ends, at least in terms of your reading of this book. I hope you've underlined or high-lighted as you've read it or, if not, that you'll do so on a second reading. This book will surprise you.

If you're new, you'll find things here with every single reading that you've overlooked. You'll be a different person professionally after as little as a month in this business, and different again at six months and a year, and at two years and ten years.

If you're an experienced search consultant, we both know there are a lot of things here you used to do, meant to do, were told to do by your manager — but that you've just drifted away from, or never fully implemented. And frankly, you too will find many new ideas here. You don't have to admit it to your business associates. But you can't kid me! You too should underline or high-light this book….and read it again once you do so at regular intervals.

This is a remarkable industry. Make the most of it! I've seen the techniques presented here and in the products I've recommended turn former secretaries and school teachers into wealthy people. Those with no business experience have become top executives running large search firms. Former engineers and IT people can become good salesmen tripling their previous earnings as a result, and those who have a good sales background already will see an industry which, once they learn it, will allow their background to translate into major money. And all of this is done while helping corporations to solve problems, corporate managers to achieve better results, and candidates of all types to a happier and more successful career! Professionally, what could possibly be finer?

If you're in a boom market as you read this, you know how terrific our industry is. My only advice is to keep learning and to improve your skills.

The reason our business experiences shrinkage in every Recession is that too many of our practitioners, to borrow on an old Wall Street joke, "confuse brains with a Bull Market". They generate a good income, think they know it all, and quit learning. Such "training" as they do is really just hearing marginal speakers…and they probably don't pay much attention even there. Don't let it happen to you.

One of the wonderful things about our industry is that it affords an opportunity to utilize all of your intellect. It seems redundant to say that what causes boredom is lack of challenge, but it is accurate. The same thing day-after-day with no sense of progress except monetary may nourish the bank account and lifestyle, but is soul-destroying at work. If intellectual and professional challenge interests you, then you came to the right place!

THE FUTURE OF SEARCH

The oldest continously owned and operated "employment agency" in the United States, B. Loehr Employment in St. Louis, is over 100 years! Still in business and still doing well.

The Employer-Paid-Fee business which predated real search and recruiting is over fifty years old.

Our business has seen some slow times during Recessions. But guess what? With no exceptions, our industry has come back stronger, better, with higher per-desk-averages, higher average fees, and higher per-office production than before the Recession...every time!

And as this is written, we stand on the verge of our greatest times ahead.

Why? No secret. Population trends. The giant Baby Boom generation of 1946-1963, 78 million of them, ain't kids any more. They currently hold down the vast majority of positions in corporate America. And following them, in the next 17-year time-frame, we have the Gen X-ers, 43 million of them, to fill the same positions now held by the 78 Million boomers. You are already seeing the leading edge of this situation. For the decade of 2000 to 2010, workers 55 and over will increase by 77%, four times the rate of those from 25 to 54. The oldest boomers will start retiring in 2008. And it will continue, fewer and fewer qualified candidates to fill corporate positions, for 17 years! Hmmmm… Long-term labor shortage, anyone?

Now it is certainly true that some factors will have minor influence on our industry. But it is also true that we always hear of "sea changes" that are going to harm our industry from nay-sayers, hand-wringers, or hustlers looking to sell a product. The reality is that these things are relevant only in specific niches rather than in the broad market of American industry or the economy at large. Our business environment will <u>always</u> be in a state of flux, constantly undergoing transition. But the skills you possess give you the ultimate ability to adapt, to adjust, to be quick-on-your-feet, and prosper greatly in <u>any</u> market!

If you were ever in a position of being in the right place at the right time in the right industry....well, welcome to the Boom Market that's coming! Congratulations!

AND IN CLOSING...

It has truly been an honor and a privilege to be in this wonderful industry for so many years. As unlikely as it may seem, what makes me happy is helping people. I did it as a Search Consultant, as Manager of multiple firms, as Director of Training for a major franchise, and as an independent speaker and trainer all over three continents. And now, as Author. Perhaps that will have even the greatest impact. You never know.....

I hope you'll read this book over and over. If you want the "real me", I do have audios, and I've recommended some other excellent products as well. Don't just be good in this business. Be great!

And here's something you can do for yourself. When you see someone who you think would be right for this business, tell him or her about it. I've recommended this business to many who have had a fine career as a result. This book will give them a much better sense as to whether they are right for this business.

The other thing you can do is help someone who is struggling in this business. You don't have to actually coach them. That's the manager's job. But we all have doubts in our early years. And a little encouragement goes a long way. I have never been reluctant to recommend the truly excellent products of others that will increase production. I do so in this book, just as I do in public speaking or training programs. You shouldn't be either. This book or other products mentioned here may spell the difference between success and failure to a struggling recruiter. Don't tell him to "read it"; tell him to buy it, and then to underline and high-light it! It doesn't hurt you to help others; it is the best thing you can do for <u>both</u> of you.

When you find something good, whether it be this book or this wonderful industry, don't keep it to yourself. Pass it on! Just as I have to you…

With confidence and warm best wishes to you personally for great success in the best business in the world,

Larry Nobles

Further Education

For information on additional material in audio, video or book formats designed to increase your production, visit the following websites:

www.larrynobles.com

www.stevefinkel.com

or call

314-991-3177

HAVE YOU BORROWED THIS BOOK?
Buy your own, and <u>Explode</u> your Production!

Search and Placement! A Handbook for Success

ORDER FORM
Please cut with scissors on dotted line or send information to below address.

TELEPHONE ORDERS: (314) 991-3177: Have Visa, American Express, or Mastercard ready.

POSTAL ORDERS: Placement Marketing Group
         P.O. Box 410412
         St. Louis, Missouri 63141 USA

FAX: International <u>Only</u>
(country code) (314) 991-5071

PRICE:
        1 – 5 Books $45.00 U.S. each
        6-23 Books $35.00 U.S. each
        24 or more   Call for quote.
                    Volume discounts available.

SHIPPING: USA <u>Only</u>.
         Per Book <u>Airmail</u> - $3.50 U.S.

         International – Airmail
         Canada, Mexico $ 7.00 U.S. per book
         Europe $ 15.00 U.S. per book
         Australia, South Africa, Asia $ 20.00 U.S. per book

Note: International shipping in 24 book (case) increments is far less expensive. Call for details.

(OVER)

Please Print Legibly

Name: _____

Title: _____

Company Name: _____

Address: _____

State: _____ Country: _____ Zip/Postal Code: _____

Phone Number: _____

Size of Firm: 1-2 _____ 3-5 _____ 6-10 _____ 11 and over _____

Sales tax: 6.5% books shipped to Missouri addresses.

MAKE CHECKS PAYABLE TO: **Placement Marketing Group**

Payment: __ Check __ American Express ___ Money Order
__ Visa ___ Mastercard

Note: On International Credit Card Orders, banks will make automatic conversion to your currency.

Credit Card Number: _____

Name on card (Print): _____

Signature: _____

Expiration Date: _____ / _____

Please process the following order:

Total:

Books _____ at _____ Each $ _____

Shipping: $ _____

Sales Tax (Missouri Orders Only: 6.5%): $ _____

Overall Total: $ _____

A GIFT FOR A FRIEND OR NEW CONSULTANT
Help Them to Succeed!

Search and Placement! A Handbook for Success

ORDER FORM
Please cut with scissors on dotted line or send information to below address.

TELEPHONE ORDERS: (314) 991-3177: Have Visa, American Express, or Mastercard ready.

POSTAL ORDERS: Placement Marketing Group
P.O. Box 410412
St. Louis, Missouri 63141 USA

FAX: International Only
(country code) (314) 991-5071

PRICE:

       1 – 5 Books $45.00 U.S. each
       6-23 Books $35.00 U.S. each
       24 or more Call for quote.
                  Volume discounts available.

SHIPPING: USA Only.
Per Book Airmail - $3.50 U.S.

International – Airmail
Canada, Mexico $ 7.00 U.S. per book
Europe $ 15.00 U.S. per book
Australia, South Africa, Asia $ 20.00 U.S. per book

Note: International shipping in 24 book (case) increments is far less expensive. Call for details.

(OVER)

Please Print Legibly

Name: _____

Title: _____

Company Name: _____

Address: _____

State: _____ Country: _____ Zip/Postal Code: _____

Phone Number: _____

Size of Firm: 1-2 _____   3-5 _____   6-10 _____   11 and over _____

Sales tax: 6.5% books shipped to Missouri addresses.

MAKE CHECKS PAYABLE TO: Placement Marketing Group

Payment: __ Check __ American Express ___ Money Order
              __ Visa __ Mastercard

Note: On International Credit Card Orders, banks will make automatic conversion to your currency.

Credit Card Number: _____

Name on card (Print): _____

Signature: _____

Expiration Date: _____ / _____

Please process the following order:

Total:

Books _____ at _____ Each $ _____

Shipping: $ _____

Sales Tax (Missouri Orders Only: 6.5%): $ _____

Overall Total: $ _____

A PERSONAL COPY FOR EVERY MEMBER
OF YOUR FIRM
And <u>Explode</u> your Firm's Production!

Search and Placement! A Handbook for Success

ORDER FORM
Please cut with scissors on dotted line or send information to below address.

TELEPHONE ORDERS: (314) 991-3177: Have Visa, American Express, or Mastercard ready.

POSTAL ORDERS: Placement Marketing Group
P.O. Box 410412
St. Louis, Missouri 63141 USA

FAX: International <u>Only</u>
(country code) (314) 991-5071

PRICE:

> 1 – 5 Books $45.00 U.S. each
> 6-23 Books $35.00 U.S. each
> 24 or more Call for quote.
> Volume discounts available.

SHIPPING: USA <u>Only.</u>
Per Book <u>Airmail</u> - $3.50 U.S.

International – Airmail
Canada, Mexico $ 7.00 U.S. per book
Europe $ 15.00 U.S. per book
Australia, South Africa, Asia $ 20.00 U.S. per book

Note: International shipping in 24 book (case) increments is far less expensive. Call for details.

(OVER)

Please Print Legibly

Name: _____

Title: _____

Company Name: _____

Address: _____

State: _____ Country: _____ Zip/Postal Code: _____

Phone Number: _____

Size of Firm: 1-2 _____   3-5 _____   6-10 _____   11 and over _____

Sales tax: 6.5% books shipped to Missouri addresses.

MAKE CHECKS PAYABLE TO: **Placement Marketing Group**

Payment: __ Check __ American Express ___ Money Order
              __ Visa __ Mastercard

Note: On International Credit Card Orders, banks will make automatic conversion to your currency.

Credit Card Number: _____

Name on card (Print): _____

Signature: _____

Expiration Date: _____ / _____

Please process the following order:

Total:

Books _____ at _____ Each $ _____

Shipping: $ _____

Sales Tax (Missouri Orders Only: 6.5%): $ _____

Overall Total: $ _____